Y0-DYG-634

English Teaching:
An International Exchange

English Teaching: An International Exchange

Edited by
James Britton
with the assistance of
Margaret Gill
(Australian Association for the Teaching of English)
William Washburn
(Canadian Council of Teachers of English)
Stuart Middleton
(New Zealand Association for the Teaching of English)
Mike Torbe
(National Association for the Teaching of English, UK)
Arthur Applebee
(National Council of Teachers of English, USA)

on behalf of the
International Federation for the Teaching of English

1984

HEINEMANN EDUCATIONAL BOOKS
London and Portsmouth, New Hampshire

MIDDLEBURY COLLEGE LIBRARY.

Heinemann Educational Books Ltd
22 Bedford Square, London WC1B 3HH
70 Court Street, Portsmouth
New Hampshire 03801
LONDON   EDINBURGH   MELBOURNE   AUCKLAND
HONG KONG   SINGAPORE   KUALA LUMPUR   NEW DELHI
IBADAN   NAIROBI   JOHANNESBURG
PORTSMOUTH (NH)   KINGSTON   PORT OF SPAIN

©International Federation for the Teaching of English 1984
First published 1984

British Library Cataloguing in Publication Data

Britton, James, *1908–*
    English teaching: an international exchange.
    1. English language—Study and teaching
    I. Title
    420'.7'1   LB1576

    ISBN 0-435-10116-1

Library of Congress Cataloging in Publication Data
Main entry under title:

English teaching, an international exchange.

    Bibliography: p.
    1. English philogy—Study and Teaching—Addresses,
essays, lectures. I. Britton, James N. II. International
Federation for the Teaching of English.
PE65.E52   1984   418'.007   84-15820
ISBN 0-435-10116-1 (U.S.)

Typeset by The Castlefield Press, Moulton, Northants.
Set in 10/11 point Linoterm Baskerville
Printed and bound in Great Britain by
Biddles Ltd, Guildford and King's Lynn

Contents

Foreword

I am very grateful for the assistance given to me by the associate editors named on the title page. Let me at the same time make it clear that the final selection was my responsibility alone. Our thanks are due also to Paul O'Dea, NCTE Director of Publications, and Keith Nettle and Heather Morris of Heinemann Educational Books.

All royalties from this publication will go to the International Federation for the Teaching of English in support of further international activities on the part of the member associations. To the twenty-three authors who have contributed to this collection, therefore, our gratitude for their generosity.

James Britton

Information on Journals

For further information regarding the journals from which articles have been reprinted, write to the addresses below:

Australian ATE: *English in Australia*, AATE Inc., PO Box 203, Norwood, South Australia 5067.

Canadian CTE: *The English Quarterly*, Tom McNeil, Faculty of Education, Brandon University, Brandon, Manitoba, Canada R6A 1A9.

New Zealand ATE: *English in New Zealand*, NZATE, PO Box 1154, Postal Centre, Wellington, New Zealand.

NATE (UK): *English in Education*, NATE Office, 49 Bromsgrove Road, Sheffield S10 2NA, United Kingdom.

NCTE (USA): *Language Arts*) NCTE, 1111 Kenyon Road,
            The English Journal) Urbana, Illinois, 61801,
            English Education) United States of America.

Part I

Parents, Teachers – and, of course, Children

We could not use language as we do, and above all we could not learn it as babies, unless we were always floating in a general willingness to make sense of it (Empson, *Milton's God*, p. 28).

I speak . . . in order to emerge into reality, in order to add myself to nature (Gusdorf, *Speaking*, p. 50).

In arranging the chapters that make up this collection I wanted to avoid stereotyping them. Rather, for example, than putting all the pieces about writing into one package and the pieces about reading into another, I hoped to preserve the kind of integration that would reflect our views of how language should operate in classrooms. Yet I wanted the juxtapositions to say something; I did not want to revert merely to random or arbitrary arrangements. As a result, I have aimed at groupings that are more like concert arrangements of muscial performances than they are like sub-heads in a library classification.

Take for instance Part I: it displays, as one focal point, an emphasis on the importance of listening. Are we aware, I wonder, of the way electronic inventions have opened up new possibilities for listening – both the social kind of listening and the art of eavesdropping? (Without tape-recorders there could have been no Watergate.) As teachers, we have already learned a great deal from the delayed and repeated listening that tape-recording has made possible – and we stand to learn a great deal more. It is not simply a matter of gains in linguistic study. Because expressive speech reveals the contours of a speaker's thinking, a listener may increasingly tune in to his modes of thought: relaxed conversation indeed is so transparent a window into a mind and disposition and personality of a speaker, that we are probably never more directly present to each other than we are in intimate conversation.

So here we have Garth Boomer bugging the bedroom of his garret in London to exhibit a pre-sleep state-of-the-nation commentary from a 3-year-old exile (Chapter 1); and Gordon Wells drawing upon a rich store of recorded speech to indicate the complementary roles that speech in the home and speech in the classroom might play in a young child's education (Chapter 2); and Anne Baker describing what happened in her primary-school classroom when she started to 'listen' to what the children wrote (Chapter 3).

Taken together, these three chapters offer a commentary on the home/ school transition. Negotiation between child and adult, the development of shared meanings in a situation where choice is offered – these are the school conditions that produce 'real writing' for Anne Baker, just as they are on Gordon Well's evidence, characteristic of the kind of talk in school that builds on and complements talk at home.

1   Piggy Nick – That's a Good Word*

Garth Boomer (*Principal Education Officer, South Australia*)

Simon, Catherine, Jean and I were living in a one-bedroom garret in a three-storey block of flats in London. We'd only been in England a couple of weeks and I noticed that Simon's pre-sleep monologues had grown to proportions that would have done credit to Cecil B. de Mille. He'd been in the habit of talking to himself back in Australia but the transplant to London seemed to have given his bedtime spiel a new impetus.

Unethically, but in the interest of science, I decided to do a Watergate on him. I planted a tape-recorder behind the bedhead. The night-time ritual was to put Catherine down in the double bed while Jean and I read or watched television in the sitting-room. When it was our bedtime we had to transfer the children to makeshift beds in the sitting-room.

Catherine, who was then 5 years old, always dropped off to sleep very quickly, leaving Simon, then 38 months, alone with himself. On the night of 2 October 1972 his only 'property' was his Teddy bear. Catherine was asleep alongside him.

What follows are brief extracts from the transcript of what he said:

[*simulated sleep noises*]
Pssh . . . Pssh . . .
[*10-second silence*]
Scratch . . .
[*assorted sounds: 2 minutes' silence*]
Prr
Daddy's the boss, Daddy's the boss, Daddy
the Daddy is the boss [*chanted*]
[*indistinct sentence: 20-second silence*]
The water bag
The hot water bag   [*Catherine has taken a hot water bag [bottle] to bed.*]
[*laughing*]
Hallo, Hallo, Halloo, Halloo
Yup the up the poo
Jiggety, jiggety jog
The mouse ran up the clock
The mouse ran down
Jiggety, Jickety – [*pause*] jock
[*mumbling, then 1½-minute silence*]
Is that Greg or Nanna or Grumpy or Alison? [*his cousin, back in Australia*]

*Adapted, by permission, from *The Spitting Image*, by Garth Boomer and Dale Spender, Adelaide, Rigby, 1976.

I haven't got any honey
Do with it to do with it
[indistinct sounds]
That won't hurt
Look at that
P'yoopy, yoopy, yoop
[indistinct whispering]
Sit down, sit down [dramatized]   [Earlier that day, Simon had fallen off the makeshift
Why you crying   swing at the back of the flats. A couple of young
Oh hosh hosh   English children from the flat downstairs had
                                                    comforted him.]
We don't mean to cry do we
No
That's right
O yeh you do
I'm happy now
[indistinct sounds]   [Here after only a few weeks in London, he does a
                                                    creditable imitation of the English accent – 'hosh'
                                                    equals 'hush'.]
We have a swing
O pee doodle
Fell off the swing
. . . clumsy   [tune of Humpty Dumpty]
Why you crying, don't cry, hosh don't
prosh will
you don't cry
Going to have a little drop . . .
Dumpy, dumpy dip   [continues humming in this vein]
Look . . . my handle
Now got lot . . . two handles
Wash it
He has enough
had enough
[indistinct sounds]
Night-time   [simulated sleep sounds and humming]
Shopping bag, shopping bag, shopping bag [chanted]
Up the dee, up the dee, up the dee
Woo b doo   [to the tune of 'London Bridge is falling down']
[1-minute silence, then extended humming]
Go to sleep now   [simulated snoring]
Night-time
[laughing]
Hallo, hallo
[laughing]
Der, der, der, der
The fire'n, the fire'n, the fire'n, the fire fire
The feer, feer, feer   [to the tune of 'The Farmer in the Dell']
The fire, fire, fire, fire, fire   [On our first day in London we took up lodgings in
. . . engine   a poky room in a hotel in Gower Street. The traffic
The fire engine   was loud. The children rushed to the window in
It boom boom   amazement when a fire engine went past at full blast.
Fire engine   Simon was really impressed by the 'different' sound.]
It boom boom
Fire engine
I broom, broom, broom
The fire's out   [glissando]
The fire's out, the fire's out   [sharp repetition]

The fire's out   [glissando]
The fire's out   [repeated more softly]
The fire's out   [still more softly]
The fire's out   [louder]
The fire's out, the fire's out   [sharp repetition]
Fire's out   [glissando]
The fire's out, the fire's out
Fire's out   [glissando]
The fire's out   [echo effect]
Fire . . . is   [pauses]
Engine, engine
[indistinct sounds; grunting]
It's night-time
It's night-time   [chanted]
The fire's out, the fire's out, the fire's out,
the fire's out
The fire's in, the fire's out   [repeated]
The fire's out, the fire's in
The fire's in
Der, der, der, der, der   [simulated siren]
* * *

Hallo Caffy, Caffy
Caffrine, Caffrin   [to sleeping sister]
[yawn]
Night Caffrine   [10-second pause]
I told you
A piggy nick
A piggy back
A piggy back on me
Right under there   [chanting]
Right under here on my head
I don't know what to do
I don't know what to do
I can't put her head
I don't know what to do
Pat her   [indistinct sounds]
Oh, no you can't
Oh, yes I can   [repeated three times]
Oh, yes I can
Oh, no I'm not   [repeated three times]
That's the slip
It is the slip to go in the water   [Friends back in Australia had a swimming
That's the water down there   pool with a slippery dip.]
and you jump
jumpy, jumpy, jumpy   [chant]
We had a piggy
A piggy nick   [sound like R, rrr . . .]
A piggy nick
A piggy nick?
Oh, that's another good word
* * *

Oh time to get up
No it's time to go to sleep
When I go . . .
Ring ding ling
Time to get up

Tired	*[mumbling]*
They're pushing me down aren't they	*[I can't resist drawing attention to the symbolism.]*
[2-minute silence: yawn: indistinct sounds]	
Sing . . . yella	
the ella sumporine	*[sings]*
We all live in the ella sumporine	*[to the tune of 'We All Live in a Yellow Submarine']*
ella sumporine	
ella sumporine	
We all live in the ella sum . . .	*[and the rest is silence]*

Simon, taking on patterns of experience and soothing words like ballast, finally dives into the subconscious of sleep. We all live in a yellow submarine. We need to lay the ghosts and demons of each day before sleep washes over us. What can I say about Simon's amazing method of rocking his own cradle?

Three years ago, inspired by the late Ruth Weir's study of the monologues of her son Anthony, I mined my transcript with a scholar's zeal, doing word counts and analyses of the metalinguistic practice of vowels and consonants. I noted the way in which he built up phrases progressively; how he punned and rhymed and played and associated and dramatized; how he tenaciously worked to reconcile Australia and England.

In seminars at the Institute of Education I used Simon to illustrate the theories of Chomsky and Jimmy Britton (Simon, in the spectator role) and Jean Piaget and Lev Semenovich Vygotsky. I used him to 'prove' that we all have a natural urge to tell stories and write poems and compose songs. Now I can't bring myself to repeat the linguistic dissections. I just want to show.

Look on his work, teachers, and despair. Despair because you cannot teach him more than the merest fraction of what he teaches himself about language and life. Relax and enjoy your children and enjoy yourselves.

2 Talking with Children: The Complementary Roles of Parents and Teachers*

Gordon Wells (School of Education, University of Bristol)

At about the age of 5, all children in our culture reach an important milestone in their development, as they move from the familiar and supportive environment of their home into the larger unknown world of school.[1] During the next ten years the aim of those who teach them will be to induct them into the skills, knowledge and values of the wider culture, and to help them to achieve independence and responsibility in the use of their individual talents, both contributing to, and receiving from, the social, intellectual and material resources of the society of which they are becoming members. However, some children benefit from their schooling much more than others, and it has frequently been argued that a major cause of differential success is the difference between children in their ability to meet the linguistic expectations of the classroom as a result of their pre-school linguistic experience at home.

Certainly, language must play a large part in the ease or difficulty with which children make the transition from home to school. For the many differences between the two environments – in size, in organization patterns and routines, in the goals that are set and in the means that children are expected to use in achieving them – impinge most strongly on the child's moment-by-moment experience through the differences in styles of linguistic interaction that characterize them. The greater the difference, the more likely it is that the child will experience a sense of disorientation, which may manifest itself in behaviour that is assessed as lack of ability or unwillingness to learn. Once labelled in this way, it may then become progressively more difficult for such children to overcome their initial disadvantage and reach the levels of achievement of which they are potentially capable.

In spite of much theorizing on this subject, however, there has been very little systematic study of the actual experience of children making this crucial transition, apart from the studies of Bernstein (1973) and Tough (1977), which have observed children in quasi-experimental situations in school and then either inferred the characteristics of home experience that preceded the performance in school or drawn obliquely upon questionnaire information. The Bristol study, 'Language at Home and at School',[2] is probably unique in following a representative sample of children through the pre-school years and into the infant school, recording regular samples of their spontaneous use of language in these two settings. In this chapter, I

*Abridged, by permission, from *English in Education*, vol. 12, no. 2, summer 1978.

shall try to describe some of the main characteristics of children's experience of talk at home and at school, as we have observed it in the recordings we have made, and I shall consider some of the implications of the differences that emerge from a comparison between them for the ease with which children make the transition.

Talk at home

If one asked parents the question 'Why should children talk?', one would probably receive an answer such as that given by one particular mother: 'It's natural. They want to join in and be like other people. They just learn from listening to and talking to other people.' And in many ways, 'naturalness' describes what we have observed. Despite wide variations in the kinds of home in which they are growing up, there is remarkable uniformity in the sequence in which children learn the main components of language and even in the rate at which this learning takes place. There are differences between children, of course, both in the age at which they begin to talk and in the stage they have reached on entry to school, but these are relatively insignificant when compared with the amount that all children learn in these early years. All but a very small minority of children reach the age of schooling with a vocabulary of several thousand words, control of the basic grammar of the language of their community, and an ability to deploy these resources in conversations arising from the many and varied situations that occur in their everyday lives. Of all the children that we have studied, there is only one of whom this claim cannot be made with confidence, and even he is by no means limited to 'a basically non-logical mode of expressive behaviour', as Bereiter (1966) would have us believe to be typical of vast numbers of children. It seems, therefore, that the child's predisposition to learn whatever language he is exposed to, together with some minimum experience of language in use, is sufficient for the child to acquire a basic linguistic competence before he goes to school.

However, there are important differences between children, particularly when looked at from the point of view of the transition to school, and these concern the uses they habitually make of their linguistic resources: the things they talk about, and the ways in which they talk about them (Halliday, 1968). Learning one's native language is not simply a matter of learning vocabulary and grammar, but rather of learning to construct shared meanings as part of collaborative activities in which the words and sentences both refer to the shared situation and reflect a particular orientation to it. As Bernstein (1971) has argued, through the aspects of common experience that parents choose to talk about, and the particular relations that are given prominence in the form of their utterances, they present to their children a particular view of the world and their place within it. For example, if objects are constantly referred to in terms of ownership, and prohibitions and permissions are justified in terms of proprietorial rights, the child will be quick to learn the grammatical markers of possession (Wells, 1974) and over time will acquire an orientation to 'property' that is very different from that of the child whose parents encourage an exploratory attitude to objects, only prohibiting an interest in particular objects when there is a risk of danger.

Differences of orientation resulting from parental emphasis are particularly common between the sexes, boys and girls being subtly directed towards different interests through the situations in which their parents choose to initiate conversations with them. In a comparison we made of conversations initiated with 3-year-olds, we found that over half the conversations with girls were in relation to household activities where the children were frequently 'helping' to carry out the task (a ratio of 2:1 compared with the boys), whereas a far greater proportion of conversations with boys were in situations where the children were engaged in exploratory play, with or without the active participation of the adult (a ratio of 3·5:1). Surprisingly enough, there were not such marked differences between boys and girls in the conversation that they initiated at this age, but by the time children start school, there are quite strong differences between boys and girls in the topics that they most frequently talk about – differences that are at least partly the result of their earlier experiences at home.

There are differences, too, in the ways in which language contributes to the structuring of experience. Everything that happens in a child's daily life is a potential subject for the sort of talk that facilitates attention, interpretation and evaluation, but parents differ in the use they make of these opportunities. In some homes, events are taken very much for granted, each one receiving the same sort of passing comment, whereas in other homes there is a much greater selectivity, some events being discussed in considerable detail and connections made with the wider context in which they occur. As a result of such different experiences, the internal models of the world that children are constructing take on their particular shapes and textures and come to be more fully developed in some areas than others.

In the following episodes we can see these subtle shaping processes in action as particular events are explored through talk. In the first example, James (aged 3½ years) has just come in from playing outside, and he is standing at the door, taking his boots off. He draws his mother's attention to a bird, and his mother takes up his interest, explaining the birds's nest-building activities:

	M: There we are	[*Mother helping James to change.*]
	There – one slipper on	
J: I can see a bird		
	M: A what, love?	[*James watching bird in garden.*]
J: See a bird		
	M: Is there? Outside? [*whispers*]	

J: Yes [whispers]
J: See [whispers]   [James points to bird.]
                                    M: Is he eating anything?
                                      [whispers]
J: No [whispers]

                                    M: Where? [whispers throughout]
                                    M: Oh yes he's getting –
                                      Do you know what he's
                                      doing?
J: No [whispers]

                                    M: He's going to the . . . the . . .
                                      paper sack to try and pick
                                      out some pieces –
                                      Oh he's got some food there
                                      And I expect he'll pick out
                                      some pieces of thread from
                                      the sack to go and make
                                      his nest . . . up . . .
                                      underneath the roof,
                                      James
                                      Wait a minute and I'll –
                                      OK wait a mo' wait a mo',
                                      James
J: That bird's gone [whispers]
                                    M: Has it gone now?
J: Yes [whispers]
                                    M: Oh
                                      Take those long trousers off
                                      because they're . . . a bit
                                      muddy in there
J: Yes, he's gone

Here we see a mother naturally entering into her child's interest and
directing it through the fuller meaning she gives to what they are looking at
together.
  In the second example, Wendy (aged 3½ years) is playing at the kitchen
sink:

W: I'm going to play   [Wendy climbs on to a
    with the water   chair at the sink.]
    again, Mummy
  Is that all right?
                                    [. . . 6 . . .]
                                                        [Mother returns to
                                                          kitchen.]
W: I'm washing this
    for you, Mummy
                                    M: You're being very helpful
                                      this morning, Wendy
                                      (appreciatively)
                                      Er. Yes (doubtfully)
                                      Don't make it TOO bubbly,
                                      love
                                                        [Mother comes to investigate.]
                                      Have you put some more – ? [Refers to washing-up liquid.]

W: I want to play –

No [= *don't do that*]
'Cos Mummy's just wiped
up all that, lovey
And I told you I didn't want
to get it too wet
Didn't I?

M: Er – no

[*Mother wipes draining board
again.*]

There we are
Now try NOT to get all the
water over there, love
Please
[. . . 19 . . .]

[*Mother continues to wipe and
put away dishes. Wendy
blows bubbles through
a straw.*]

W: See those bubbles!
Come and see those
bubbles

M: Just a minute, love
And I'll come right away

This time the child's interest doesn't entirely fit in with Mother's plans, but the mother accepts the child's intentions before setting restraining conditions on how the activity can be carried out.

Finally, Jacqueline at the much younger age of 2¼ years brings a book to show to her mother:

J: Look at those balls, Mum
I show you

[*Jacqueline holds out book.*]

M: Show me what, darling?

J: I show you all the balls
I show you balls

M: You're showing me the balls
in your book, are you?
Let me see then
Where?

J: Balls

[*Jacqueline shows the
picture.*]
[*Mother asks about other
picture.*]

M: What's this?

J: That's a doggy

M: What's this?

J: That's a pussy cat

M: And who's this?

J: That's Lulu

M: Hasn't she got a lovely
kitten?

J: Lulu's putting the –
Pussy cat's

M: Lulu's putting the pussy
cat's hat on, yes

J: Lulu's – pussy cat's –
Lulu's – putting pussy
cat's hat on

11

Mother's questions here are first to check that she has understood the child's intentions correctly and then to invite her to go on talking about the pictures. We can see here how the mother guesses Jacqueline's meaning intention and provides her with the complete form, which Jacqueline is then able to say herself. In all these examples of 'home-talk' we can see a number of important qualities that characterize the sort of conversational experience that leads to effective use of language by children:

1. A warm responsiveness to the child's interests and a recognition of the child as an autonomous individual with valid purposes and ways of seeing things.
2. Negotiation of meaning and purpose in the joint construction of an intersubjective reality.
3. An invitation to the child to consider the immediate present in a wider framework of intention and consequences, feelings and principles.

Such conversations also have, albeit loosely and sometimes imperfectly, a reciprocity and cohesion which results from both participants attempting to understand the meaning intended by the other and to express their own meanings in ways which will be understood against the background of shared information that has either been made explicit or can be taken for granted.

There are a number of further characteristics which distinguish such talk from that which is most typical of schools. Firstly, most of the conversations are initiated by the child (70 per cent was the figure we found in one analysis); secondly, it is sporadic, arising spontaneously from the interest of the moment, and it is almost completely lacking in a didactic pressure to teach particular facts or skills; and thirdly, it ranges widely over the whole of the family's shared experience, both inside and outside the home.

Talk at school

All the children quoted above are making excellent progress at school. Indeed, Jacqueline has made such good progress that she has been moved into the junior school well before her seventh birthday, and James is the most advanced reader of the children we have been following up in the project 'Children Learning to Read'.[3] The following extract, which shows how confidently Jacqueline is coping with the routines of school life, is taken from a recording made when she had been in school less than a term. She has just drawn a picture of Jack Frost, and is about to dictate a story to go with it:

T: What're we going to
   write here today?

J: This . . . is . . . a –   [*J. dictates to T.*]
Boy: Jack
J: No

T: What's his name?   [*J. plays with T.'s pendant.*]

J: Jack Frost

T: Jack Frost

J: Here . . . is . . . Jack Frrro –   [*J. dictates to T.*]

T: Jack   [*T. writing*]
   What's Jack Frost doing?

J: Frosting the grass

T: He . . . is . . . frosting
   He's frosting the grass

J: With –   [*J. continues to dictate*]

T: With – oh with whom?

J: His wand

T: With his wand [*sounding
   surprised*]
   What's he doing to you?   [*J. looks at her fingers.*]

J: Nibbling my toes and my –
   and fingers

T: He's nibbling?

J: Yeah

T: Nibbling? Right

J: My . . . toes –

T: Nibbling –   [*T. writing.*]

J: – and my –

T: – my –

J: – fingers   [*J. holds up her fingers.*]

T: And my – ? What else did
   you say?

J: Chin

T: Chin
   Oh you're going to write –
   Have to write this line very
   little, won't you?
   Now . . . d'you remember
   how you do it?

J: Yeah

T: That line goes along there   [*T. shows J. in which
                                     direction to write.*]

J: Yeah [= *Yes, I know*]

T: Do you want me to put the
   dots for you or can you
   do it without the dots?

J: I can do it without the dots
   [*with assurance*]

The final story, which was written with great concentration, read as
follows:

Here is Jack Frost.
He is frosting the grass with his wand.
He is nibbling my toes, my fingers and my chin.

From Jacqueline's point of view, it seems that the answer to our question 'Why should children talk?' is that it is both enjoyable and interesting. She has confidence, because her experience has led her to form expectations that people will take her seriously as a conversational partner and will be interested in what she has to say. And indeed, watching her with her teacher, it seems that her expectations are justified.

Not all children make the transition to school so easily, however, and some, lacking confidence and fluency, may be so tongue-tied and monosyllabic that they give the impression of being almost without language at all. Teachers certainly have the impression that many children enter school with a 'linguistic deficit', and those who are unwilling or unable to respond to the linguistic demands of the classroom apparently lend support to this impression. How serious, then, is the problem? Certainly there are children who have little or no command of English on entry to school, but these are, almost without exception, children of non-English-speaking parents: their problem is not lack of language, but lack of English, and they need the special provision of appropriate second-language teaching. These children apart, the number of children of English-speaking parents who have not acquired a basic command of English by the age of five is very small indeed. However, the particular dialect of English they have learnt, or the uses they habitually make of language, may be different from those most valued in school and as a result, they may find it difficult to communicate successfully with strange adults, who are unfamiliar with their expectations.

[*The author goes on to suggest that poor speaking performance in school may often be in part a result of the nature of the demands teachers make, in particular 'the remoteness of those demands from direct personal involvement in shared or self-initiated activity'. He criticizes teachers for over-using closed questions − an approach that tends to turn discussion into 'guessing what's in teacher's mind'; and suggests that they should employ a variety of types of interaction in accordance with the nature of the task in hand, and in particular in accordance with the degree to which the goal of the task is predetermined. He continues as follows.*]

To find an example of exploratory talk where the outcome was not determined in advance, I had to turn to a class discussion of 'The Pobble who has no Toes' in one of the recordings analysed in Margaret Hocking's study (1977). The teacher's purpose in this case was specifically to encourage the children to make a personal response to the poem, while still remaining faithful to the meaning of the text:

> T: Shall we just read that bit
>   again?
>   'His Aunt Jemima made
>   him drink Lavender
>   water tinged with pink.'
> C_1: What's lavender water taste
>   like?

T: I don't know
I've never tasted it
Have you?

C₂: We have a drink and it's
pink and it's strawberry
And the first time I had it I
didn't like it so the next
time I put sugar in and I
liked it

T: Do you think you would
like lavender water?

Chn: No

T: Why not?

C₃: Because when Mummy tells
me would you like
lavender water I says no
thank you

T: I wonder why you
wouldn't like it though

{ C: I expect it tastes horrid
  C: Like sea water
  C: Nasty
  C: Salty

T: You think it would be
salty?
What do you usually do
with lavender water?

C: I don't know
I don't know what it is

T: It's a perfume
Lavender water is a scent
that ladies put on

C: Ugh!

T: It wouldn't be very nice,
would it, to drink?

C: Maybe that's why his toes
came off

T: Maybe that did make his
toes come off
He certainly lost them
T: What about the things he
ate?
Would you like them?
'Eggs and buttercups fried
with fish?'

Chn: No
C: I like the fish and eggs

T: What about the
buttercups?

{ C: I wouldn't like them
  C: I don't like fish
  C: I don't like flowers and that

T: You don't like flowers
Don't you normally eat
flowers?

Chn: No

15

T: The things that are green
The flowers that are green
yes

T: We don't eat the grass
but some animals do

T: That's right
They like it

C: Don't you eat cabbage?
And cabbage is a flower
C: Yes and you eat cauliflowers
C: You'd not eat flowers that
bloom

C: Can we eat the grass?
Chn: No
C: But the grass is green

C: The cows eat it
C: Cows
C: Guinea pigs

The whole discussion is in this style: the children contributing ideas from their own experience and the teacher helping them to maintain the thread, by picking up the most relevant aspect of each child contribution and using it to extend the exploration. Naturally, there are a number of digressions, such as the discussion of herbivores above, but in the process, as Hocking points out, the children are learning the beginning of the critical method in an interaction which, significantly, is child-initiated and mainly child-sustained.

It *is* possible, therefore, to develop a style of interaction that is relatively undetermined and open to pupil contributions, yet at the same time appropriate to the chosen task. And because it can embrace spontaneous pupil contributions, it is surely the most effective way of complementing the talk of the home, by building on the foundations that have already been laid in the free-ranging, child-initiated conversations that have been the experience of the vast majority of children before they come to school. At the same time, such talk looks forward to the larger goals of formal education, by introducing the criteria of conformity to experience, internal consistency and relevance, in relation to curricular tasks selected by the teacher.

Since these are the qualities that one would expect teachers to be endeavouring to develop in children's talk, why is it that this style of interaction is so rare in children's first experience of school? A number of explanations might be suggested. The most obvious is that teachers do not, after all, place as much value on these qualities as their public pronouncements would have us believe; at heart they are only concerned to train skills and to drum in facts. However, I do not believe that this is, in fact, the case. More probable, it seems, is that they do value such qualities but in a rather diffuse way that does not fully inform their moment-by-moment interactions in the classroom. Other pressures, such as the desire to be seen to be efficient, and to keep to a well-prepared programme of work, take on a greater priority, and control of the class – or the loss of control that is feared if children are allowed to take the initiative in task-related talk – assumes an overriding importance. It is certainly true that a high proportion of children's spontaneous contributions to class or group discussion are in varying degrees irrelevant to the immediate task, and thirty or more children all wanting to develop their own line of thought pose a serious threat to the teacher's control over the discussion. But before we accept this explanation at face value, we should stop to ask 'Irrelevant to whom?' Not to the child, presumably, since he is prepared to speak out in front of his peers, and struggle to make his meaning clear. The irrelevance must, therefore, be in the mind of the teacher, who has planned in advance the course that the children's learning should take. But what is relevant to the teacher may be irrelevant to the child, unless he is helped to relate his personal experience to the task in hand, and the teacher's control may be bought at the expense of the full and active involvement of the child.

Relevance in talk is only a particular case of matching means to ends, procedures to goals, and in many spheres of activity children have already achieved considerable competence of this sort, particularly where the goal is self-chosen. What makes talk a special case, however, is that it is a reciprocal activity, in which both participants have to be prepared to negotiate their meanings towards the attainment of a shared goal. Relevance in talk is thus essentially a matter for negotiation. But it is through such negotiation of meaning that language is first acquired, with parents helping children to match utterances to the understanding they both have of a shared situation. By the time they come to school, children already have some understanding of relevance in talk, as can be seen in the conversations that they themselves initiate. What schools should provide, therefore, is the opportunity to develop and extend these conversational skills by putting them to use in the exploration of the new ideas and experiences that the more formal curriculum provides. However, this is only possible if at least some curriculum tasks adopt a style of interaction which is truly reciprocal, and where the goal of the task is sufficiently open-ended for the relevance of the children's contributions to be negotiated as the talk proceeds. Only in this way will children develop the confidence and skill to use talk as a means of understanding and controlling the world in which they live. Our problem as teachers is to learn how to maintain the supportive responsiveness of parents, while at the same time complementing it with a clear sense of the skills and knowledge that we wish to make available.

Notes

1. This paper is a revised version of an address to the Pre-School Commission of the Annual Conference of NATE, Norwich, April 1977.
2. Details of the research programme are available from the Secretary, 'Language at Home and at School', School of Education, 19 Berkeley Square, Bristol BS8 1HF.
3. See note 2 above.

References

Bereiter, C. *et al*. (1966) 'An academically oriented pre-school for culturally deprived children', in *Pre-School Education Today*, ed. F.M. Hechinger, New York, Doubleday.

Bernstein, B. (1971) *Class, Codes and Control: Vol. I*, London, Routledge & Kegan Paul.

Bernstein, B. (ed.) (1973) *Class, Codes and Control: Vol II*, London, Routledge & Kegan Paul.

Halliday, M.A.K. (1968) 'Language and experience', *Educational Review*, vol. 20, no. 2, pp. 95–106.

Hocking, M. (1977) 'Verbal interaction in the infant classroom and its place in the learning process', unpublished PhD thesis, University of Bristol.

Tough, J. (1977) *The Development of Meaning*, London, Unwin Education Books.

Wells, C.G. (1974) 'Learning to code experience through language', *Journal of Child Language*, vol. 1, no. 2, pp. 243–69.

3 Real Writing, Real Writers: A Question of Choice*

Anne Baker (Clifford Bridge Primary School, Coventry)

. . . we have nothing to rely upon in making our choices but ourselves (Richards, 1929).

Writing and reading are part of everyday reality in our society. They are ways in which we relate, share our thoughts and feelings, live and learn. I am writing, now, because I have something to say; you are reading, now, to find out my meaning. If we couldn't write, or read, we would be social cripples.

Writing I meet requires me to feel, to think, to act, to reflect, to refer, to know, to notice. It appears in the shape of bills, forms, statements, signs, adverts, newspapers, magazines, reference books, novels and so on. It actually makes a difference to how I live my life. I have responded to a political census, a tax return and an application form by filling them in; I have believed that what a newspaper tells me *is* the news; I have been persuaded by an advert into buying a certain product; I have had confirmation of what I know in a piece of information; I have been moved by a narrative. Whether I read a little, or a lot, my life is influenced by writing.

As a reader, it seems to me that writers have a certain power, which lies most obviously in their ability to communicate their purposes to me, perhaps to change me. As a writer, I feel that the possible power to change other people is significantly less important than the power which comes from actual involvement in writing. I write, and therefore have a way of thinking and feeling, and a way of looking at and finding out about life, which amounts to a way of living.

I am involved in writing, now, to search for and discover what I mean and believe to be true about writing. My thoughts emerge, slowly, on to paper, and then I ponder them to decide if I've said what I really intend. I think my written thoughts over, go away and come back, if necessary, and they are still there, holding my meanings steady. If I want, I can rewrite my thoughts, which is to rethink them, and so, gradually, through writing, discover my meaning, what the truth is, for me. I live through, and let go of, my thoughts and feelings as I write; I get to know myself a bit better, I learn and I change.

*Reprinted, by permission, from *English in Education*, vol. 15, no. 3, autumn 1981.

The whole point of being a writer, it seems to me, is that you change as you write, you change yourself, you change the way you think (Lessing, 1980).

Real writing is purposeful communication by writers to their readers. Real writers are those involved in writing for the purpose of communicating their own thoughts and/or feelings to their readers, which may include themselves. When they write, real writers participate in a process which I understand to be a question of choices made by the writers themselves. The process for each writer, whatever their stage of development, is something to do with the following decisions:

deciding you have something to say to yourself, to someone, or to some people;
making up your mind to write something;
deciding on the form your writing will take;
allotting the time you need to write;
discovering by writing just what it is you have to say;
getting what you have to say right before letting go of it;
choosing whether, or not, to publish what you have written, and where;
entrusting what you have written to your reader, or readers.

People usually learn to write at school when they are children, because as children they have to go to school and schools elect to teach writing. Schools have tremendous potential for being the right sort of places for real writing to happen. Each school is a miniature society with a life of its own that is different from home and different from outside society, a kind of meeting place of the two, the private and the public. Each school is a local and therefore known community of children and adults, the individual and the group, in richly complex relationships. Just the sort of place where children can use writing very much as real writers do in society as a whole, to live with, to learn with, to relate, to share.

That is, they will, if the life of the school is right, if it is concerned with children's own learning, if it provides a context in which children can participate in the writing process. Such a context is one in which children are free to do their own writing, to make their own choices. When they decide they have something to write, they are given the time and opportunity to carry out their purpose, to explore what they think and feel through writing, and to find out what they mean, at their own pace. They can invent, or discover, for themselves the form that does most justice to their closest concern. They can publish if they please. They can learn to trust their authentic voices and to entrust what they have written to the eyes of their readers. Such a context is one in which teachers assist children in their writing, rather than direct what they must do. They do this by emphasizing to children that the only reliable choices in writing are those that they make for themselves. This is the context for real writing, in which real writers best grow. This is the context in which children, from first freely making marks on paper, can develop as real writers along a continuum of real writing that could stretch throughout their lives. It is also the context in which teachers, by paying a real attention to what children do, can come to accept and respect children, as of right, for what they are, what they are interested in and what they have to say.

Unfortunately, in spite of the fact that schools place an enormous emphasis on writing, so that apparently 60 per cent of children's time is spent in writing in school, much of the school writing I see isn't real. It isn't real because it isn't generated by the purposes of its writers, but rather by their teacher's. It isn't trying to do the things I know writing can do: change, persuade, move, influence, inform. It doesn't reflect the living nature of writing going on in our society, of which schools are, after all, a part. It isn't real, and, if the writing isn't real, then neither are the writers.

When I inquire what is happening in schools where the writing isn't real, I find that the context for writing is very different from the one I have described and the procedure used for getting writing is opposite to the writing process as I understand it. Crucially, in schools where the writing is directed, children are not consulted as to whether they have anything to say, and, if and when they have, it is not considered to be of central importance. 'Deciding you have something to say' and 'making up your mind to write something' are key choices in the writing process, because on one, or the other, or both of them, rest all the other choices to be made. If children aren't allowed to make the key choices, but are forced to accept someone else's decisions as to what is going to be said and written, then the writing process is crippled and any other decision not worth making. Interestingly enough, in schools where the writing isn't real, children aren't allowed to make any other choices, anyway. It is the teacher who makes most of the decisions about writing, the school organization seeing to the rest, and it is the teacher and her, or his, teaching that are the focus of attention.

What are the differences between schools where there is an awareness of the way in which the process of writing involves the writer in making a series of choices and decisions, and those where the teacher makes all the decisions?

Instead of children deciding they have something to say, the teacher decides what is going to be said by presenting a stimulus, a topic, a theme or an interest. Or, the teacher sets an exercise, or worksheet; or gives notes; or requires feedback on what she, or he, has taught. Or, the teacher prepares an examination or a test. The teacher is then the only audience for whom the children write. She, or he, collects the 'work' and reads it.

Instead of children making up their minds to write something, the teacher decides children will write in the writing lesson, when they do write.

Instead of children deciding on the form their writing will take, the teacher, either explicitly, by saying so, or implicitly, by directing children to exercises, dictates form. So there are thirty stories, thirty poems, thirty adverts, thirty letters, thirty essays. There are language laboratories, course books, source books, workbooks and worksheets.

Instead of children allotting the time they need to write, the school timetable and other organizational constraints determine when the lessons are, and children have to write in these lessons which start and end at certain pre-set times.

Instead of children discovering just what it is they have to say, much of their writing is carried out in the form of exercises which the teacher decides upon. There is such a thing as 'writing practice'.

Instead of children getting what they have to say right, through as many drafts as are needed, before letting go of it, stories, letters, poems and so on are usually produced as 'one offs', or else written once in 'rough' and then in 'neat'. They are then 'marked' and corrected as finished products, judged by the teacher as right or wrong, good or bad. Paper, and its use, is strictly limited.

Instead of children choosing whether, or not, to publish what they have written, and where, the teacher chooses 'neat' copies of children's writing to put on the walls, and sometimes, any and all kinds of writing go on the walls. The teacher asks for writing to go into children's notebooks, which are then put away into desks or trays until the books are full. The books are then kept in cupboards, or on offer to be taken home, or placed in the bin.

Instead of children entrusting what they have written to their reader, or readers, the teacher reads children's writing and endorses it with ticks, or crosses, and maybe makes a critical comment and adds a score. She, or he, notices those children who cannot cope with the conditions set for writing, and perhaps describes them as 'slow learners', or lazy, or lacking in concentration, and prescribes more of the same thing to remediate the situation. She, or he, perhaps praises those children who can cope with the conditions, and describes them as hard-working and 'bright', and uses their success to justify continuing to teach in the same way.

In schools where the writing isn't real, where the teacher or the school makes the decisions at every stage of the writing procedure, children are expected merely to practise and perform. They are not involved in making choices for themselves, their purpose isn't their own, they are not real writers. It seems to me, in such schools, the teacher spends too much time trying to teach writing to children, and not enough time helping them to write. To keep writing real, it must be used. More than that, a person's language can't be separated from them, the living person is in their language. So, to try to impose a language process, such as writing, from the outside, as a thing to be taught, to be transmitted, is to misunderstand the nature of language, and of people.

In my present school, the priority is 'getting real writing going in real situations where a real commitment to meaning becomes possible' (Burgess, 1973). The children are free to choose when to write and for how long. Children who want to write for themselves do so, and their privacy is respected. Children with a story to tell, narrate it and have it typed into their story book if they wish, to be placed on the shelf and read along with commercially produced books, or presented to the person for whom it was written. Children who want to communicate with people outside school write letters, post them and receive replies. Labels are written by children to accompany objects they have brought in to display. Experts at gardening, bird-watching, or dinosaurs, write what they know into books and folders and posters, for themselves, or as a resource for other children to use. Favourite books generate reviews recommending they be read. Notices for clubs, their registers and planned activities appear. Experiments are set up with accompanying instructions for carrying them out. Notes are made, and compared, as observations are carried out on snails, worms, flowers, insects, or whatever the children find arouses their curiosity. Here, Steven, aged 9, uses writing for a very personal reason, to come to terms with the death of two birds. He writes in his Nature Notebook, which he lets other children read, and me:

> Today me and Paul buried the second bird that we found. And I feel responsible for the little fellow's life, but he isn't alive anymore, so I can't feel responsible, but I do anyway. So there, to everybody who's there.

And again:

> And yesterday we found a dead bird, but we didn't get a look in when Mrs Minns said some of her class could bury that one. But I suppose I was just feeling responsible for it.

And finally, he writes to me in a book he uses to evaluate what he has done each week, and to which I reply:

> I loved doing the piece on the Swan and the dead birds. I think I have got rid of my responsibility for them.

Steven's confidence in his own written voice, here, is an example of what happens when children have 'a way of interpreting life for themselves and a tradition of writing for themselves that has more chance of surviving than an everlasting insistence on writing to a formula' (Rosen, 1973).

It is hard to change from being a teacher who makes all the decisions about writing, to being one who lets the children choose. The professional change, for me, came with the beginnings of personal change. It involved seeing children as individuals at the centre of their own lives, as people with something to say, and capable of making up their minds to say it and with the right to do so. It involved removing myself from the focus of attention in writing (and, incidentally, in everything else). I still had ideas, but I stopped walking in with an idea for all and tried to let my ideas be responses to the children's needs. I encouraged the children to be their own resource, and to look to themselves and each other for inspiration and support, as well as me. I got out from being their audience, unless they actively chose me, when I replied, and I helped children to think of other people they might have something to say to in writing. I started listening to them, trying to get behind their heads to see the way they were coming at what they were trying to say. I began to let them make their own minds up and value their own judgements, because in the end they have nothing to rely on in making their choices but themselves.

In his book *Freedom to Learn*, Carl Rogers says:

My experience has been that I cannot teach another person how to teach. To attempt it is for me, in the long run, futile (Rogers, 1969).

As teachers, we can reflect, perhaps wryly, on his honesty, for none of us were taught how to teach. We know we learned to teach by teaching. Real writing, the sort that is part of everyday reality in our society, the sort that can help children to make discoveries about themselves and their relationships with other people, is like teaching. It cannot be taught either. Real writers learn to write by writing.

References

Burgess, C. *et al.* (1973) *Understanding Children Writing*, Harmondsworth, Penguin Education.
Lessing, D. (1980) *Interview With Doris Lessing*, BBC2.
Richards, I.A. (1929) *Practical Criticism*, London, Routledge.
Rogers, C. (1969) *Freedom to Learn*, Columbus (Ohio), Merrill.
Rosen, C. and H. (1973) *The Language of Primary School Children*, Harmondsworth, Penguin Education.

Part II

Learning to Read-and-Write

Writing, which allows one's depths to speak . . . (Gusdorf, *Speaking*, p. 115).

To use language in speech, reading and writing, is to extend our bodily equipment and become intelligent human beings (Polanyi, *Knowing and Being*, p. 148).

The Soviet psychologist L.S. Vygotsky died in 1934. Yet one of the most interesting commentaries on acquiring mastery of the written language to be published in recent years is certainly his chapter 'The prehistory of written language' in the posthumous publication, *Mind in Society* (1978). Traditionally, the teaching of reading and the teaching of writing have appeared as strategies for the cultivation of two distinct sets of skills. Vygotsky would replace them with a natural learning process that begins with gesture, moves through the symbolisms of play and drawing to the point where a child discovers that he 'can draw not only things but also speech' – the point of entry into the symbolic behaviour that operates in the two modalities of reading and writing. Vygotsky's account is tentative, incomplete, admitting that much has yet to be discovered.

There is a similar tentativeness in the four chapters concerning reading and writing that comprise Part II: they share a recognition of the value of turning one's powers of observation and of listening upon one's own behaviour as learner or teacher; they share a kind of professional humility, and an honesty in self-questioning.

It is widely recognized (after Vygotsky) that spoken language and written language represent distinct functions, stem from different origins. Nevertheless interaction between the two modes is in practice close and constant – and this is something that is featured by each of the four contributors to Part II. For language development to be 'natural' and for reading and writing to count as 'real', they must, particularly in the early stages, be seen to float on a sea of talk. It is talk of this kind that turns common experience into shared experience – the shared experience that Vygotsky secs as distinguishing human learning from animal learning: 'human learning presupposes a specific social nature and a process by which children grow into the intellectual life of those around them' (*Mind in Society*, p. 88). The contribution to that growth made by a child's ability to use the written language can hardly be overestimated. It is an important insight on Vygotsky's part to see writing and reading, in association with talking and doing, in this context of the broad social/intellectual development of the child; and that is the perspective on literacy that informs the work of the contributors to Part II.

4 Child Language Research and Curriculum*

*Diane DeFord (Southern Illinois University) and
Jerome C. Harste (Indiana University)*

An untested assumption underlying many initial literacy programmes in this country [the USA] is that reading and writing, unlike oral language, require formal instruction and direct teaching in order to be learned. To accent both the fallacy and the reality of this assumption, Frank Smith (1978) was led to conclude that teaching takes place, all too often, in the absence of learning. It is our contention that reading and writing curricula can be designed such that children are provided with the freedom to explore language and grow as language users in much the same way they learned oral language.

Recent language and literacy research (Halliday, 1975; King, 1977, 1980; Heath, 1982; Ferreiro, 1980; Harste, Burke and Woodward, 1981; Harste and Carey, 1979b; DeFord, 1981) has identified three concepts relative to how children learn language which we believe affect curriculum:

1. Classrooms as contexts of literacy simultaneously offer constraints and potentials that affect language learning.
2. Meaningful language settings, where transactions are allowed to occur naturally, are the most conducive settings for literacy learning.
3. The best data upon which to make instructional decisions come from watching learners in supportive and functional language settings.

Classrooms as contexts of literacy

In order to understand the cognitive and linguistic processing operations involved in literacy, one must do so in light of the context in which that processing takes place. Goodenough (1957) pointed out that children and adults, in order to know whatever they need to know to operate in a manner acceptable to others in society, must understand what forms of verbal and non-verbal behaviour are appropriate in what social settings.

Theoretically in making an acceptable response a language user must orchestrate a variety of constraints: where the communication takes place (home, school, playground, etc.), under what conditions the communication is encountered (a sermon, school lesson, an accident), and the

*Reprinted, by permission, from *Language Arts*, vol. 59, no. 6, September 1982.

relationship between the parties involved (teacher–student, parent–child, and the like). The situational context, then, imposes constraints, but because of the generative relationship between text and context, offers certain communicative and meaning potentials.

The significance of *what is communicated* in the classroom is a result of complex processes of interaction among educational goals, background knowledge, and what various participants perceive over time as taking place (Gumperz, 1981). It is the teacher's knowledge of language and language learning that directs actions and decisions made within the ongoing instructional environment. In order to understand instruction, however, the child's interactions within the specific contextual constraints and potentials must be considered.

Two examples will illustrate the importance of teacher and pupil interactions within the context of the instructional setting. The first comes from a study carried out by DeFord (1981). One of the teachers had consistently stressed the necessity of decoding when her readers were reading. While this teacher had indicated that gaining meaning was an important goal of her curriculum, 7-year-old Laura's responses to the 'Burke Interview' (Burke, 1977) give consistent testimony not only to what the pupil had perceived the teacher as having communicated but how such perceptions affected cognitive and linguistic processing:

When you're reading and you come to something you don't know, what do you do?
We sound out the first two letters. After I gots that I try to see another word – if it has three syllables.
Do you ever do anything else?
If I do all that and I still don't get it, I try my vowel rules.
Who is a good reader, and what makes them a good reader?
Rusty, he is a good reader because he always tries the first two letters.
Do you think he ever comes to something he doesn't know when he's reading?
Sometimes he misses periods [full stops]. Even I miss periods sometimes.
What do you think he does then?
If it's a word, a real word we aren't used to, he tries the first two letters, or tries to find a little word.
If you knew that someone was having difficulty reading, how would you help them?
I would try to whisper to them to try the first two letters.
What if that didn't help?
I would pray that God will help them find the word.
What would your teacher do to help that person?
She would say to tell them to use the vowel rules, or look for a small word, or try the first two letters.
Who helped you learn to read?
Sister —— especially, and my kindergarten teacher, my kindergarten teacher taught me some of the consonant sounds. Sister —— taught me consonant digraph sounds and they helped me a lot.
What would you like to do to be a better reader?
I would study my vowel rules and my phonics a lot because that's mostly reading.

Can there be any doubt what her instruction has been?

Nor is this an isolated instance. Jeff, age 6½, carefully drew a picture (see Figure 4.1) when asked to write a story (Harste and Carey, 1979a). He then shared his story about himself and his sister and the things they like to do at home: 'Play Star Wars and go to the zoo'.

Researcher: But, Jeff, we wanted you to write your story.
Jeff: But I don't know how to write. I can't even read yet.
Researcher: I'll bet you do; why don't you go and write the names of what some of the things are that are in your picture.
Jeff: But I can't spell.
Researcher: Just spell them the way you think they are written.

Jeff returned to his seat and wrote the words shown in Figure 4.1. As he wrote *tree* (JRE), he transformed the /t/ sound into a /j/. Charles Read (1971) explains that sounds produced at the same point of articulation are

Figure 4.1 Jeff – uninterrupted story writing

often interchanged in the written text. As he finished his labelling of *tree*, he added the letter 'y' with 'I'll bet there's a silent 'y' on the end of that word'.

In writing *house*, Jeff spelled H-O-S. As he looked up, he said, 'I'll bet there's a silent 'e' on the end of that word,' and he added the final 'e'. This same procedure was followed with T.I.E. Fighter (TIFOTORE), sun (SUE), and x-wing rocket fighter (S-WIGROGOTFORE). Then, in spelling *cloud*, Jeff wrote KLD, stopped and said, 'I'll bet there's a silent 'l' on the end of that word.'

In both Laura and Jeff's cases, it is apparent that what they learned was not what their teachers had believed they taught. None of the teachers were consciously saying that: (i) if you can't spell, you can't write, (ii) pronouncing words is what reading is about, or (iii) language is full of little tricks. However, Laura and Jeff as learners in these language situations were doing what our language learning principle tells us; namely, making contextually orchestrated and appropriate responses. There can be little doubt that these unnatural language behaviours and others are learned via the demonstrations available in classrooms (Smith, 1981).

Language learning data such as these highlight two myths that undergird most curriculum:

Myth 1: Reading and writing processes operate independently of the contexts in which they occur.

Myth 2: Because it is a language generalization, we ought to teach it.

It is important for teachers to have an understanding of what they believe about language and language learning. Instruction, be it by design or default, is theoretically based. Teachers must come to understand how their beliefs affect what children believe about language and language learning. (In Figure 4.2 the arrows that join the teacher circle and the

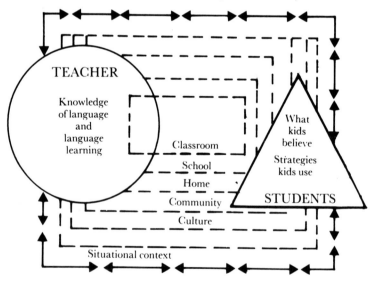

Figure 4.2 Teacher, context, and students: towards a transactional view of literacy instruction

students triangle capture this predictive relationship.) The various contexts surrounding classroom instruction can support or not support the specific instructional context as defined by the teacher. (In Figure 4.2 the boxes represent alternate contexts which affect instruction by heightening or diminishing the teacher variable.) It is through understanding contextual constraints and their relationship to literacy and literacy learning that we can identify, tap, and develop the necessary resources of literacy instruction and literacy learning. In spite of or despite one's particular theoretical position on language and language learning, a first step towards improved curriculum is recognition of this relationship between instruction and learning.

Literacy learning through natural language transactions

'I'm not going to let these kids write another word until they learn to spell.' While this quote from a teacher reflects a certain frustration, it also reflects several important misconceptions about learning: (i) the conventions of language can be learned and practised outside the process and then integrated, at a later date, into the process, (ii) growth is measured through control of convention, and (iii) the learner enters into proficiency through progressive stages of perfection. These misconceptions do not allow us to see literacy as a transactive event.

In Louise Rosenblatt's (1981) words, 'Transaction means, not the interaction between two separate and distinct things, but a creation of a new element by a merging of two elements . . . it is like hydrogen and oxygen merging into water, something new.'

Eight-year-old Robert's writing exemplifies transaction (see Figure 4.3). In attempting to capture the ire of a king on paper, he wrote: 'I don't care how you do it, just do it! I am ruler of this land. If you don't do it, you will be *axlacutted*, if you don't' (Harste, Burke, and Woodward, 1981).

The enjoyment and wonder of language that emerges with the child's invention of 'axlacutted' is as important as was James Joyce's initial use of stream of consciousness writing; it manages to create something unique from the coming together of past and present.

All writing is and must be functional at the point of utterance. The mind, Robert shows us, with his first crossing out of 'axlacutted', is far ahead of hand. The mind–hand span is the reason functional writing is not a stage but a keep-going strategy for all of us. If teachers overfocus on convention and correctness, children begin editing text before they produce it (Atwell, 1980). 'I can't spell' becomes the excuse; failure to engage in the process the result.

Parents and teachers typically allow language exploration with the very young in learning oral language. The child that spoke 'I willn't do it anymore, Mummy,' was rewarded with a hug and a kiss. The parent listened with full understanding of what was meant. In school, all too often,

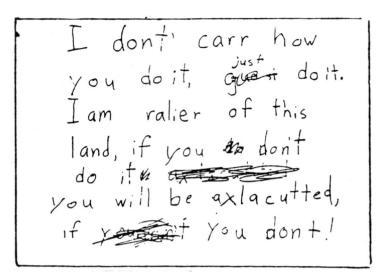

Figure 4.3 Robert – uninterrupted story writing

children's attempts at writing and reading are responded to in quite a different manner.

What we haven't understood is that it is the search for text unity – a search for contextual appropriateness, and orchestrated sign – that is the driving force of literacy. Children's responses to literacy are textual and orchestrated events. It is through the process of self-correction that the reader and writer demonstrates this sensitive understanding of the subtleties of language. In Figure 4.4 the corrections that Zack initiated in the re-reading indicate an understanding of the functional differences between an oral story and a written story. 'There are planes . . . . They're having a dog fight' is an oral language form. 'They are airplanes . . . . They are having a dog dog fight' is the more formal written language form, and reflects Zack's knowledge of how written language texts differ from oral language texts.

It is natural language settings that allow children the opportunity to test their most sensitive language hypotheses. Meaningful language settings, where transactions are allowed to occur naturally, are conducive to language learning. As educators, we cannot condone practices or programmes that: (i) place convention before language expression, (ii) take the meaning and functional purposes of written language out of the learning setting, or (iii) evaluate growth and quality through progressive stages of perfection. On the contrary, the child is the informant. Within this perspective, littering the environment with meaningful print in settings that allow freedom of exploration fosters literacy learning. Teaching, rather than intervening in this process, is best viewed as supporting the learning that is already taking place.

Key:

$\dfrac{\text{They}}{\text{There}}$ = substitued they for there when reading.

Λ = repeated phrase in reading.

Figure 4.4 Zack (age 6) – dictated language experience story and first reading

Evaluating learners in natural language settings

Our contention is that we know little about children's understanding of language from tests and testing settings that constrain and isolate language into 'measurable behaviours'. The myth involved here is important enough to mention early on in this section: If something can't be measured, it isn't worth including in instructional programmes.

33

A good example of this myth is found in many pre-school and kinder-garten programmes. If you ask teachers of young learners if they let the children write messages, the general response is: 'We practise our letters and writing our names.' The belief here is that because the children can't write conventionally, their writing can neither be understood nor measured. The problem with this position is that it is wrong, as is evident when the writing of children as young as 3 and 4 is examined (DeFord, 1980; Harste, Burke, and Woodward, 1981).

David, aged 3, and Dawn, aged 4 (see Figure 4.5), already demonstrate an impressive understanding of the written form of their language. They not only understand the nature of messages but know how to represent their meaning utilizing appropriate conventions (linearity; left-to-right, top-to-bottom directionality; uniformity of size and shape, etc.). Ofer and Chang,

Figure 4.5   David and Dawn – uninterrupted letter writing

both aged 4 (see Figure 4.6), reflect the influence of culture; how their respective Hebrew and Chinese influence written language growth and development. To look at young children's writing and see only scribbles is to miss the socially orchestrated event they represent. What can you find in a scribble? Harste (1982) maintains that in addition to convention, one can find intention, invention, organization, orchestration, experimentation, context, and the list goes on.

Teachers and pupils are in a better position to understand the shortcomings of current testing than are researchers, as they are situated where the evidence is. The curricular question that evaluation must answer is: 'In light of what we know about language, language learning, successful

Figure 4.6 Ofer and Chang – uninterrupted
multicultural writing samples

language users, and written language growth and development, how are
these language users performing?' Recent research with young children
clearly demonstrates that our best evaluative data are provided when we
observe real language users in real language settings using real language. It
is in this functional and naturally supportive environment that we can
decide which of all the resources available the language user used or elected
not to use and on the basis of this information make our best instructional
decision.

Often our best language truths may go untaught, but not unlearned
(Burke, 1980). It is the non-assumptive evaluative stance of open-ended
literacy events that permits us to understand why this might be so.

Implications

The implications for curriculum development are clear. First, classrooms
must become natural language environments. We often seemingly go out of
our way to make classrooms unnatural language settings.

Second, what we believe about language and language learning does
make a difference. Theoretically based instruction is a given. Effective
language arts teachers must continue to grow in their understanding of
language, language learning, successful language users, and how language
users grow and develop. From a position of understanding, searching, and
reflection, teachers can develop classrooms that promote experimentation,
growth, and search among their students.

Third, we must redefine proficiency. The belief that learners enter into proficiency through successive stages of perfection has stifled language production. Literacy is neither a monolithic skill nor a glorified state. One doesn't either have it or not have it. Evaluation must assess situational context, constraints, and transactions. An isolated analysis of conventions stresses the maintative, rather than the generative aspects of literacy, and fails to offer the forward look embodied in Emig's notion of literacy and freedom (1982).

Fourth, curriculum and instruction must be centred around various contexts of literacy. An understanding of the contexts in which we read and write consitutes the basis of curricular structure. Often we see the problem with skill instruction as being a problem in transfer of learning rather than as a problem with the model of language which undergirds that approach to instruction. The teacher who notes that readers are having difficulty reading content area materials must develop print expectancies for content materials in the early years by providing opportunities to encounter science and social studies materials.

Finally, classrooms at all levels must litter their environments with print. Available choice and ready invitation are two natural components of any good literacy learning setting.

References

Atwell, M. (1980) 'The evolution of text: the interrelationship of reading and writing in the composing process,' unpublished PhD thesis, Indiana University.

Burke, C.L. (1977) 'The reading interview,' in *Reading Comprehension Handbook*, ed. B. Farr and D. Strickler, Bloomington, Ind., Indiana University, Language Education Departments.

Burke, C.L. (1980) 'A comprehension-centered reading curriculum: videotape,' in *Reading Comprehension: An Instructional Television Series*, directed and produced by D.J. Strickler, Bloomington, Ind., Indiana University, Language Education Departments.

DeFord, D.E. (1980) 'Young children and their writing,' *Theory into Practice*, vol. 19, pp. 157–62.

DeFord, D.E. (1981) 'Literacy: reading, writing, and other essentials,' *Language Arts*, vol. 58, September, pp. 652–8.

Emig, J. (1982) 'Literacy and freedom,' speech presented at the Conference on College Composition Annual Meeting, April, San Francisco, California.

Ferreiro, E. (1980) 'The relationship between oral and written language: the children's viewpoints,' paper presented at the annual meeting of the International Reading Association, May, St Louis, Missouri.

Goodenough, W. (1957) 'Cultural anthropology and linguistics,' in *Report of the Seventh Round Table Meeting on Linguistics and Language Study*, monograph Series on Languages and Linguistics (vol. 9), ed. I.P. Garvin, Washington DC, Georgetown University Press.

Gumperz J. (1981) 'Conversational inferences and classroom learning,' in *Ethnography and Language in Educational Settings*, ed. J. Green and C. Wallet, Norwood, NJ, Ablex, pp. 3–24.

Halliday, M.A.K. (1975) *Learning How to Mean*, London, Edward Arnold.

Harste, J.C., Burke, C.L. and Woodward, V.A. (1981) *Children, Their Language, and World: Initial Encounters with Print*, NIE Final Report no. NIE-G-79-0132, Bloomington, Ind., Indiana University, Language Education Departments.

Harste, J.C. and Carey, R.F. (1979a) 'Classroom constraints and the language process,' in *Cognitive Psychology and Reading Comprehension*, ed. J. Flood, Newark, NJ, International Reading Association.

Harste, J.C. and Carey, R.F. (1979b) 'Comprehension as setting,' in *New Perspectives on Comprehension*, Monograph in Language and Reading Studies, ed. J. Harste and R. Carey, Bloomington, Ind., School of Education, Indiana University, October, pp. 4–22.

Harste, J.C. (1982) 'What's in a scribble?' speech given at the Seventh Annual Lester Smith Conference on Educational Research, February, Bloomington, Indiana.

Heath, S.B. (1982) 'Protean shapes in literacy events: ever shifting oral and literate traditions,' in *Spoken and Written Language*, ed. D. Tannen, Norwood, NJ, Ablex.

King, M. (1977) 'Evaluating reading,' *Theory into Practice*, vol. 14, pp. 407–18.

King, M. (1980) 'Learning how to mean in written language,' *Theory into Practice*, vol. 19, pp. 463–9.

Read, C. (1971) 'Preschool children's knowledge of English phonology,' *Harvard Educational Review*, vol. 41, pp. 1–34.

Rosenblatt, L. (1981) 'Focus on literature,' paper presented at the 4th Annual CELT Rejuvenation Conference, May, Rochester, Michigan.

Smith, F. (1978) *Understanding Reading*, New York, Holt, Rinehart, & Winston.

Smith, F. (1981) 'Demonstrations, engagement and sensitivity: a revised approach to language learning,' *Language Arts*, vol. 52, pp. 103–12.

5 Do We Teach the Way We Read?*

Lola Brown (English Adviser for the Central Northern Region of South Australia)

Recently someone told me about *A Candle for Saint Anthony* by Eleanor Spence. Told me enough, that is, for me to want to read it. So I did.

In the last few years I've spent a lot of time thinking about children's reading and writing, partly because I've been working with two groups of teachers, one examining reading and the other examining ways of connecting reading and writing. Along the way, we've been delving into articles about reading and trying to come to some conclusions about what the act of reading 'literature', in its broadest sense, really entails.

Like most people, I have to find things out for myself. With that focus, I tried to jot down the impressions that remained with me most powerfully after I'd finished *A Candle for Saint Anthony*: the things I'd noticed while I was reading and those I'd remembered afterwards. This is the collection I was left with:

The whole 'rich man's' suburban life: swimming pool: clothes: mostly a flavour rather than details.	(The frantic pursuit of idleness I see in some young people – sun, pleasure, fun – yes, that's how it is.)
The plane journey to Europe – all the details: I'm not even sure which ones are the book's and which ones are mine.	(Vivid memories of my own first experience of this; I loved every moment of it.)
The Vienna woods – damp, overgrown – 'the gentle northern light' (I can even quote!)	(I remember, poignantly, my English country childhood.)
The relationship between the two boys.	(Like some deep attachments in the adolescence of both my children, and mine – perfectly natural and transient – but new and individual in the book.)
The contrived ending.	(I remember wondering, about thirty pages before the end, how the writer would resolve it: there didn't seem to be anything further to be done or said.)
The two boys, as people.	(Facets of each one reminding me of a host of young people I've known.)
The mother, left in Australia with her adolescent son in Europe.	(I wouldn't be able to cope with that kind of separation, not knowing it would end.)

*Reprinted, by permission, from *English in Australia*, no. 62, October 1982.

Now I was saddled with some highly uncomfortable reflections, as a teacher of English in secondary schools of some twenty years' experience:

a novel has in it: { people events places/contexts; material and emotional landscapes } as I read, I'm adding stories and comment { I remember... That's the way things are... That's not the way things are... What if... suppose that... (in relation to me and my life and to the characters and their lives). }

And this is what I have to conclude:

1. I've never *read* a book in the way I '*teach*' it. That is, what I select to talk about in class is the product of *retrospective vision*, while students are still involved in the process of acquiring the author's world. A mis-match!
2. Only one of my responses had a literary bent, yet what I select to talk about is often related to the literary devices, conventions and forms the author uses to construct this 'reality'.
   These I've absorbed subconsciously, as I've reconstructed it for myself. My actual dialogue with the author has been at the level of *remembering, speculating, associating*.
3. No one else on earth could read this book in the way I did.

Two particular articles I'd read recently came to my mind at this stage. In one, by James Britton, I was struck by this comment: 'Active response to a work of literature involves what might be called an unspoken monologue of responses – a fabric of comment, speculation, relevant autobiography' (Britton, 1968, p. 36).

That crystallized what I'd just found out about my own reading of fiction. One way in which I'd made Eleanor Spence's world 'real' was by filling it in with details from similar experiences of my own.

In another article, 'Using story structure in the classroom', Stephanie McConaughy (1980) demonstrates how the ability to process story items develops from child to adulthood, and how this is a crucial factor in determining the way in which a story is comprehended. That article suggested to me one reason why children reached different conclusions about a shared novel, and why some simply couldn't perceive the complex connectedness of events that would lead them to see what I wanted everyone to see!

Uncomfortable reflections on past practice. 'Write a character study of A'; 'Explain how the author's handling of time reinforces the theme of the novel'; 'Discuss the importance of setting in this novel!' What relation does this sort of writing bear to the things I'd just found out? It ignores totally the reality of the experience of reading a novel – or anything else of a literary nature, for that matter. It also ignores the fact that, if children haven't reached the stage of the then-automatic adult processing of a story's parts to perform the balancing act that goes on in the mature mind in connecting and ordering those parts relatively to one another, they aren't in a position to make sensible statements in response to those questions.

I can. Perhaps because, after thirty years of reading stories with the trained expectation of applying conventional literary criteria to them, the habit is ingrained. To ingrain it in my students, of course, I always have to go back; reread; make the patterns explicit. I don't do it when I'm reading for me. The two ways of reading, the 'unspoken monologue of responses' and the processing of story items, must be occurring simultaneously in my mind, and reinforcing one another. But the powerful one – the one that leaves reverberating echoes when the novel's finished – is undoubtedly the first, when I'm reading for me.

What can I do about this in a classroom? I can't ignore what I think I've found out. Of course I want my students to have the equipment they need to perceive an author's messages and intentions. So I have to find out how they are coping with the 'processing' individually, even if it is a shared class novel, and then devise strategies to enable them to develop and refine that ability. First, though, I need to know how they're doing it.

But I also want my students to know that what's really happening as they read is what's really happening to every reader. More importantly, I want them to know that it's *legitimate*! Writing is the most common means by which we, as teachers, endow anything with legitimacy. It's our seal of significance. So I have to have some of the personal 'comment, speculation and relevant autobiography' written down.

This is what I might do.

I might have a class keep two running commentaries as they read a novel. I might ask them to use the left-hand side of a book for recording what happens in the story, progressively, and set aside 5–10 minutes at the end of each lesson we spent on the novel for them to do this. Any notes, any direct comment on new things that have happened in the story, would go on the left-hand page. On the right-hand page, all through the study of a novel, I might make the writing a kind of response–journal, composed of the sorts of things I described at the beginning of this chapter.

I think I would have to do it myself and show them, to start with, because if I am to be faithful to the point made earlier about the individual nature of response, I couldn't determine for the whole class which of these possibilities of remembering, speculating and associating would operate most powerfully for any one child during the reading of a particular chapter or passage. I might have to structure and direct more, but I wouldn't want the writing to seem like a series of carefully placed set essays.

I would expect the talk in the classroom to support this approach too. It strikes me that if our ability to make the world of a novel 'real' depends very much on the experiences we bring to it, sharing those experiences might trigger appropriate ones in other people or fill in the gaps where they have none to bring.

At the end, I'd like to see what happened. I'd be interested to read the completed direct commentary on the book side by side with the personal, journal-type writing. I think I'd also know a lot more about why individual students were receiving different messages from the novel than I'd find out from comprehension exercises on it or from set essays. At the end also I would quite probably spend a lesson or two telling them, or asking them to find, the literary conventions, because I like them. Some of them might, too. But only when the real reading was finished.

References

Britton, J. (1968), 'Response to Literature' in J.R. Squire (ed.), *Response to Literature*, Urbana, Illinois, N.C.T.E.

McConaughy, S. (1980), 'Using Story Structure in the Classroom', *Language Arts*, 57 (2), February, pp. 157–65.

6   The Teaching Craft: Telling, Listening, Revealing*

Donald M. Murray (The University of New Hampshire)

The mirror surprises. The grey beard has turned white. The apprentice teacher is asked to speak as a master. The amateur who came to teaching late teaches teachers, and what was chutzpah is confirmed by rank. I have fooled them all.

But not myself. I am still apprentice to two trades which can not be learned: writing and teaching. I am thankful for the anxiety of each blank page, the stagefright before each new class.

I spend my time looking ahead to what I have not tried, to what I have not learned. But when I am asked to look back over my shoulder I discover reason in what I had believed was accident. I seem to have done three kinds of teaching, each new stage building on the one before, as if my progress had been calculated, not the result of tossing away my notes after every class.

Teaching by telling

When we begin to teach we have to learn to teach standing up. When I came to teaching nineteen years ago I thought the classroom a casual place where we would converse. Of course, I would do most of the conversing. They would listen, and they would learn.

I found myself on a stage playing to an audience that did not particularly want to listen or to learn. I was expected to stimulate, motivate, entertain, perform.

I found I had two hands, enormous hands, and no place to put them. Sometimes my right hand got tied in the cord of the window blind and I was tied to the window on the right side of the classroom. I would dismiss the class and try to get untied before the next class arrived. One of my colleagues confessed he took home a lectern and practised letting go. He had been frozen to the lectern for each entire class.

I found that I chewed on a right knuckle when I spoke. It did not clarify my mumble. At times I spoke so fast I could not even follow what I was saying myself, and at other times the silence rose in the room like an irreversible tide. I think it was at least a year that I only taught the upper left-hand corner of the ceiling, another year before I faced the blurred faces, a third year before they turned to people. It took me longer to have the

* Reprinted, by permission, from *English Education*, vol. 14, no. 1, February 1982.

courage to turn my back on the class and use the blackboard. I was certain if I turned away from them they'd leave – or attack.

I had to learn to pace the class. Remember that wonderful scene in the film *Starting Over*, when Burt Reynolds teaches for the first time, tells the class everything he knows about writing, and dismisses the class? Then a student raises his hand and says that only five minutes have elapsed.

To teach well standing up we have to be able to see through the complexities of the subjects we have learned to the unifying simplicities. We have to learn to repeat without seeming to repeat, to hear the question asked instead of the question expected, to read the audience, to teach by telling.

In teaching teachers many of us, myself very much included, advocate inductive methods of teaching, forgetting that we had to learn to teach by telling first, to perform, to get attention and hold it, to command the classroom. Teaching standing up isn't easy; it's an art in itself. And we have colleagues who make a respectable career of teaching by telling. But after approximately five years of teaching standing up I was moved to a new classroom, and I found I had a new craft to learn.

Teaching by listening

The chairs were not in rows, and there was no desk at the front of the room. There was a great rectangle of tables. I would have to learn to teach sitting down.

I couldn't do it at first. I had in the old classroom occasionally, towards the end of the semester, slid out from behind the lectern and leaned against the front of the desk trying to appear casual. And there had been moments when I had even perched on the desk, but I was still looking down at my students. I was not really teaching sitting down.

At first I brought a lectern into the classroom and used it at the head of the table. And then for a semester or two I hopped up and down, sometimes standing, sometimes sitting. I found it was an enormous challenge to teach sitting down.

When at last I found I could remain in my seat, sitting at the same level as my students, I listened in a different way, and perhaps they were able to speak in a different way when I was not looking down at them and they were not looking up at me.

I still needed to be able to teach by telling. I did not discard that discipline as much as I built on it. I knew my students would not leave or attack, even if they should. I knew how to pace and clarify. I knew how to read their faces. At last I could begin to listen to what they were saying. When I did listen I found that they were discovering in their writing and their reading what I had been telling them, and they found it before I told them. Somehow I had developed an environment in which we wrote writing and read writing and in which we were able to share what we were learning.

At times I was a bit worried, perhaps a bit hurt. I remember once when I was called out of the room, the discussion had not been going well, but when I came back in the discussion was going very well indeed. I slipped back into my seat; they didn't notice I was there. But after a while I was able to enter into the discussion and share what I was learning from the text and from them. I hadn't been excluded, just the opposite; when I was able to listen they were able to include me in their learning.

I had a new role to play. I could still teach by telling. My students seemed to appreciate the times I told, but I noticed they were much shorter lectures, hardly lectures at all. They would sometimes be opening remarks, the establishing of a topic to be discussed; or concluding remarks, the summing up of what had been discussed, an effort to put the discussion into context.

My preparation for class changed. It focused more on my own learning through my own reading and writing, so that I was able to enter into the discussion of what we were learning during the time of the course. My teaching was more fun, more spontaneous. I learned from my students, and they were excited that I was learning from them as they learned from me. I became quicker on my feet sitting down than standing up – the apparently contradictory metaphor was accurate. I learned to react quicker and better, to take advantage of the accidents that led to learning. And as my class gave me more time to learn I gave them more time to learn.

It took me at least ten years to learn to teach sitting down. I felt I had at last learned teaching by listening when Tim said at the end of a class, 'That was the best class we've had.' And I was able to answer, 'I know. I didn't speak for the first fifty minutes.'

Teaching by revealing

In the past few years I have found that I am exploring a new form of teaching. It has seemed a natural evolution. I still at times teach by telling and I still, even more of the time, teach by listening. But I also realize that I have become comfortable enough to teach by revealing my own learning.

This is related to what Frank Smith calls 'demonstrations'. He has pointed out the importance of showing how something is done in a number of his articles and in his book *Writing and the Writer* (New York, Holt Rinehart & Winston, 1982). But demonstration can and should be an effective way of telling. The teacher shows the student how to do a particular kind of writing, or demonstrates a particular method of reading. The focus is on showing how to do something properly.

The same connotation holds in the modelling by teachers that Richard Beach and others are interested in studying. It is important for the teachers of teachers, especially, to model the kind of teaching they advocate. Too many of our education courses are taught by methods and attitudes that contradict what is being taught.

I suppose that I am demonstrating and that I am modelling, but I feel that I am at least extending these activites as I am learning how to reveal myself learning.

More and more I teach by writing in public. I have even, when invited to do a 'reading', responded by offering to do a 'writing'. This, in part, brings the beginner's terror back to my teaching and keeps me from being bored by the sound of my own voice. But I think it does something more than that. Both writing and reading are essentially private acts, but if we are to teach them we must find ways to make them public.

When I face the blackboard to write in public I do not know what I will hear myself say. I re-create the experience of the blank page. I write to find out what I will write. It does not matter whether I write badly or well. Mistakes can be more productive and instructive than writing without mistakes. On my page alone I often see a breakdown in syntax at the point of a breakthrough in meaning. I am not looking, however, for correctness or incorrectness; I am looking for what Maxine Kumin calls 'the informing material'. I am listening for voice; I am seeking the hint of an order.

And then, another time, I am working in public to make a text come clear. I cut, I add, I reorder. I follow the conventions of language, or I ignore them, if that is what I have to do to make the meaning clear. My students share their search for meaning with me. We teach each other by learning.

We read a text together, following false scents, racing down trails that suddenly stop, losing our bearings, helping each other find meaning in the prose and sharing with the writer, who may be teacher or may be student, the many ways that meaning may be found in a text and made clear.

I no longer know what I will teach or what I will learn in a class, or from a class. I am never sure, in fact, what has been learned. But I do know that learning is taking place, for I am learning, and my students are learning, and we are revealing our learning to each other.

7 Talking About Writing: A Classroom Experiment*

Phil Cormack (*Language Arts Advisory Teacher, Wattle Park Teacher's Centre, South Australia*)

This is not a success story, but it does have a happy ending!

My conferencing[1] ideas failed, but from that failure came the important lesson that, as a teacher, I often underestimate children's ability to teach each other. A second principle has also emerged: through experimenting with children in a classroom, both teacher and students can develop a feeling of learning together and as a result school work becomes more meaningful in the eyes of the children.

Beginning

My action research project began as an inquiry into teacher–student conferencing but soon expanded into many other areas of classroom practice and philosophy. I sometimes felt like the person who picks at the thread of a jumper and keeps on going until he realizes the whole garment is being unravelled.

My initial aim was to discover whether the strategy of setting up a predictable structure for student–teacher conferences about writing would enable the student rather than the teacher to control that conference. I also wanted to test whether the particular conference strategy of the teacher not reading the student's work and thus forcing students to talk about their writing or at least read it out loud, would be beneficial in helping them to redraft. My underlying belief is that a 'conference' should be a *two-way* problem-solving, idea-sharing meeting – in this case between one student and the teacher.

I was going to evaluate these hunches by the 'before and after' technique – compare the draft before the conference with the redraft after. I suppose my vision, no doubt fostered by my adolescent magazine reading, was of a weak spindly first draft before the 'Miracle Charles Atlas Conference Course' followed by the strength and poise of the post-conference piece. That's not how it happened, but, thanks to the enthusiasm and good sense of the children in my class, all was not lost.

Plan of action

This is how I began. I had been working on a classroom scheme where the children wrote, often on topics of their own choice, within a restricted time.

*Reprinted, by permission, from *English in Australia*, no. 58, December 1981.

My first moves were to set up a classroom structure that would enable me to talk to the children individually – something that I could not do under the scheme as it was. I explained to the children that there would be five 15-minute periods a week exclusively for writing. One of these would be reserved for teacher input only: new ideas, forms, techniques, workshops. In addition I carded story starters, word play ideas and suggestions so there would be no lack of ideas for writing. The other four sessions were, in the main, the children's writing for whatever purpose they chose. Within these periods I asked the children to keep me informed of what they were writing and with whom, if sharing a task, by keeping a 'writing record card' that they showed me when starting a new piece.

Next came a rather intensive re-education course on the 'process' of writing where I attempted to wean the children off the idea of one-shot drafts or, almost as bad, one-shot drafts which were capitalized, checked for spelling and rewritten 'neatly'. Relying heavily on articles by Donald Graves and Don Murray, I presented writing as a three-stage process of pre-writing, writing (the first draft) and re-writing, before you had something worth publishing. We studied, as a class, each of these in turn.

Pre-writing

In looking at pre-writing, I stressed that ideas for writing are found anywhere and everywhere. The class enjoyed brainstorming nifty titles, breathless opening lines and embarrassing or funny situations. Of particular value was Mike Dilena's idea of asking the children to write down everything *they* knew about – hobbies, unique occurrences, interesting or happy or sad situations they had been in. We had sessions where the children just tried their hand at noting ideas, rough plans and outlines for stories. I particularly remember one session where I struck a chord with the children through describing how I avoided sitting down to begin writing a college essay or article, and assured them the experience of not knowing how to begin was not unique to them. I made the point of legitimizing talk as a basic pre-writing activity.

Thus my first conferencing objective was to talk to the children to help them to decide what to write about and to 'rehearse' their writing before they set pen to paper. However, I noticed the children in these conferences did one of three things. Some children came to the conference resenting that they had to think too much about the story before it began: they were members of the school of 'let the story unfold as I write' – a legitimate technique. A second group was basically out to please me and went through the motions rather than seeing it as a means to improve their writing. The third group had, horror of horrors, cheated by talking to their friends and decided about their writing before the conference. These conferences were marked by pained expressions on the children's faces as they made it clear I was holding up the writing.

Uneasy that all was not going to plan, but pleased with the children's enthusiasm for writing, I moved on to the easiest of the three stages to tackle, the writing of the first draft. Heartened by the reaction to my self-revelations in the pre-writing section, I brought to school and displayed as many old first drafts and rough copies of my own writing as I could lay my hands on.

I had also been writing with the children occasionally, and displayed these stories. Once again, through seeing scribbled margin notes, untidy writing and scratchings out, the children saw that their experiences were not unique. When doing first drafts I encouraged the children to write as fast as possible in order to get down all their ideas and information. They reponded enthusiastically to this idea though a few tended to 'stew' over the right way to begin, or correctness.

Redrafting

We had come to the point where I felt the experiment proper would begin – looking at redrafting. It is a fairly common experience among teachers that it is difficult to get children to be enthusiastic about and see the value in redrafting. Forewarned by similar experiences myself I felt that the use of one-to-one conferences would provide a means to making redrafting easier and meaningful for the children. Rather than introduce the idea of redrafting on a whole-class basis, as I had done with pre-writing and writing first drafts, I explained to the children that any piece of writing from their writing sessions that they wished to make a good copy of for display or performance, had to be first discussed with me in a redrafting conference. I therefore tackled it mainly on a one-to-one basis. My only whole-class session was to tell the children that they needed to come to the conference with a question they wanted to ask about their story – the idea being that they opened the conference with an issue of their own, not mine.

My conferencing strategies were never to read the children's work at that stage and to help along discussion with questions like, 'What are you trying to say?' or 'What's the best part of your story?' My basic hunch was that redrafting would never be meaningful to the children if done on the teacher's terms. My whole approach would be to throw the responsibility for assessing the work on the writer.

The results were disappointing. A few children, the successful writers mainly, used the conferences to sort out issues in their own minds and proceeded to improve the first draft on their own terms. For the others it failed, and exploring the reasons has given me a list of mistakes not to repeat:

1. Many children have no experience of questioning their work to find out if it says what they mean it to say.
2. Many children, confronted on their own by a teacher, redirect their

thinking to agree with what the teacher is saying or to what they think he wants them to say.

3. A teacher who tries to discuss work with every child ends up with very long queues of bored children.
4. Most children have no idea of how to improve their writing because they have no concept of what makes good writing.
5. Because the children were writing for their own purposes they were mainly writing for themselves or their peers. By discussing it only with me they weren't having contact with their audience.

In spite of the fact that my conferencing experiment was not successful, I sensed that many children were becoming interested in the self-evaluative approach to redrafting. So following my instincts I set out in new directions. I was able to do this quite comfortably because I had been stressing all along to the children that the conferencing and writing periods were an experiment from which I hoped we would all learn.

New directions

In casting about for material to help me overcome the shortcomings I have mentioned, I found Moffett and Wagner's book *Student Centred Language Arts and Reading K-13* and Murray's article 'What makes readers read?' most useful. Moffett's enthusiasm for the small group process provided a means of overcoming the problems of teacher domination as well as the long queues of bored children:

> Most group work in conventional schooling fails to foster exchanges between peers because the group is too large or the teacher dominates (p. 35).

> If learners don't process each other's work in groups they cannot gain enough experience with the language arts to become good at them. When a teacher has to process everything that's written, students can't possibly write enough (p. 35).

I now talked to the children about responding to each other's group work rather than bringing it to me. I asked at a class meeting for suggestions as to how 'writing conference' groups could be organized. Their ideas boiled down to:

1. Consider one person's writing at a time and that person is the group leader.
2. Find something good to say about the person's writing.

To these I added my own:

1. Make criticisms, but always with a suggestion for improvement.
2. The person whose writing is being considered must lead discussion by

asking for any help he wanted. I gave these examples:

- Is this clear?
- Do you like my ending?
- I don't know how to put . . .
- What's a better word for . . .?

3. You must listen to others' criticisms and suggestions, but remember it is you who decides which to act on and which to reject, it is *your* piece of writing.

We had the 'writing conferences' twice a week for 15 minutes in groups of four children.

I felt the introduction of these groups needed to be combined with a consideration of 'good' writing and writing techniques if the children were to have any criteria by which to judge their own or others' writing. Using Murray's 'What makes readers read?' and Rosa and Eschholz's 'The writer's checklist', I came up with a 'beginners' list' of criteria by which to judge their own writing and which they could relate to their own experiences in story-writing:

1. Writing needs to be clear – the writer should know what he wants to say and see that it comes through.
2. The title needs to be effective or appropriate – a lure to the reader.
3. The opening needs to be effective or appropriate – to encourage the reader to continue.
4. The ending should 'fit' and not feel tacked on.
5. Readers like detail – the flash of the dagger, the flow of blood in battle.
6. Readers are people and people like to know about other people and how they think and act – particularly in unusual or stressful situations.

While acknowledging that the list is by no means complete, I found it a particularly useful starting point.

Response to the new scheme was generally more positive and purposeful than before. The small groups with clear guidelines gave all children plenty of experience of reconsidering their writing. As children were often writing for their peers, they were getting immediate verbal and non-verbal feedback about their stories direct from their audience.

To help the children in their groups and to reinforce the points mentioned in the list, I often asked volunteers to put first drafts on overhead projector transparencies and held whole-class conferences on them, focusing on one aspect only, e.g. the opening or use of detail. One particular favourite of the class, and a technique for which I never had a problem with volunteers, was a 'fishbowl' conference between myself and a student with their writing on a transparency while the whole class listened and later commented. In these I would plead for more information about certain characters or be positively ghoulish in my desire for a more bloodthirsty and detailed account of the battle or criticize an ending for not fitting with my reading of the story. All of this was taken in good humour by all concerned and, I felt, improved the group work, although I had to beware they didn't go overboard for a particular style or approach just because I had stressed it.

Some children still wanted to see me about their stories and with them I had meaningful conferences because it was through their choice. Sometimes I sat in on writing workshops as a group member – especially if I had written with the class – although I had to be wary of not dominating the group. I found a one-to-one situation particularly valuable with children lacking in confidence. They found that immediate response from me on lack of clarity in their thoughts, and the increased speed with which their thoughts were written down, most useful.

By the time end-of-year commitments ended our writing sessions, I felt we had discovered some promising lines of attack for next year. Certainly the children were approaching the task of writing with greater optimism and flair now that they felt they had some understanding of the writing process. They also had a greater sense of control over their writing because they decided what to write about and evaluated, on their own terms, its effectiveness and quality. Of course, not all was rosy. Some children were setting themselves patently low standards and others tended to lock themselves into one particular style – the 'funny fantasy' particularly springs to mind – which tended to limit their writing experiences.

Further plans

Given these pluses and minuses I have new plans and approaches for the new school year with the same children:

1. Continued discussion about and emphasis on: group skills, listening, responding, staying on task.
2. Teacher modelling of group behaviour and conference techniques.
3. Looking at literature for models of style and technique:
   - ending chapters on exciting note
   - how people react under stress
   - introducing and describing characters
   - use of dialogue
   If tackled in an experimental, 'have a go' mood, even mimicking authors' styles might prove illuminating.
4. Now that confidence has been established, more teacher intervention to raise expectations and standards. 'I know you can do better – you *will* do better' before redrafting. Once a child has gone through the strenuous process of drafting, redrafting and proofing, I accept their work without criticism and with praise.

From my experience, one point has emerged above all others as most valuable. When I set out to try my conferencing ideas in writing, I did more than simply test a teaching technique. By involving the children in the than simply test a teaching technique. By involving the children in the experiment and inviting them to join with me in investigating writing, I unwittingly removed one major barrier to children improving their own work. If I may be forgiven for re-using my earlier 'Charles Atlas' analogy: teachers so often are bullies who go around kicking sand in children's faces. We communicate in so many words 'I know I am the expert and judge concerning what is good writing'. So rather than encouraging them to flex their own writing muscles, we often as not deflate their egos and offer pat answers rather than challenging questions. By admitting that I too was a learner-writer and then indicating some paths we could explore together, I gave the children power over their own learning. Of course my job has not ended there. I now have to encourage the defeatists to try, help steer some out of blind alleys, and ensure enough variety to challenge the bravest among the children. All of this will probably lead me back to ways I can valuably conference individually with children.

As the school year ended I felt it might be valuable to see what insights the children had gained into writing. I therefore asked my principal, who has a most un-principal-like relationship with the class, to talk to them in small groups about writing.

I conclude with some of their ideas about writing:

Q. What are you getting out of the writing programme?
A. It's worth the struggle because you're rewarded at the end.
A. We found out how or what authors are like and how hard it is for them to write a book.

Q. What part of writing do you most enjoy?
A. Finishing it!
A. I like thinking about it.
A. I don't like the second bit [writing].
A. [Writing the first draft] because at first you've got all these ideas you can write down. Then before you know it, you've finished.

Q. What's the difference between getting help from your friends and help from Mr Cormack?
A. Well, Mr C. might . . . he's only one person . . . might give us ideas that we don't like and where there's a lot of people we get different choices.
A. Yeah, because most of the children are our age and they might like the things that we like and they can give you more ideas.

Q. Who are you writing for?
A. When you're doing it for yourself you're really proud of it and you're doing it for other people as well.

Some comments on sharing stories:

A. The thing I really like is because when you do the story – in grade one I used to remember everyone used to say 'Oh that is good!' and it wasn't and now you can get their honest opinion on the story you are writing.

kids help you out and then you go back and write it out very good –
you know the parts you missed out.
.A. Sometimes you don't get a true opinion about your writing.
Sometimes people go 'It's all right' – they've got other things to do.

Note

1. 'Conferencing' is a term that has gained currency since Donald Graves's visit to
   Australia in 1980. Graves uses the term to describe discussion between teacher
   and pupil at the draft stage of writing.

References

Moffett, J. and Wagner, B.J. (1968), *Student-Centred Language Arts and Reading, K–13*.
(Second Edition), Boston, Houghton Mifflin.
Murray, D. (1979) 'What Makes Readers Read?', *English Journal*, May.

Part III

And Gladly Teach

A Clerk there was of Oxenford . . .
Noght o word he spak more than was nede . . .
Souninge in moral virtu was his speche,
And gladly wolde he lerne, and gladly teche

(Chaucer, *Canterbury Tales*, Prologue).

In what ways will children in my classroom learn? How, in consequence, shall I teach? When we consider how deeply the practice of teaching draws upon the individual resources, the *personality*, of a teacher, we might well ask whether there are any helpful generalizations to be made about it. If, as DeFord and Harste suggest (pp. 27–37 above), English teachers have harboured the delusion that wherever a generalization about language exists they must teach it, I would guess a similar charge about pedagogical generalizations could be laid at the doors of teacher-educators.

Nevertheless, an important general inference arises from the three accounts of teaching that follow: a teacher must remain responsible for the teaching and learning that goes on in his or her classroom and cannot relinquish that responsiblity to any outsider: programme or kit or textbook or administrator. Teaching/learning consists in interacting behaviours and a teacher must be free to interact. I think this point is very clearly made, and further developed, in the report of case studies published under the title *Beyond Surface Curriculum*, by A.M. Bussis, E.A. Chittenden and M. Amarel. To launch into further generalizations, these authors divide teaching styles (and types of curriculum) into four categories according to the degree to which (i) teachers, and (ii) students in the class contribute to decisions as to *what* is taught and *how* it is taught. Traditional *unidirectional* education (teacher contribution high, child contribution low) needs in their view to give way to an *interactive* model (teacher contribution high, child contribution high) – the product, clearly, of teacher/class negotiation. But the heaviest losers in the fourfold classification are the *laissez-faire* classroom (child contribution high, teacher contribution low) and the classroom where the teacher has abdicated responsibility – the users of teacher-proof kits or prescriptive programmes (teacher contribution low, child contribution low).

Individualized instruction may at one time have seemed to offer us an ideal: but the ideal of the interactive classroom is not that. There we must balance a degree of individual learning with the benefits of corporate learning: teacher and students become a community in which *they learn with each other and from each other*; in which communal experiences maintain a sense of community that allows individuals to work happily on their own separate tasks and interests: but also a talking community where interests are shared, where enthusiasms are infectious – and where talking has scope enough to become a major mode of learning.

8 Demonstrations, Engagement and Sensitivity: The Choice Between People and Programs*

Frank Smith (Lansdowne Professor of Language in Education, University of Victoria, British Columbia)

In an article in *Language Arts* entitled 'Demonstrations, engagement and sensitivity: a revised approach to language learning' (Smith, 1981), I discussed the proposition that children's brains learn constantly. Everything demonstrated to children by act or by artefact is likely to be learned by them. Educators should not ask why children often do not learn what we believe they are taught, but rather what they might be learning in its place. Teachers may not teach what they think they are teaching.

In this chapter I shall consider some implications of the view that children are always likely to learn what is demonstrated to them. In particular I shall argue that the critical question confronting teachers of language arts today is not how writing, reading and other aspects of literacy should be taught, but what we want children to learn. This is not a question for research to resolve; the relevant evidence is available. Rather the question requires a decision, upon which the future of teachers and of literacy may depend.

The decision to be made is whether responsibility for teaching children to write and to read should rest with people or with programs, with teachers or with technology. This is not a matter of selecting among alternative methods of teaching children the same things. Different educational means achieve different ends (Olson and Bruner, 1974). The issue concerns who is to be in control of classrooms, the people in the classroom (teachers and children) or the people elsewhere who develop programs. Different answers will have different consequences.

The argument will cover the following points: (i) that programs cannot teach children literacy (though they may be extremely efficient at teaching other things), (ii) that programs and teachers are currently competing for control of classrooms, and (iii) that teachers will lose this contest if it is fought in terms of those things that programs teach best. Of course, I must be more explicit about what I mean by 'programs'. But first I shall briefly restate some relevant points from the first of these two articles.

The ever-learning brain

Analysis of the enormous complexity and essential arbitrariness of the conventions of language that all children master who succeed in using and

* Reprinted, by permission, from *Language Arts*, vol. 58, no. 6, September 1981.

understanding the familiar language used around them led to the proposition that children's brains strive to learn all the time. Children cannot tolerate situations in which it is not possible for learning to take place. Boredom or confusion are as aversive to brains whose natural and constant function is to learn as suffocation is to lungs deprived of the opportunity to breathe.

Learning occurs in the presence of *demonstrations*, and what is learned is whatever happens to be demonstrated at the time (or rather the learner's interpretation of the demonstration, the way the learner makes sense of it). Learning never takes place in the absence of demonstrations, and what is demonstrated is always likely to be learned. Demonstrations are continually and inevitably provided by people and by products, by acts and by artefacts. A teacher bored with what is being taught demonstrates that what is taught is boring. A reading or writing workbook containing nonsensical exercises demonstrates that reading and writing can be nonsensical. Demonstrations can also be self-generated; they can be constructued by imagination and reflection in the privacy of the mind.

Learning is an interaction, a concurrent event rather than a consequence of a demonstration. Learning is immediate and vicarious, the demonstration becoming in effect the learner's own learning trial. I termed this interaction *engagement* to indicate the intimate meshing of the learner's brain with the demonstration.

Engagement with a demonstration will occur if there is *sensitivity*, defined as the absence of expectation that learning will not take place. The expectation that learning something will be difficult, punishing or unlikely is itself learned and can be devastating in its long-term consequences. Like all other learning, the expectation that learning will not occur is established by demonstrations.

To learn to read and to write, children require (i) demonstrations of how reading and writing can be used for evident meaningful purposes, (ii) opportunities for engagement in such meaningful uses of reading and writing, and (iii) freedom from the unnecessary undermining of sensitivity. Obviously teachers are able (or should be able) to provide such demonstrations and opportunities for engagement. The question is whether programs can also meet the three requirements.

The nature of programs

Programs appear in a number of educational guises – as sets of materials, workbooks, activity kits, guidelines, manuals, record sheets, objectives, television series, and computer-based instructional sequences. The history of instructional programs is probably as long as that of education itself, but they began proliferating during the present century as experts in other fields (such as linguistics, psychology, computer science, and test construction) and other external agents increasingly asserted views about what and how teachers should teach. The assumption that programs could achieve educational ends beyond the capacity of autonomous teachers grew rapidly in North America with the educational panic that followed Sputnik in 1957 and the coincidental development of management systems and operational techniques for the solution of logistical problems. (A senior official of the International Reading Association once announced gratefully that the National Aeronautics and Space Administration would help to eliminate literacy by contributing the technology that had delivered men to the moon.) The pervasiveness of programmatic approaches to education is now expanding further and faster as the development of microcomputers makes a new technology available for the delivery of pre-packaged instruction.

Despite their manifold variety in education, programs have a number of common elements, the most critical being that they transfer instructional decision-making from the teacher (and children) in the classroom to procedures laid down by people removed from the teaching situation by time and distance.

Children and teachers can be programmed in the same way that computers are programmed, with all goals and activities specified in advance and procedures provided for every decision to be made. Unprogrammed decisions made by computers are regarded as random behaviour likely to divert or derail the entire program, and the same attitude is taken in the programming of teachers and children. At least one commercial reading program specifically admonishes teachers not to answer questions asked by children that the program has not anticipated. Some programs are explicitly 'teacher proof'; others merely warn teachers not to improvise or to tamper with their procedures. No program, however 'individualized', asserts: 'This program should only be used by a sensitive and intelligent teacher capable of exercising independent judgement about whether it makes sense to use this program with a particular child on a particular occasion.' Instead there is an assumption that the program will be more sensitive and intelligent than the teacher, that instructional decisions will be better made in advance by individuals who do not know and cannot see the child who is supposed to be learning from the program (and who in turn cannot see, know, or question them).

Educational programs share a number of other characteristics, all deriving from the fact that they strive to make decisions in advance on behalf of teachers and children. All of these common characteristics constitute constraints or limitations on what the program can achieve, yet paradoxically they are frequently claimed to be virtues of the program. For example, it is a critical limitation of programs that they cannot demonstrate what reading and writing are for. Teachers can demonstrate the utility of literacy by ensuring that children observe and participate in written language activities that have a purpose – stories to be written and read for pleasure, poems to be recited, songs to be sung, plays to be acted, letters to be sent and received, catalogues to be consulted, newspapers and announcements to be circulated, advertisements to be published, signs to be posted, schedules to be followed, even cribs to be concealed, all the multiplicity of ways in which written language is used (and taken for granted) in the world at large. None of these purposes can be demonstrated by programs, which can only demonstrate their own instructional intentions. Reading and writing are *human* activities, and children learn in the course of engaging in them. Programs must assume that children will learn to read and write before actually engaging in these activities, which means that programs demand learning for which no utility is evident.

The virtue claimed for programs in face of the fact that their instruction is decontextualized and bereft of evident purpose is that they are 'skill-based', that they teach basic or sub-skills with an implied promise that isolated fragments of skill and knowledge will one day fall into place and the learner will suddenly become able to participate in the new and hitherto unexplored activities of reading and writing. Because programs are more concerned with exercises than purposes, their activities bear little resemblance to any normal, motivated, selective act of reading or writing. Therefore program developers tend to depend on theories that reading and writing are inherently unnatural and difficult (e.g. Mattingly, 1972; Liberman and Shankweiler, 1979), to be learned by rote rather than by the meaningfulness which is the basis of spoken language learning (Smith, 1977).

All programs fractionate learning experience. Because learners cannot be left free to wander at will through (and out of) the program – which would then not be a program – tasks have to be broken down into small steps without evident relationships to each other or to reading and writing as a whole. Because learners can have no intrinsic motivation to perform such tasks – there is no evident reason for doing one thing rather than another – the order in which tasks must be approached and mastered is narrowly prescribed. This is totally unlike the way in which infants are immersed in the environments of meaningful spoken language, to be progressively understood in the manner that makes most sense to each individual child. The virtue claimed for the highly artificial and arbitrary sequencing of programmatic learning is that it is systematic and scientific, although it could equally well be characterized as a systematic deprivation of experience. The responsibility assumed by prescribing the exact nature and order of experience that each individual child requires in order to reach an understanding of reading and writing is awesome, analogous to restricting a child's exploration of the visual world to glimpses of pre-determined events paraded past a slit in an enveloping curtain.

Also, because of the purposeless and decontextualized nature of programmatic instruction, the program itself must decide whether the learner is right or wrong. When language is employed for meaningful uses, the context provides clues that not only indicate what the language is probably about and how it works but also whether the learner is right or wrong (Smith, 1975). There are only two kinds of mistakes in such meaningful language, those that make a difference and those that do not. A mistake that does not make a difference does not make a difference. A mistake that makes a difference becomes self-evident and is the basis of learning. But with meaningless programmatic instruction every deviation from the literal path is an 'error' although the only difference it can possibly make is that it is not permitted by the program. Mistakes are to be avoided rather than accepted as opportunities for learning. Nevertheless, learners are constantly moved towards difficulty because tasks that they can accomplish without error are regarded as 'learned' and no longer relevant. The virtue claimed for these constraints is that learning can be promoted, monitored and evaluated every step along the way. There is 'quality control' of both the learner and the teacher, no matter how insignificant the mistake or irrelevant the learning task.

As programs have become increasingly more systematic, greater restrictions have been placed on both the time and possibilities available to teachers to introduce activities of their own. Programs dominate classroom activities. The virtue claimed for this limitation is that programs become total 'management systems' for delivering instruction to children. Instruction is seen as a manufacturing process, with the learner as raw material, the teacher a tool, the instruction as 'treatment', and a literate child as the product delivered at the end. Few program developers are as frank as Atkinson (1974), who admitted that his own elaborate computer-based program began with phonic drills because these could be most easily programmed on the computer. The importance of comprehension in reading (but not in learning) was acknowledged by the characteristic programmatic strategy of treating comprehension as a set of skills to be acquired rather than a state which is the basis of all learning (Smith, 1975).

Because programs are by their very nature piecemeal, unmotivated, standardized, decontextualized, trivial and difficulty-oriented, it would often not be appparent what they were supposed to be teaching if they were not clearly identified. Teachers often say they are teaching reading or writing (or spelling or comprehension) because this is the label attached to the program that happens to be in use. And programs are typically not modest in their claims, particularly those that insist upon being the most rigorous. A widely promoted program of 'direct instruction' claims that 'any child can learn if he's taught in the right way', the right way being the 'carefully developed and unique programming and teaching strategies' of the system. To continue quoting from the promotional materials, 'The teacher knows exactly what she has to teach. And how to teach it. All the steps for presenting a task, evaluating student responses, praising and correcting the children are carefully outlined.' Having made every decision in advance, including when it is appropriate to praise, the program claims that 'the teacher can concentrate fully on teaching', though what is left to be taught (apart from the program) is not specified. A more frankly commercial program combines mutually incompatible vogue words with hyperbole to claim that 'The needs of the gifted, the average and the perceptually handicapped child are all met through [the program's] psycholinguistic approach. . . . Pupils are introduced to reading through the multisensory-motor method . . . combined with intensive audio-visual activity.' Also not untypically, this program claims to be indebted to eminent neurologists who had emphasized 'the central role played by the integrative areas of the brain' and 'the functional grouping of neural units in learning', as if the activities laid down in the program had some kind of unique neurophysiological status.

The relevance of research

Another egregious characteristic of programs in education is their claim to be based upon research. The more elaborate and restrictive the program, the more its developers are likely to assert that its content and successes are validated by empirical evidence while instruction that is based on teacher insight and experience is likely to be dismissed as naïve, intuitive, and primitive. 'Child-centred' is used as a derogatory label.

However, despite all the claims and assumptions there is no evidence that any child ever learned to read because of a program. And probably there never could be such definitive evidence because no child (one would hope) is ever exposed to a 'controlled' situation of only programmatic instruction without other access to written language in its manifold purposeful manifestations in the world. On the other hand, there is abundant empirical evidence that children have learned to read without the benefit of formal instruction, either before they came to school or by interaction with teachers who were independently self-directed (Clark, 1976; Torrey, 1979). Often such children have few social or intellectual advantages; they are precisely the children for whom programmatic instruction is supposed to be particularly appropriate.

Research has yet to look closely at the manner in which children frequently learn to read and write without or despite formal instruction, or indeed at what children actually learn as a consequence of such instruction. Instead, research has tended to concentrate only on whether children learn whatever fragmented skills particular programs happen to teach. The research paradigm often contrasts an experimental group that receives a particular program with a 'control' group that does not. Both groups are then tested on the specific instruction and the experimental group naturally does somewhat better. Alternatively, one program is compared with another, generally to show minimal difference between them (Bond and Dykstra, 1967; Stebbins et al., 1977; House et al., 1978). The advantage of whatever such programs actually teach seems to wash out after Grade 3 (Williams, 1979; Chall, 1967) when matters of comprehension begin to assume inescapable proportions.

Considerable research remains to be done on how exactly children succeed in learning to read and write, but it will not be done by researchers who believe that such learning is a matter of mastering programmatic reading and writing skills. Instead there is a great need for longitudinal and ethnographic studies of how children come to make sense of print and its uses, such as those of Goodman (1980), Ferreiro (1978), and Hiebert (1981), demonstrating for example that pre-school children can understand functions and the general character of print long before they receive formal instruction.

Much more research could be done into what children can and must learn about reading and writing without recourse to programs, into how programs do and should relate to this prior knowledge, into what teachers who succeed in helping children learn to read and write actually do, into what exactly children who have learned to read and write have learned (from teachers and from programs), and also into what children who have failed to become readers and writers have learned. On the other hand, the fact that research demonstrates that readers have particular skills that non-readers do not have should not be interpreted to mean that non-readers will become readers if drilled in those particular skills, which may be a consequence rather than a cause of reading. Such has been found to be the case for knowledge of letter-names (Samuels, 1971) and for familiarity with the conventional language of reading instruction (Downing and Oliver, 1973–4).

Teachers versus programs

With their inevitably limited objectives, programs teach trivial aspects of literacy and they can teach that literacy is trivial. Children are learning all the time. Rather than demonstrate the utility of written language, programs may demonstrate that reading is nonsense and ritual, that writing is boring, that learning is threatening, that children are stupid, that teachers are puppets, that schools cannot be trusted and that children's own interests, cultures and insights into language can be ignored. Teachers can demonstrate all these things too, but programs do so more efficiently.

The proliferation of programs in education today is unnecessary, irrelevant and dangerous. Programs are unnecessary because millions of children have learned to be literate without the contemporary technology of instructional development and there is no evidence at all that the employment and enjoyment of literacy have increased with the growing reliance upon programs. There is no evidence that children who have difficulty becoming literate do better with impersonal programs (although they may exhibit irrelevant and limited learning from what the programs teach). Rather, it is the children who have the least success in learning who most need personal contact, to be reassured of their ability to learn, and of the utility of what is to be learned. I am not saying that teachers cannot on occasion make independent use of material provided with programs, but that teachers should not be used by programs.

. Programs tend to be irrelevant by their very nature. They demonstrate tasks rather than purposes. There is widespread anxiety today because many students leave school with poor writing and reading abilities. But the real tragedy is that competent readers and writers as well as the less able leave school with a lifelong aversion to reading and writing, which they regard as purely school activities, as trivial and tedious 'work'. Students of poor ability who are interested in reading and writing will always have the possibility of learning. But those who detest the activities are lost; they have learned from the wrong demonstrations.

Programs are dangerous because they may take the place of teachers. The issue is more critical today than ever before because more people seem to believe that the way to improve education is to operationalize it even further, and because the technology now exists to make teachers redundant. It is widely believed, especially among those who promote computer-based instruction, that children can 'do all their learning' at a console, that microcomputers are cheaper than teachers (which is a fact) and that they are more efficient than teachers (which is true for what such devices teach best). It is perhaps ironic that dissatisfaction with the performance of teachers has tended to grow as education has become more systematized, yet the 'solution' to the perceived decline in literacy and teacher effectiveness has continued to be the increase of program control at the expense of teacher autonomy.

Teachers are an endangered species. While being given less and less freedom to teach, they are being held more and more accountable. And in the comparison with technology teachers are being put at a crucial disadvantage. Teachers are not evaluated on whether children enjoy reading and writing, on how often and extensively children independently engage in reading and writing in their everyday lives, nor even on how fast they learn when the learning is relevant to their own individual interests. Instead, children and teachers are evaluated on what the programs teach best, on standardized, decontextualized, fragmented 'skills'. The majority of reading tests favour programs, since they are restricted to measuring the same kinds of things that programs teach best, isolated facts and skills that can be dealt with one standardized step at a time.

The problem is also that while programs make teachers look ineffectual, teachers (and children) make programs look good. A teacher tells a child to spend an hour on worksheets and at the end of the day there will be time for independent reading. At the end of the year the child can read and the teacher gives all the credit to the worksheets. The way most teachers are trained not only leads them to be dependent upon programs but to give programs the credit for success, though not the blame for failure.

The Martian test

Imagine a Martian space traveller sent to earth to investigate the nature and utility of the reading and writing that earthlings find so important. Suppose the Martian decided that classrooms would be the best places to gather information. What would the Martian conclude reading and writing to be from the materials available and from the activities of teachers and children under the influence of programs? Could a reasonable report be sent back to Mars? As I said in my earlier article, the problem may not be that children do not learn in school but that they learn all the time. And like the Martian they will learn exactly what is demonstrated. Should we expect children to be any less misled than the Martian?

Conclusions

The critical issue confronting education today is not which programs are best for teaching children to read and to write, but what children will learn. Teachers can teach that literacy is useful, enjoyable and attainable, provided they are left free to teach in an unprogrammed manner. Programs will teach something else – that literacy is what programs demonstrate.

I am not arguing against technology. I think microprocessors and every other aspect of contemporary technology should be important tools for learning – like typewriters and calculators – but not control devices for teaching. Children should learn to use technology but not to be used by it. The question again is, 'Who is in charge?'

Many people can think of teachers who override programs and who engage children in productive language learning. Many teachers believe they themselves are exceptions. And of course such teachers exist. My concern is that they may be losing the possibility of teaching. Programs are being thrust upon them, not only by school and political administrations but by parents and the media, all seemingly convinced that programmed education is a universal panacea. It will not help if teachers also believe that programs can only be benign.

Teachers as well as literacy are threatened. And only teachers can resist the threat. They can resist by asserting their crucial role in teaching literacy against all who assert otherwise. In the present decade, the most important educational function of teachers may well be outside the classroom rather than within it.

References

Atkinson, R.C. (1974) 'Teaching children to read using a computer', *American Psychologist*, vol. 29, pp. 169–78.
Bond, G. and Dykstra, R. (1967) 'The cooperative research program in first-grade reading', *Reading Research Quarterly*, vol. 2, pp. 5–142.
Chall, J.S. (1967) *Learning to Read: The Great Debate*, New York, McGraw-Hill.
Clark, M.M. (1976) *Young Fluent Readers*, London, Heinemann Educational Books.
Downing, J. and Oliver, P. (1973–4) 'The child's conception of "a word"', *Reading Research Quarterly*, vol. 4, pp. 568–82.
Ferreiro, E. (1978) 'What is written in a written sentence? a developmental answer.'

Journal of Education, vol. 160, pp. 25–39.

Goodman, Y. (1980) 'The roots of literacy', in *Claremont Reading Conference Forty-Fourth Yearbook*, ed. M.P. Douglass, Claremont, Calif.

Hiebert, E.H. (1981) 'Developmental patterns and interrelationships of preschool children's print awareness,' *Reading Research Quarterly*, vol. 16, pp. 236–60.

House, E.R., Glass, G.V., McLean, L.D. and Walker, D.F. (1978) 'No simple answer: critique of the follow-through evaluation', *Harvard Educational Review*, vol. 48, pp. 128–60.

Liberman, I.Y. and Shankweiler, D. (1979) 'Speech, the alphabet and teaching to read,' in *Theory and Practice of Early Reading*, (vol. 2), ed. L.B. Resnick and P.A. Weaver, Hillsdale, NJ, Erlbaum.

Mattingly, I.G. 'Reading, the linguistic process, and linguistic awareness?' in *Language by Ear and by Eye*, ed. J.F. Kavanagh and I.G. Mattingly, Cambridge, Mass., M I T Press.

Olson, D.R. and Bruner, J.S. (1974) 'Learning through experience and learning through instruction,' in *Media and Symbols: The Forms of Expression, Communication and Education*, ed. D.R. Olson, Chicago, National Society for the Study of Education, 73rd Yearbook, Part 1.

Samuels, S.J. (1971) 'Letter-name versus letter-sound knowledge in learning to read,' *Reading Teacher*, vol. 24, pp. 604–8.

Smith, F. (1975) *Comprehension and Learning*, New York, Holt, Rinehart & Winston.

———— (1977) 'Making sense of reading – and of reading instruction,' *Harvard Educational Review*, vol. 47, pp. 386–95.

———— (1979) 'Conflicting approaches to reading research and instruction,' in *Theory and Practice of Early Reading*, (vol. 2), ed. L.B. Resnick and P.A. Weaver, Hillsdale, NJ, Erlbaum.

———— (1981) 'Demonstrations, engagement and sensitivity: a revised approach to language learning', *Language Arts*, vol. 58, pp. 103–12.

Stebbins, L.B., St Pierre, R.G., Proper, E.C., Anderson, R.B. and Cerva, T.R. (1977) *Education as Experimentation: A Planned Variation Model: Vol. IV-A An Evaluation of Follow-Through*, Cambridge, Mass., Abt Associates.

Torrey, Jane W. (1979) 'Reading that comes naturally: the early reader', in *Reading Research: Advances in Theory and Practice* (vol. 1), ed. T.G. Walker and G.E. MacKinnon, New York, Academic Press.

Williams, J. (1979) 'Reading instruction today,' *American Psychologist*, vol. 34, pp. 917–22.

9   Instructional Scaffolding:
Reading and Writing as Natural
Language Activities*

Arthur N. Applebee (*Associate Professor of Education, Stanford University*) *and*
Judith A. Langer (*Visiting Scholar, University of California, Berkeley*)

Discussions of how to teach reading and writing skills have usually focused
on specific skills assumed to be important components of adult
performance. This perspective has led to extensive taxonomies of
questioning techniques, to legions of workbook and textbook activities
providing 'practice' in one or another component skill, and to outlines of
ideal lesson sequences focused around such categories as motivation,
introduction of new concepts, practice and application.

We will argue here for a different focus in planning and analysing
instruction in reading and writing. Rather than extensive analysis of
component skills, we wish to focus on the language task to be carried out by
the student, and the instructional support, or 'scaffolding' (Bruner, 1978;
Cazden, 1980) that is needed in order to carry the task through successfully.
In this model, the novice reader or writer learns new skills in contexts where
more skilled language users provide the support necessary to carry through
unfamiliar tasks. In the course of this process, the structure provided by the
skilled reader and writer is gradually internalized by the novice, who thus
eventually learns to carry through similar tasks independently.

This model of learning to read and write is based on recent studies of how
young children first learn the complex patterns that structure spoken
language. Michael Halliday (1975), for example, has provided some
interesting analyses of how his son Nigel developed complex structures for
organizing and describing events. One example that Halliday presents
occurred after a visit to the zoo. During the visit, Nigel and his father had
watched a goat try to eat a plastic garbage can lid, and had seen the
zookeeper intervene to take the lid away. The incident obviously made an
impact on Nigel, who returned to the topic later in the day:

Nigel: try eat lid.
Father: What tried to eat the lid?
Nigel: try eat lid.
Father: What tried to eat the lid?
Nigel: goat . . . man said no . . . goat try to eat lid . . . man said no.

Then, after a further interval, while being put to bed:

Nigel: goat try eat lid . . . man said no.
Mother: Why did the man say no?

*Reprinted, by permission, from *Language Arts*, vol. 60, no. 2, Febuary 1983.

Nigel: goat shouldn't eat lid . . . [shaking head] good for it.
Mother: The goat shouldn't eat the lid; it's not good for it.
Nigel: goat try eat lid . . . man said no . . . goat shouldn't eat lid . . . [shaking head] good for it.

The story is then repeated as a whole, verbatim, at frequent intervals over the next few months (p. 112).

This example is an excellent illustration of the ways in which a more skilled language user provides a scaffold that allows a novice to carry out a more complex task. Nigel's parents are building on his already-developed skills in dialogue to enable him to develop and maintain a brief narrative. Several aspects of their interaction are particularly important for our purposes, providing a model of examining language learning in school contexts:

1. The parents' questions are embedded in the child's attempt to complete a task that he has undertaken but cannot complete successfully on his own; Nigel responds well to the questions because they serve his own intentions.

2. The questions are structured around an implicit model of appropriate structure for a narrative; they solicit information that will make the child's narrative more complete and better formed.

3. At times, the parents directly model appropriate forms that Nigel is in the process of mastering, recasting or expanding upon the child's efforts without 'correcting' or rejecting what he has accomplished on his own.

4. Over time, the patterns provided by the parents' questions and models are internalized by the child, and are used without external scaffolding in new contexts. In turn, the scaffolding the parents provide can be oriented towards the next steps in Nigel's growth as a language user.

School learning can also be studied as a series of problems to be solved in a context where new strategies and skills are learned in interaction with others. When direct interaction with an individual student is not possible or appropriate, much of the scaffolding has to be provided in more public, less individual forms – through the structure of the lessons, the framing of exercise and textbook material, and the focus of the teacher's comments and discussion. Thus 'instructional scaffolding' can occur in two ways, either in direct interaction with individual students or in group-oriented instruction. Teachers approaching instruction from this perspective must (i) determine the difficulties that a new task is likely to pose for particular students, (ii) select strategies that can be used to overcome the specific difficulties anticipated, and (iii) structure the activity as a whole to make those strategies explicit (through questioning and modelling) at appropriate places in the task sequence.

The scaffolding provided allows the novice to carry out new tasks while learning strategies and patterns that will eventually make it possible to carry out similar tasks without external support. Although we have not usually thought of the teacher's role in this way, in fact scaffolding can be a powerful analytic tool in examining what teachers do to help students learn to read and write. The concept of scaffolding is as relevant to students' initial encounters with written language as to their later struggles to master the more complex forms peculiar to particular subject areas (e.g. book reports, lab reports, themes).

If we generalize the natural language learning processes described by Halliday (1975) and others, we can derive a set of criteria for judging the appropriateness of the instructional scaffolding that teachers provide for particular school tasks. These criteria emphasize five aspects of natural language learning: intentionality, appropriateness, structure, collaboration, and internalization:

1. Intentionality: The task has a clear overall purpose driving any separate activity that may contribute to the whole. Eventual evaluation of students' success can be cast in terms of what they intended to accomplish.
2. Appropriateness: Instructional tasks pose problems that can be solved with help but which students could not successfully complete on their own. The most appropriate tasks will be those that involve abilities that have not yet matured but are in the process of maturation or, in Vygotsky's (1962) terms, abilities that are not so much 'ripe' as 'ripening'.
3. Structure: Modelling and questioning activities are structured around a model of appropriate approaches to the task and lead to a natural sequence of thought and language.
4. Collaboration: The teacher's response to student work recasts and expands upon the students' efforts without rejecting what they have accomplished on their own. The teacher's primary role is collaborative rather than evaluative.
5. Internalization: External scaffolding for the activity is gradually withdrawn as the patterns are internalized by the students.

What students do in school

If we use the notion of scaffolding as a way to conceptualize school tasks, many current practices do not fare particularly well. Rather than helping students carry out more complex reading and writing activities, our instructional apparatus either ignores the problems posed by the new task, or adds new and irrelevant steps along the way. These steps generally segment the task in ways that require students to deal with small bits (e.g. definitions of words, statement of the main idea) in isolation from broader concepts. The following excerpt from a study guide developed for a sixth-grade unit on energy is typical of many reading/writing activities:

From page 18:
1. _____ is the basic renewable energy source.
2. YES NO Are solar energy collectors a new idea?

3. Why is the idea of using solar energy coming back?

1. _____% of the energy used in this country is used to produce _____ heat to warm _____ and heat _____.

Such activities focus attention on isolated or fragmented aspects of knowledge rather than engaging students in purposeful tasks through which they could learn to deal with both new content and the patterns of argument and evidence they will need as they read and write in their subject classes.

Classroom approaches to writing instruction have been desribed in a number of recent studies (Applebee, 1981; Graves, 1978; Petty and Finn, 1981). Though we will examine some examples of better practice in a moment, most student writing about new learning takes one of two forms: (i) essay questions designed to test whether students have learned material covered in textbooks or class discussions, or (ii) highly structured exercise material in which important concepts or new skills are highlighted in multiple-choice, fill-in-the-blank, or similarly restricted formats.

If we examine these two approaches as examples of scaffolding, we find that they represent opposite extremes. The typical essay question assumes that no support should be provided: the students' task is to recite material that they have already mastered rather than to explore new and more difficult forms. As an assessment device such questions have their place, but as the locus of instruction they are clearly inadequate. The 'scaffolding' provided in the typical practice exercise, on the other hand, is all-pervasive. The exercise material usually takes over all of the problems inherent in structuring text, leaving the student to do little more than slot in whatever information is missing. Rather than being helped to complete tasks more complex than they would otherwise be able to carry through, students find themselves completing exercises simpler than those they would ordinarily do on their own. They are required to fill in 'school language' – bits of information related to the concepts the teacher wants the students to learn. There is neither the need nor the opportunity for the students to reflect on new ideas, to integrate or apply them in new ways, or to make them their own. That they are often bored and frustrated seems hardly surprising.

Classroom approaches to reading instruction are very similar. In her recent study of comprehension instruction, for example, Durkin (1978–9) found that virtually all of the comprehension activities in middle-grade classrooms tested students' comprehension of what they had read, rather than providing strategies or skills for approaching more complex reading materials. The brief excerpt from the study guide on energy, quoted above, is typical of what Durkin found. Rather than helping students deal with new material, the activities are designed to test recall of isolated facts from students' texts.

An alternative model was suggested in a recent report from the National Assessment of Educational Progress (1981). Rather than testing comprehension, the NAEP report suggested that effective comprehension activities would build upon students' initial interpretations through writing or discussion activities that confront readers with alternative views. In defending their initial judgements and reconciling opposing arguments, readers would progress towards a fuller understanding – and to reinterpretation where necessary. Unfortunately, results from the National Assessment suggest such approaches are rarely used in American schools.

Some positive examples

Studies of 'typical' approaches obscure the many interesting activities that fill the classrooms of our best teachers. In these classrooms, teachers use many different forms of instructional scaffolding to support students' attempts at more difficult language and thinking tasks. Many of these activities are quite traditional, providing pre-reading or pre-writing activities, 'guides' to structure comprehension or writing, and discussion or revision sessions to expand upon and develop students' initial work. The particular way the activities will be framed depends upon the particular subject area and the skills that the students bring to the task. The examples that follow, drawn from the science lessons of teachers trying to develop more effective approaches as part of a district curriculum development project, will illustrate how the notion of instructional scaffolding can help us analyse and better understand the activities we develop for our students.

Example 1

The first example comes from a fourth-grade class studying the concept of convection in a larger unit on weather. As part of the lesson, students were guided through a simple experiment demonstrating the effects of convection. At this point in the year, both the concepts involved and the conventional 'pattern' of a science experiment were new to the students. To help them with the task, the teacher discussed the steps while they were being carried through in class, and provided a worksheet with the following questions:

1. Complete the following sentence: I think the winds are caused by . . .

   Hot versus Cold. You will be given directions for an activity using hot and cold water. Follow these directions carefully and then complete the following:
2. Describe what you did. (PROCEDURE)
3. Complete the picture of the jar on the right to show what happened. Describe what happened below. (OBSERVATIONS)
4. CONCLUSIONS – We will do together.
   What word describes what has been happening in the jars with hot and cold water?

If we examine this activity in the light of our criteria for effective scaffolding, we can see both strengths and weaknesses. First, the activity clearly meets the criteria of intentionality and appropriateness. It involves a purposeful language task and builds on the students' knowledge towards a new form that is more complex than they could complete successfully on their own.

Because the lab report format is new, and the students' initial efforts are still quite awkward, Ellie's description of the procedures she followed parallels those of others in the class. Unfamiliar with the form, she draws heavily upon her knowledge of how to give instructions (and the language of the teacher in discussing what to do) to complete this part of the task:

> Take the cup of frozen green water and remove the tape. Dip it in a bottle of hot water. Watch what happened to the cold water.

As Ellie and her classmates become more familiar with the lab report form, their descriptions of lab procedures will rely less on their teacher's language and more on their own.

The fit between the activities suggested and an overall model of appropriate approaches to the task (our criterion of structure) is somewhat less comfortable. The three middle questions on the worksheet model an appropriate organizational format for a lab report and successfully segment the task. Students can complete each section separately yet end up with a final report structured around 'Procedures', 'Observations' and 'Conclusions'. Because the students are so unfamiliar with this format, the teacher in this case uses class discussion to provide further support for the final section (conclusions), rather than leaving the students to complete the task on their own. It would have rounded out the activity more fully, however, if the teacher had then asked the students to write up the conclusions, in their own words, as a last section to their lab reports.

The first and last questions on the worksheet are somewhat out of place in the overall activity. The final question is reminiscent of restricted comprehension questions, reminding students to remember definitions of key words without requiring an understanding of the underlying concept. While the vocabulary being emphasized is certainly appropriate, it has been tagged on at the end rather than integrated into the task as a whole.

The role of the opening question is less clear. It may be intended as a kind of 'topic sentence' for the lab report, or as a pre-writing activity to orient students before they begin to write. The format adopted, however, defeats either of these purposes, drawing attention away from the problem to be addressed in the experiment, towards a restatement of concepts drawn from the teacher's earlier presentation. Ellie responded in kind, with a tightly packed 'school response': 'I think the winds are caused by high pressure and low pressure and convection.' This answer is technically correct, but there is no indication that Ellie understands the implications of 'convection' for winds and weather.

The opening question in a follow-up experiment developed by the same teacher provides an interesting contrast. It begins: 'What are you trying to find out in the next activity? (PURPOSE).' Here the students' attention is focused foward towards the activity, and the question is integrated into the lab report as a statement of purpose. This time, Ellie responded with her own words instead of echoing the teacher's: 'What would happen if you put hot water into cold water?'

From the assignment itself, we cannot judge whether the teacher adopts a collaborative role in responding to the students' work or whether the scaffolding provided is withdrawn as the students internalize the underlying structures.

Example 2

The second example comes from a fifth-grade class which had been studying about states of matter. Students in this class were familiar with the patterns of science experiments and with lab report formats. The teacher could therefore rely upon students' knowledge of these forms rather than building those patterns into the structure of the lesson. In this case, the students carried out the experiments with teacher guidance. She then put the words 'procedures' and 'outcomes' on the board and reminded the class to use these as headings for their reports.

Mark's report is similar in quality to those of his classmates; it is incomplete and represents an awkward mix of his own language and the instructions given by the teacher as the lesson progressed:

I. Procedure – First take 2 Ice cubes out of the freezer and put them in a pot while they are solid. Put them on a hot burner.

II. Outcome – The ice turned from solid to liquid. Now put the lid on the pot for 2 min. Take off the lid and quickly turn it over fast. Look at the lid it is all wet with water because when you put the lid on you trapped the steam on the top. It will turn back into solid if you put it in the freezer.

Again, this task meets our criteria of intentionality and appropriateness. The students have as their overall purpose a presentation of the experiment – what they did and what happened as a result. At the same time, their performance on the two-part writing task suggests that the activity does extend beyond what the students can successfully complete on their own. Mark knows that lab reports are made up of discrete sections, that two of these are 'procedures' and 'outcomes', and that the writing of these sections can be approached as a series of one-paragraph tasks.

For the procedures section, Mark has used his own words. However, like Ellie in the first example, he has turned his own experiences into directions for someone else to carry out. He does not yet understand that a lab report requires him to recount his own actions. Further, his presentation is incomplete, particularly in his confusing second paragraph. In the outcomes section, Mark skips from the first outcome back to the successive procedures he followed – and continues to change voice from experimenter/narrator to teacher/instruction giver. In his last two sentences, Mark recognizes the need to formulate some conclusions, although he is somewhat awkward about it.

Although her removal of other forms of scaffolding was appropriate, this teacher has not complied with our criterion of 'collaboration' rather than evaluation in response to students' early efforts. Her comment on Mark's paper – 'good' – was typical of her responses, although Mark and his classmates clearly needed further support in recasting and expanding their first attempts to find an appropriate form for their reports.

Example 3

Our final example comes from an eighth-grade class which had been studying electricity and how electric tools and appliances work. After conducting a series of electricial experiments, the students were told to select a tool or appliance, to examine how it worked, and then to write a report about it. To help them visualize the placement of the parts they would refer to in their reports, the students were told to begin the report with a diagram. While this task as a whole complies with our criteria of intentionality, appropriateness and structure, the writing produced by the students suggests that more scaffolding activities were needed if they were to complete the task successfully.

Jeff's paper is similar to many others in that it is driven by his personal experience in completing the task rather than by a sense of appropriate expository structure:

Electric Knife

Once you plug in the electric knife you push down on the switch to make the electrical connection which make the motor run which turn the worm gear which turns the circular gear which makes the knife go back and forth – see diagram.

Although Jeff's information appears to be technically correct, he does not follow a report format, but rather blurts out his observations using the narrative form with which he is more familiar. While Jeff uses some of his knowledge of reports, this clearly is insufficient. There is no introduction or general statement of purpose. There is no elaboration, and there is no conclusion. The drawing of the diagram seems to have solved one of the problems that the teacher anticipated; it led Jeff to focus (appropriately) on the internal structure of the electric knife, rather than on its typical uses. As is clear from Jeff's paper, however, he also needed support in structuring the language of the report. Although this could have been provided in the teacher's responses to Jeff's work, in this instance the teacher's comments were evaluative rather than collaborative. For the most part they focused on the bits of information Jeff omitted (and which lowered his grade) rather than helping him present his findings in a more appropriate way.

Conclusions

The examples we have discussed were selected to illustrate the kinds of instructional scaffolding that can be provided within one area of the curriculum; each led students through the thinking and language tasks involved in school science experiments. The framework we have used to discuss these tasks, however, is generalizable; it can be appropriately applied to reading, writing or discussion activities in any area of the curriculum. The particular skills that will need instructional support will vary from grade to grade and subject to subject, but effective activities will meet our five criteria of intentionality, appropriateness, structure, collaboration and internalization. Rather than separating students' learning of subject-area content from their developing thinking and language skills, such activities integrate new learning with ways in which students express their knowledge. The processes of learning to read and to write become intertwined in mutually supportive natural language activities.

References

Applebee, A.N. (1981) *Writing in the Secondary School*, Urbana. Ill., National Council of Teachers of English.

Bruner, J. (1978) 'The role of dialogue in language acquisition', in *The Child's Concept of Language*, ed. A. Sinclair, R.J. Jarvelle and W.J.M. Levelt, New York, Springer-Verlag.

Cazden, C. (1980) 'Peekaboo as an instructional model: discourse development at home and at school,' *Papers and Reports of Child Language Development*, vol. 17, pp. 1–29.

Durkin, D. (1978–9) 'What classroom observations reveal about reading comprehension instruction', *Reading Research Quarterly*, vol. 14, pp. 481–533.

Graves, D. (1978) *Balance the Basics: Let Them Write*, New York, The Ford Foundation.

Halliday, M.A.K. (1975) *Learning How to Mean*, New York, Elsevier North-Holland.

National Assessment of Educational Progress (1981) *Reading, Thinking, and Writing*. Denver, Col., Education Commission of the States.

Petty, W.T. and Finn, P.J. (1981) 'Classroom teachers' reports on teaching written composition', in *Perspectives on Writing in Grades 1-8*, ed. S.M. Haley-James. Urbana, Ill., National Council of Teachers of English.

Vygotsky, L.S. (1962) *Thought and Language*, Cambridge, Mass., MIT Press.

10 Writing Something to Somebody*

Jerre Paquette (Calgary teacher, doctoral student at the University of London Institute of Education)

Part I

There must have been moments when you regarded me as a disembodied typewriter, or as an Irish name on the title page of a book, or as a kind of animated sentence ejector (George A. Kelly, 'A brief introduction to personal construct theory', *Perspectives in Personal Construct Theory*, ed. D. Bannister, London and New York, Academic Press).

JUNE, 1979

this person in qwezon is named tony, He likes the sun he's is allways talking about the wether when it is summing out he is in a good moud. he seemes to be experience broblems in most of the classes' it sounds like he and he's teacher are not on speecing trerms. He notes are a mess harter any order. but thing sem to get beter as they go. He seems to like to play sports mostly cotaked rugby and football. he does not have a lot of confidence in he school work. He's writing are not the best Ive seen, He work in school is so differnent from the thing he say about sports he very wereyed about what people say about him. Writing is not hes favorit thing in most of he gornal the first time say and I quite this famus words (I do not feel like writing) he work has improved 100 percent

So went the final piece of sustained writing Tony will ever do and the most carefully worked out one he ever did. He felt good about this writing and, smiling broadly, handed it to his teacher after 1½ hours of effort and twelve years of training. As far as can be told, this is the only piece of his writing that has been kept and it is one of only ten pieces of writing he did all year in all his courses (excluding two-sentence entries in his English journal). And he did indeed improve 100 per cent.

Tony was very worried about what people, mainly teachers, would say about him; for the only meaningful expression of himself as a complete person was the body of writing that had accumulated under the watchful and stern eyes of his assessors. And he knew well what kind of a writer he was and what that meant to the teachers. The accumulation, if it has been stored, is rather small, in fact, and in terms of the schools' standards, of a very miserable quality indeed. Yet, once we are freed of our roles as examiners, it is not very difficult to be moved in this passage by the presence

*Abridged, by permission, from *Teaching Writing*, The Canadian Council of Teachers of English, 1981.

of a most perceptive and socially motivated and inclined young man of apparent skills and interests, all unfortunately peripheral to the serious demands and interests of the school.

It should be noted, too that upon presenting his writing to his teacher, Tony left the classroom and left school for ever, neither demanding nor expecting a response of any sort from his teacher. He was of two minds about it: on the one hand he knew he had completed his final assignment and, as assignments go, knew that they require only the response of the evaluator, which was a matter out of his hands; on the other, he was clearly satisfied and even proud of having made something, of having said something in print of personal worth, which needed no supporting teacher response. The objective point of view he adopted to write his self-analysis suggests that his writing was really a dialogue between the objective observer implied in the line 'this person in qwezon . . .', and himself. His teacher-audience was secondary in one sense and was likely the observer whose role he had adopted for the occasion. That is, his writing here was representative of a modulating frequency between some person whose identity and style he had come to know and assimilate, and his own personality or self. Hence, this passage is really a written dialogue held internally over a period of 1½ hours and made manifest in writing: what appears to be a rather simple and pathetic piece of writing reflects a most elaborate operation of interacting skills on a highly abstract level, albeit poorly developed.

A teacher asked Tony to write this passage. Nobody else would have asked him to attempt such a thing, particularly in writing. And it was to a particular teacher that Tony directed his work. If, by chance, a friend or parent or employer or some other teacher had demanded this of him, what would the results have been like? Would the tone, content, style, length, editing, format, grammatical structures, lexicon and general appearance have been altered in any way? And if there had been differences, what would they have said to us about his writing abilities that this passage does not? In as much as we are all generally aware of how the identity of the person to whom we are speaking affects how we are speaking and what we are saying, certainly it is fair to assume that the audience to whom we perceive we are writing must affect our written language in similar ways. And we are also generally aware that the wider the experience one has with a variety of listeners or partners in dialogue, the more adept we become at adapting the elements and units of our oral language system: restrict the variety of partners in dialogue, so also restrict the range of language structures and styles we come to develop. We thereby also restrict what we may each perceive the power of language to be. Herein lay Tony's principal problem with language in the written form.

What Tony seems to have accomplished, as demonstrated by the passage quoted above, is not so much in terms of his improved grammatical and semantic structures as in terms of the skill in assimilating a particular-*cum*-generalized audience to whom his language system has adapted. I wish we could have hung on to him a while longer in order to explore this development further, but he didn't feel he belonged. And it was largely through his experiences with writing that he came to feel this way.

While it is not the principal purpose of this chapter to explore theories of audience, I do hope that Tony's writing impresses upon you as it does upon me our crucial need to understand the influence of audience upon the written forms of language. We do not, in fact, have any such theory available to us. Audience does not often even appear as a concern in the questions relating to the problems of writing. Where it is discussed or explored, audience is treated simply as an external object towards which we direct our thoughts. But what if the matter of audience is really something that has to be construed as an aspect of internal language development rather than, or as well as, an external influence? Then we must not talk about language directed *at* or *to* somebody, but rather language that emerges internally from out of the process of dynamic social interaction – somewhat like talk without the partner present. That is not to say that talk and writing are the same thing; but, more importantly, that writing owes its existence to the same influence as talk: the overwhelming human need to say something to somebody. In writing exists a special instance of the need and difficulties of having a clear sense of audience if the language is to express effectively the precise intentions of the individual in the given context of social interaction.

Writers do not write in solitude any more than speakers speak in solitude. The private act of writing on paper should not be construed as a vision of solitary man, for the act of writing is the act of sharing shaped meaning with real and construed others who influence the shaping by their incorporation within the self of the writer. For teachers, this is an essential concept to be considered unless we are to be happy with the notion that writing is merely a production of autonomous language devoid of the need for human context and contact. Writing may have life only if there is a strong and clear sense of two or more people being involved in the process; if there is within the writer the ever-present influence of a construed audience that may render him mute, articulate or verbose, and which is all-pervasive throughout the entire writing process, dictating choices at all levels of language use. Writing may be said to be dead when it is filled with meanings not wanting to be said to somebody who doesn't want to be affected by them. In this sense, perhaps teachers read more dead writing than anybody else in the world.

Part II

How can I tell what I think until I see what I say? (W.H. Auden).

I want now to discuss a specific way of providing students with a more meaningful and productive experience with the teacher as an audience.

While we might rather discuss ways of employing different audiences and therein chat about the uses of pen-pals, peer-group writing, activity-associated writing, and so forth, I feel that it is essential to realize first the potential of the teacher himself or herself as a genuine partner in written language. Most of us already employ highly inadequate tricks to get students to write to a range of 'real' audiences: 'Pretend you are writing to the president of the Automobile Association and . . .' Those tricks don't work because the students know only too well who the real audience is in fact – the teacher-examiner, of course. So pervasive is this teacher-audience that, as Robert, a 15-year-old successful writer puts it, one need not even pay attention to the matter of to whom the writing is being directed:

> In school we write not to anyone . . . we just give information. Not to someone, we just write information down on paper and whoever happens to be reading it soaks up the information.

In a taped discussion, he goes on to distinguish between 'real' audiences and teacher-examiner audiences:

> Oh yeah, there's definitely a difference because when you're writing to someone you always, you're careful, you're careful what you say. You know, you have to think 'How can I put it so he understands it' . . . but when you write an essay you think, 'I can put the information down, it doesn't matter . . . who's reading it, they all understand it'. But when you think of you're writing to somebody about something then it's, I think it's easier to write to somebody about something.

Robert finds the teacher-examiner an unsatisfactory and unstimulating audience for whom it is difficult to write in spite of the fact that he fully knows how to fulfill the requirements of such an audience. Yet, it seems to me, the audience most capable of being stimulating in a consistent and helpful way remains the teacher. But not the teacher as 'nobody', rather the teacher as 'somebody'. And for the teacher to emerge as a particular somebody for the writer, a way must be found to redirect the teacher's and the student's preoccupation with the surface features of language to the embedded, shared meanings for which language is intended.

Journal writing done on a daily basis has the potential of overcoming many of the negative associations students have for writing and establishes it as a genuine means of sharing ideas and information with somebody who is genuinely interested. For the student, journal writing to and with a teacher makes possible one kind of private contact with an adult that has the potential of being extended in useful and exciting ways into the business functions of writing with which schools must eventually be concerned. That is, through journal writing, which is free of the demands of an evaluator and in which a student may explore a vast range of subject ideas and writing styles and techniques, the student may come into much more contact with a variety of language devices, systems and styles as a consequence of the teacher becoming a participating particular while not forsaking his generalized role of classroom instructor and examiner.

A daily journal may consist of a number of features and may be approached in any number of ways, depending on curricular and timetabling restrictions. However, there are some features that I would deem essential to the goals implied above:

1. As their name suggests, they should be kept on a daily basis in a routine fashion in order that they become part of the accepted scheme of things.
2. They should be kept as a matter between the teacher and student with nobody else having access to their contents.
3. The teacher should be prepared to respond to each child's writing on a regular basis, however brief the response may be. Here the teacher must decide on the importance to a student of the frequency and length of responses. Some students need little response, some continual, most need just a sentence or two much of the time.
4. Students must become convinced that the journals are read without examination being an intention of the teacher. Hence, the teacher must respond on a personal level, in writing, and he must resist the temptation to circle errors: his own written responses serve well as a model.
5. In the main, the subject-matter of the journal should be decided upon by the student with the teacher helping the student extend, explore and shape through his questions, reactions and own writing samples.

Usually, a controlled time-period of 10 minutes at the start of each class period is an ample amount of time for writers of all abilities to make a statement, continue a thought, respond to a teacher comment, extend a poem, tell a joke, or introduce a problem. Frequently, out of the journal dialogue will emerge a specific formal assignment topic or at least (or best) a direction for the kinds of topics or subjects or writing styles appropriate for the specific student's course work and evaluation.

Best of all, however, journals enable the student to have dialogue with a teacher in a rich and varied framework of personal subject-matter. The dialogue-in-writing may not last long in each instance, but neither does most teacher/student dialogue. In the journals, however, the written form allows for later extension and continuation or later reflection and recapitulation. Indeed, the accumulation of shared teacher–student comments that may be reviewed and reconsidered at leisure is the other major advantage of the journal: it becomes a record of generally meaningful exchanges which have likely undergone some sort of significant development over the year or semester. And very frequently, through the 10 minutes of writing a day, even the 'poorest' writers will take off on a self- or mutually-discovered writing project for its own sake. And others, like Tony, may make a statement otherwise never attempted or even thought.

And it doesn't need to be marked!

But having said that (and having hinted at a promise for a little magic, I suppose), I must also admit that journals take up a lot of time. My colleagues and I who have worked with journals extensively for many years now, both in elaborate and simple ways, have frequently had to take off a whole day simply to respond to journal entires made over a period of two weeks or so. Yet, there are ways of coping with the problem of time, and the results do show up clearly in many ways in the regular matter of course work. Most students end up doing more writing cumulatively in 10 minutes a day over a semester than they do in their regular course work. Many students are able to write a page and half in that 10 minutes a day; other students may achieve only two sentences at a time; others extend their journals in their 'own' time. Very few write nothing at all. In the end, students and teachers have come to know one another really quite well, and new possibilities for thought through writing have been explored and realized.

The transition from success in the journals (defined simply as the student's acceptance of writing as a way of saying something to somebody) to improvement in writing in general is made largely through the assimilation of an audience with the self: In the course of writing that major formal assignment for the teacher, the student is able to borrow from her experience in writing to the teacher/particular in order to make meaning to the teacher/general. After all, writing is simply a way of saying something to somebody. Having the way and the something, but not the somebody, is to have nothing at all but empty form.

Journals work. I should say that again. Journals work! But it takes time to make them work. And teachers have to be fairly well organized if they are not to become discouraged and depleted of their energy and will; they have to exploit the help that is inherent in the social milieu. And help there is: in the capacities of peer and senior students to become partner respondents in association (or not) with the teacher, inherent in the co-operation from teachers from other departments; inherent in the flexibility of our systems to formally meet the articulated needs of the teachers and students.

With these latter points in mind, then, I would like to turn to the matter of how to deal with journals and briefly describe approaches I feel are effective and workable.

Part III

Can I say what I want, or do I have to write an essay? (Student journal-writer).

Certainly it is important to keep in touch with what a student is saying in a journal, but often an oral response is more, or as, appropriate a way of responding and sharing as writing, particularly when you are simply pressed for time or energy. The important thing is to be certain of establishing for the young writer a genuine audience from and with whom he or she can learn to share thoughts and feelings in writing and from whom he or she can develop an internalized sense of audience which can be called upon when the occasion to write presents itself.

I would like now to describe a more prestructured and controllable method by which to assure the development of the kind of audience I have just mentioned. Thus far, it has been my intention to focus on the capacity of the teacher to be that genuine audience. But, obviously, there is an equally important and more readily available resource from which to draw. That is, handled and developed carefully, the students themselves may become constructive, genuine and sensitive audiences for one another and may draw from one another a range and quality of writing the adult audience may not.

To do this, to be mutually helpful in extending one another's expressive abilities and inclinations, there needs to be not a simple casual relationship between the students involved, but one that provides a degree of positive tension between reader and writer which enables both to feel challenged without feeling threatened. One approach is to draw upon students from senior grades to act as 'writer-respondents' to one's classroom students. This may be organized in several ways and may involve very complicated student–student–teacher relationships or may be very simple and involve simply a regular exchange of journals with individuals from separate classes. It is to the more complicated situation, however, that I want to draw your attention.

For several years I have worked with students assigned the label 'Teacher-aide'. Often I have had to change the name to suit the constraints of local union policies, but I prefer this name because it places the students involved somewhere between my concerns and those of the students to whom they are assigned. Simply put, students from outside of my class (usually) are selected to become 'journal partners' for my students. Their task is to respond on a daily or near-daily basis to the writing done by my students in the first 10 minutes of my class. Added to this basic responsibility is the task of identifying for me those strengths and weaknesses in language that journal writers may be exhibiting in their daily journal. This input into writing profiles that I build up for each student is added to what I have already included from regular English work and serves to offer me a more comprehensive and positive view of my students' writing abilities.

Programs of this sort may get very complex indeed – but also very exciting. They may include, for example, making the teacher-aides part of a fully credited course designed to offer them growth and insights into human relationships, growth in their communications skills, and growth in their own teaching abilities. What begins as a focus on the growth of skills of student writers readily gets shifted to a focus on and interest in the development of 'teaching' skills in the senior student. If you want it to, that is.

The basic procedure in developing such a program is worth describing in brief. It involves selecting senior students on the basis of their own writing skills and interest in human dynamics (for want of a better term) and personal characteristics (reliability and sensitivity being paramount) to work with teachers within the English department on matters relating to journals. Most often, for each English class taught a teacher ia assigned three senior students whose task is to respond to the journals of five or six students (depending on the size of the class and the number of students teachers want to respond to themselves) according to carefully worked-out guidelines and under the general supervision of a 'teacher-aide instructor'. Effectively, the department has offered 'Teacher-aiding' as an English option and has developed a course appropriate to the department's and students' needs. 'Communications' is often chosen as a name for the course. It involves a training period of about three weeks with the TA instructor (an English teacher) and includes discussions and case studies of writing problems specifically and human relationships generally. Once the TAs are assigned to regular English teachers, however, the TA instructor is freed of regular class duties and is responsible for supervising the TAs from an appropriate distance, including having weekly or bi-weekly meetings with them as a group.

It is tempting to get very specific at this point (and difficult not to), but to describe the program in all its detail would be to be inappropriately lengthy, especially since each department would have somewhat different constraints and demands than those in which I have worked. Clearly, however, such a program does have much potential for the learning of all the students involved and it is not the case that one is being exploited for the sake of the other. Neither does this teacher–student relationship detract from the responsibilities or effectiveness of the classroom teacher. Rather, it extends both. And what it does for the writing abilities and self-concepts of the students involved is most impressive indeed, extending as it does both the range and sheer volume of meaningful and varied writing opportunities for the students, a volume no individual teacher could respond to or hope to elicit without involving other people.

The teacher's concern becomes, in all this apparent busyness, to transfer the writing development observed in the journal to regular course assignments, a feat accomplished in the first instance by continuing to be the sort of genuine audience the students have experienced in their journal writing and through whom they have achieved confidence and experience; in the second instance, by assisting the students in understanding the particular writing demands placed upon them by the change in subject-matter and situation and audience. What may be achieved, to the students' advantage, is that they will come to see themselves as writers with a problem of technique, rather than as non-writers (and often therefore as non-people in the school context) with all the overwhelming problems that that implies in a system that *apparently* values only the competent writer.

Part IV

With the combined pressures of numbers and accountability, it becomes a simple matter for teachers to view the writing process largely as a mechanically induced language system which serves the students' needs mainly because it serves the needs of the schools. But that is such an unnecessary and limiting concept of the usefulness of a writing system. Certainly writing may be seen as an artificially contrived language (there remain a few cultures that have not even felt the need to develop such a system for themselves). But that is not to say that it may only serve artificially contrived purposes such as those that seem to describe school curricula: writing is a language not unlike talking in its capacity to serve the natural and changing social needs and personal development of the individual and community. That capacity may be realized through the structured use of personal journals. Thereby, the mutual exchange of ideas and feelings through writing that is not intended merely for the examiner can be realized in its turn.

Part IV

The Common Pool

In using the word culture I am thinking of something that is in the common pool of humanity, into which individuals and groups of people may contribute, and from which we may all draw *if we have somewhere to put what we find* (Winnicott, *Playing and Reality*, p.99).

The old adage that child's play is imagination in action must be reversed: we can say that imagination in adolescents . . . is play without action (Vygotsky, *Mind in Society*, p. 93).

To be co-opted as partner in the make-believe play of a 4-year-old is, I believe, to be in a position to explore the origins of literary experience. For the child there is a powerful motive for this play – pressure to escape from a reality that is a network of other people's purposes into a world of unquestioned autonomy for her. What she wants, goes: and I am allotted my changing role – her 4-year-old, her 14-year-old or the father of her two Teddy bears – on that basis. Under her direction we enact a story; no matter what the sources of the material – family events, her own wild hopes or fears, or some familiar nursery story – it is *we* who *enact it*.

Vygotsky's comment on imagination as play without action is a neat example of his general thesis that human consciousness results from the internalization of shared social behaviour. The co-operative activity of make-believe play, he suggests, is the only form that voluntary imagination can take in the young child: and 'imagination' is the later effect of internalizing that play. Developed imagination has many uses, but the use that most closely parallels its origins in play must surely be its role in producing and responding to works of verbal art. Here is the link we have felt between play and the arts; here we can accept the close affinity between reading a story and writing one; and here in its origins we can appreciate the *social* nature of individual literary experiences. 'Initially, an emotion is individual, and only by means of a work of art does it *become* social' (Vygotsky, *The Psychology of Art*, p. 243).

Story reading, as Margaret Spencer indicates (Chapter 11), satisfies a powerful intention because it derives from the autonomy-seeking of make-believe play, and similarly offers alternatives to reality. All the writings in this section work to extend as well as deepen our conceptions of a literary work. Barbara Hardy (Chapter 12), sees novels as 'pieces of living' and would have us bring to a text, where appropriate, 'all our knowledge of playing and loving and being young'. And Mike Torbe

(Chapter 13), provides time and encouragement for his students to develop in talk and writing a web of associations that ties the work of fiction into the reality of their own lives: it is thus that we 'find somewhere to put' what we are able to draw from 'the common pool of humanity'.

11 The Place of Literature in Literacy: 'Dip a Finger into Fafnir'[1]*

Margaret Spencer (University of London Institute of Education)

I realize that we are here to discuss a topic that is bound to challenge every generation of teachers because it renews itself as society changes and education evolves. Literacy, once the privilege of the few, has become in our day, or so we like to think, the right, the obligation, the burden of all as our social organization assumes its prevalence and counts on its efficiency. There can be no argument about the importance of literacy. An illiterate person is a social outcast, if only because that is how he sees himself. But the optimism that once made buoyant our belief that enough teachers, enough books, good research into methods, and the effective training of teachers would make all children and adults able to read and write has given way to desperate anxieties. At this time when, globally, education is once again the battlefield for even more profound social and political problems, the drive for literacy is generally urged as the most important single issue. All our hopes for curriculum reform, the enlightenment brought by inspired theorists, the growth in language studies that has made teaching the mother tongue a significant interdisciplinary activity – all are dashed by reports of unemployed teenagers applying for jobs for which they are not fitted because they are said to lack 'the basic skills' of reading and writing. The failure of so-called progressive, open-plan, integrated-day teaching is urged and thumped about by the formalists who demand 'back to the desk', 'children must be taught skills', 'down with discovery'.

Our long-awaited, conscientiously written Bullock Report (HMSO, 1975) found *no* decline in attainment over the years in the lowest achievers among 15-year-olds. Yet it is given much less credence in the UK than a well-marketed publication of some inadequate research which proclaimed the failure of progressive methods (Bennett, 1976). Literacy is being linked in people's minds with public discipline just as it was when, in the nineteenth century, Robert Raikes took the children of the English poor into Sunday Schools. From time to time in the matter of the education of the people we have to engage in the activity that Coleridge called 'rattling the fundamentals'. Our problem is that, outside the arena of our educational endeavour, only certain answers may be acceptable. It is, for example, no longer the time for massive book-buying programmes as a way out of our difficulty. Research can no longer assume that finance will be forthcoming. 'Work', applied to the teaching of reading and writing, has a more sombre

*Reprinted, by permission, from *The English Quarterly*, vol. IX, no. 4. winter 1976–7).

sound for both teachers and students.

I state all this at some length because I believe that these are matters of common concern on both sides of the Atlantic, and because it would be easy to brush away what I am going to say next as the idealism of someone who is out of touch with contemporary reality. If anything, the reverse is true. I spend part of every teaching week with the adolescents who cause concern. Far more evidence of their problems and their reading difficulties are logged in the tape-recorded lessons of these gifted teachers who are my students than has hitherto been generally available. From this evidence it is clear that we have been too simplistic by far in assuming that the teachers, the taught and the book are the main elements in this situation. I have listened for hours to the stumbling and straining that give way to ease and confidence in one student and to blank despair in another. I comb the research for hints as to what gives the 4-year-olds superb confidence and great pleasure, and as to why the 14-year-olds may not even want to try. If I have anything significant to say it is because my life as an English teacher has never let me leave this reading business alone, from the child setting out to the twelfth-grader and the Diploma student.

The only years I regret are those I spent arguing about methodology. What Jeanne Chall called 'The Great Debate' about how to teach reading has led us up too many blind alleys. By concentrating on method, by believing that the teaching mattered more than the learning, we obscured what we needed to see: that some of the best readers are successful without any pedagogic intervention. We have ignored the fact that, whatever their incentive or their socio-economic status, hundreds of children teach themselves to read in spite of what we tell them to do. They devise a means of taking on the written form of language that *makes it mean* something.

Now that we look at reading and writing in the total pattern of language development, as forms of symbolic representation, other possibilities emerge: for example, that we should examine what the successful reader of any age does when he moves with ease through our print-laden world, and how the learner sets about the job he has to do. When Frank Smith linked the child learning to read with the child learning to talk, he unpacked the theoretical log jam we had got into. Before *Understanding Reading* helped us do just that, our model of reading was the hierarchy of skills one. We worried about the child's acquisition of visual acuity, aural acuity, fluency in spoken language, and his progress in putting them all together. We saw his failure to learn as a deficit in a system which then had to be retrained by the application of special materials, so we bent our energies to remedying the deficits. Given all the reading research that exists, the business investment in every device from medical technology to books and paper, we could claim that we have given much conscientious attention to this literacy business, attention, that is, to the teacher's role. But the skills model of literacy has failure as its matrix. The research of two decades has looked at what children and adults can't do, and devised tests to prove that they are deficient. Before Frank Smith, only a few outsiders like Ronald Morris

(Morris, 1971) and the remarkable Huey in 1903, looked at success before failure.

In so far as we have urged the teaching of literacy skills because they are useful, we discounted the evidence of those who read because reading and writing were something more than useful tools. In school we have kept the idea that literacy is first trained then used, so that we have produced a well-documented pathology of *illiteracy*. Its very vocabulary accuses us: semi-literate, reluctant reader, reading-arrested, remedial education. We still cling to these ideas as if to challenge them were to call in question the expertise of the teacher and the teacher of teachers. I suggest that we have stared into this abyss of failure far too long and that the result is, as Goethe suggested it would be, the abyss is now staring into us. As I have already said, there is no denying the importance or the necessary usefulness of literacy, but this definition is too narrow, too nineteenth-century for our times when reading and writing will only be successfully taught if these activities are firmly grappled to the life purposes of the learner.

We need, first, some guidelines for a definition of literacy in our day. That is easy to say, difficult to produce. The Bullock Report shirked but acknowledged the difficulty. 'The level of literacy required for participation in modern society is far above that implied in earlier definitions', it states, and adds, 'as society becomes more complex and makes higher demands in awareness and understanding of its members, the criteria of literacy will rise.' In teachers' minds is this idea of society 'making demands' like the rising school leaving age, or endless postgraduate examinations. But the fully literate do not simply meet prescribed norms: they create their own place in society. They contribute to what is written to be read. They are not victims of official papers, but users of language for purposes which they define. To the literate, as Paolo Freire says, '[it] is not a true act if it is not at the same time associated with the right of self-expression and world-expression, of creating and recreating, of deciding and choosing and ultimately participating in society's historical process' (Freire, 1972, p. 30).

At each stage in becoming literate there is 'creating and re-creating'. A 30-year-old auto worker who had screwed up his courage to get help said, 'Before I started [to learn] I always used to buy a newspaper because I wanted to learn to read it, and felt I didn't look a fool if I had one. But I was always frightened to pull it out of my pocket in case someone leaned over my shoulder and said, "What's that?" Now it's not so bad. I can actually open a paper and read it.'

For this man, reading is not decoding the print: it's counting as a person in a world where reading counts: *seeing himself as a reader* is the reward. No study of literacy can ignore the context of the reader's situation and his intentions. The illiterate adult doesn't see himself as someone who can't do what other people can do. He sees himself as a different kind of person.

If you ask a group of successful young readers how they learned, they can separate the literacy of their surroundings, which is social and useful, from *stories*, the solitary commitment to the book. Those who arrive at school almost or completely able to read construe themselves as readers. They are clear that there is something in it for them that has to do with what they are reading and want to read. Recent research into *Young Fluent Readers* (Clark, 1976) makes it clear that we shall have to revise the folklore that surrounds their success. The support of an enthusiastic reading adult is the key factor in most cases, but Margaret Clark says, 'the richness of support for education which these families were providing was not measurable on scales such as social class, father's occupation, father's education, mother's education or even the number of books in the house'. The crucial factor was a shared enjoyment of what was being read, which engages the powerful element of consent to a lot of solitary practice.

The auto worker and the children know, in completely different ways, that it is useful to get information from reading and to pass it on by writing, but it is also crucial to grow as a person. This includes taking on meaning in its printed form. It involves asking the right questions about the relation between language and print. What these questions are and the kind of answers the children give themselves are the things we simply don't know enough about and would do well to find out.

The reason we haven't asked the right questions about reading may lie in the fact that some of them have nothing to do with teaching as we have understood it. How do children take on the conventions of the written language as distinct from what they hear in speech? The rhetoric of literature is highly particularized language and is far removed from talk, yet some children accept it without batting an eyelid. How do young readers bypass the surface structures of the text – vocabulary, sentence length, unfamiliar words – to get to meaning? How do they learn to link episodes, evoke characters that have no counterpart in life as they know it (e.g. a princess)? How do they not only read the text but get the message? How do they make up stories from pictures? The evidence from adult non-readers is clear: they have little or no experience in reading related to the necessary pleasure of story-telling. The evidence from the successful children is equally clear: they want to read stories above all. The reason is strangely simple: they tell stories all the time. The context of the child's situation is that he uses narrative as the form that best matches his world and his experience of it and he looks to stories to confirm and extend his experience. Where he meets stories in a book he learns *how to make them mean*, in every sense.

Adults, always organizing things according to the logic of usefulness, see stories as the necessary beginning. Then, when children seem competent, they switch their reading to books of information as this appears to make them autonomous learners. Thus the usefulness notion of reading is reinforced. School proceeds on this assumption. Secondary school teachers bewail the reluctance or incapacity of students to read the textbooks and the conflict is intensified. Then we have studies that show that even children who can read seem to read less and less as they grow older. The activity grows less attractive and we wonder why.

The remedy is at the root of the matter. In the early years of reading the lucky children may be given the *Children's Britannica* for Christmas, but they generally have stories read to them where the experience and the language are one:

Long ago in a far-eastern city lived a poor woman, widow of Mustapha the tailor, and her son named Aladdin. The woman made a meagre living for them both spinning cotton, for the boy, a lad of idle and carefree nature spent all his time from dawn to dusk in play with youths of the streets.

One late afternoon, while Aladdin was loitering with his companions in the market place, a strange merchant came that way. For a while he watched the youths intently and then, calling a young boy, questioned him about Aladdin, his name and kindred, his address and occupation, and all else relating to his circumstances. Now this merchant was in truth an evil sorcerer.[2]

And off we go, in the way that was hallowed even before Sir Philip Sydney described the enchantment that draws 'children from play and old men from the chimney corner'.

The pace, the flourish, the formula of the fairy-tale stay in the head as splendour and magic at a time when development is psychic and linguistic, inextricably linked. When I shopped last week in the Portobello Road where I live, I lingered by some fake antiques to watch and listen to some children – all under 6 I guess: two Greek Cypriot girls, two East African Asian boys and a West Indian boy, much smaller, playing and singing that genuine antique London air 'Oranges and Lemons', word perfect, action perfect, over and over again. I wondered who taught them – other children of course, school perhaps. Then they danced around and sang something I'd never heard: their own lore, TV jingles, the pop songs of now that are the street rhymes of later.

Why do we underestimate the linguistic variety of children? Why do we so discount the joke, the best short story form of all, the pun, the counting rhymes, the richness that the Opies found by listening to the children talking? As for singing, I'm constantly amazed by the way we ignore the whole business of language rhythms, the natural action that is song. The language of children at play always seems to me so much more varied and experimental than the adult-dominated classroom exchanges that emerge from well-meaning but often poorly conceived attempts to reform their so-called language inadequacies.

We should be less anxious about 'real' book language, for instance, if we attended more to the kinds of 'storying' children do when they play. It has all the conventions, rules and variety for reprocessing experience. Narrative is part of a child's thought process before he knows what a 'story' is. He uses it as a holding device for experience. Because narrative is the most common and effective way of ordering experience, children come to school as experienced story-tellers. They need teachers who understand that we all construe reality by telling ourselves stories about the world. The children begin to learn that there are different ways of going about explanations. Looking at a picture-book with a child and talking isn't the same activity as watching the hamster and talking. 'Once upon a time' isn't just the opening of a story, it's an invitation to see how language differentiates it. Thus in listening to stories the children have both the 'virtual experience' (Langer, 1953) of the characters and actions (the naughty princess, the valiant little tailor) and the literary experience of the telling. The rhetorical devices and conventions, even in the plainest tale which seeks to avoid all but the simplest effects, contribute to the understanding.

Perhaps it is because I move in two worlds that never sufficiently overlap, those of children's books and of English teaching, that I am persuaded that being literate in our day needs to be built on the child's desire to read in order to read stories. The hosts of talented writers for children offer, at all stages, the great diversity of styles and kinds on which contemporary literacy must rest. We have acknowledged them, but as a kind of minor cult for adults, or as the reward for children who have climbed the ladder of the basal reader. We have yet to regard literature as the best reading scheme we have, and to use it to confirm our children as readers.

Let me show you one or two – out of the many – things we neglect. We bewail the dominance of TV instead of looking at the kind of visual experience the best of it offers children. They learn early to make sense of symbols, and of ways that evoke meaning and feeling, narrative, character and response. Elizabeth Cook (Cook, 1976) points out that, 'mythic stories characteristically evolve from seen ritual images and a peculiarly visual quality survives in most of the forms in which they have come down to us. In reading the story of Jason one is . . . *seeing* a space between a whirlpool and a monster, or a witch and a warrior standing beside a tree and a serpent coiled round it and a golden sheepskin hanging from it.' Quite early, children can differentiate pictures that tell a story not in the text from those that reinforce the text. What use do we make of all that in early teaching? It may be true that the dominance of visual ideas means that we have to work harder to help children listen more intently, but it is also true that TV dialogue helps them to follow meaning from the most laconic utterances in modern writing.

Secondly, I think we underestimate the strength of the bond a child makes with a real author and the intuitive rightness of skilled authors' judgements about children. This is another aspect of the way the storying the child is doing for himself meets the story he is told. We are so busy looking for material that is 'suitable' for children because the nineteenth-century preoccupation with didacticism has given way to a post-Freudian notion of vicarious experience. The fact is, we know very little about the affective and moral development of children. But I want to read them *Where the Wild Things Are* not because it is about guilt and restitution, which it is, brilliantly and beautifully symbolic, but because Sendak is a great story-teller who names the unnameable. His audience responds by saying, 'Yes, that's how it is because that's how it feels.' The good author gives the children a credible secondary world to practise growing up in. The continuum from this to adult literacy is clear and direct. Literature is a mode of apprehending experience and language is its medium.

So why, in teaching children to read and write, do we give all our attention to the surface structures of language and ignore the differentiations the learner can make, if we let him, between ways of saying? Our passion for simple texts has confused simplicity with over-simplification. 'And it was still hot' at the end of *Where the Wild Things Are* is a loaded statement which includes 'And my Mother loved me just the same'. There is nothing rhetorically poetic about Sendak's language, yet between the first sentence and the last the reader has 'dipped a finger into Fafnir' and 'traded another's sorrow for his own'.

Consider in contrast, 'This is Peter, this is Jane', which has nothing but a common declaratory mode to which little response is possible, which holds out only a tentative invitation and promises no play. The prevalence of the common declaratory mode in early reading books seems to the child to be the only value placed on the activity. Very early he distinguishes between real books and reading books. It isn't that I am advocating the rhetoric and fantasy of the fabulous against the everyday writing of the ordinary. ' "Where is father going with that axe" said Fern one morning at breakfast' still seems to me one of the most powerful first sentences ever written. But it now seems clear that growth in literacy has to come from a wealth of kinds of discourse. The young fluent readers are highly self-critical when they write, for example, because of the force exerted by the models of sentences in their aural and visual memories.

If we offer children a share in our belief that language is a mode of apprehending they will respond to a great many ways of telling. 'Literacy is useful' is an idea like 'communication' that ignores language as a means of growth. The virtual experience of the sequence and salience of literature, language 'in the spectator role', however defined, extends and confirms the inner fiction which is our way of interpreting the world. As the world grows more complicated and our handling of it more necessary, the transcultural mode of writing more prevalent and more threatening, so we need readers who know that print gives them power, otherwise we may find we have children who can read but don't, – who assume that they are society's victims.

I know only too well the temptations that beset those who (generally women) concern themselves with this reading business. We all seem to be borrowing Rimbaud's phrase: 'j'ai seule la clef de cette parade sauvage'. I have no key, no method, only a tape-recording of a West Indian boy in a class for new readers reading *The Iron Man* with passionate ritual intensity, which confirms my conviction that literature is not the reward of learning to read, but the way by which the successful sometimes teach themselves and the way most teachers have most neglected. It might be time to call in all these powerful allies who have been waiting in the wings or on the shelves far too long and give them a turn on the centre of the stage.

Notes

1. Randall Jarrell, 'Children selecting books in a library', from *Collected Poems*, New York, Farrar, Strauss & Giroux, 1969.
   In Scandinavian mythology Fafnir was a magician who turned himself into a dragon to guard the ill-fated hoard of the Nibelungs, hidden in a cave. The poet seems to use Fafnir to refer to the place.
2. *Aladdin*, retold by Naomi Lewis, London, Bodley Head, 1968.

References

Bennett, N. (1976) *Teaching Styles and Pupil Progress*, London, Open Books.
Clark M. (1976) *Young Fluent Readers*, London, Heinemann Educational Books.
Cook, E. (1976) *The Ordinary and the Fabulous*, Cambridge, Cambridge University Press.
Freire, P. (1972) *Cultural Action for Freedom*, Harmondsworth, Penguin.
HMSO (1975) *A Language for Life* (The Bullock Report).
Langer, S. (1953) *Feeling and Form*, London, Routledge & Kegan Paul.
Morris, R. (1971) *Success and Failure in Learning to Read*, Harmondsworth, Penguin.

12 The Teaching of Literature in the University: Some Problems*

Barbara Hardy (*Professor of English, Birkbeck College, University of London*)

One of the chief problems for the teacher of English who is a literary critic, is one arising constantly in the universities, though of course less often in schools and colleges. But all teachers of literature are critics when they think and teach, and even those teachers who may, for better or worse, lack critical aptitude or interest, find themselves exposed to the influence and findings of literary criticism.

Like the teacher in a good infants school, the university teacher of literature will *as a teacher* be interested not chiefly in his own relation to his subject but in his pupils' relation to the subject. There are three sets of human particulars in a teaching situation: the particularity of the work and the author, the particularity of the teacher, and the particularity of the student. No one of these is an authority: they are or were all people.

In a paper given for a NATE conference[1] I described a student's response to Thomas Hardy's poem 'During Wind and Rain'. He rejected the idyllic presentation of family order, peace, happiness and creativity by calling it Victorian and complacent. I had previously responded to the way the poem faces the harsh facts of mutability and death and uses the family-idyll as a symbol of human transience and futility, and had never questioned its presentation of the family as a symbol of harmony and joy. When the student showed me his response, my reaction was to see the poem as changed itself by history, in a way we all theoretically acknowledge to be possible but seldom catch happening. I also appreciated the exercise of this particular judgement as a useful example of a student's use of literature to impersonalize strong personal feelings about families and institutions. While I gladly lost the poem – or what I had possessed as the poem – in the interest of tolerating the student and learning things about teaching, I was learning something else about the poem. At the time I didn't recognize this, absorbed as I was in the interest of the teaching situation, having moved from Hardy to thoughts of the student and the (Victorian) college and my teaching. But some months later, partly through discussing my 'lost poem' with a Hardy scholar, I came to see that the student was not just rejecting the poem for the sake of his necessary personal and social protest, but was seeing something in it that I had missed. He was seeing, as my friend pointed out, that the poem shows the sentimentalizing sieve of memory. It is not simply saying that these happy days had been and were no more, but

*.Abridged, by permission, from *English in Education*, vol. 7, no. 1, Spring 1973.

also saying, more subtly, that when we look back, in spite of the inexorable passage of time, and because of it, we select the candle-light and family music and sunny days and bright new house. The images chosen are not just joyful moments shown exposed to the storm and loss and death, but peculiarly ironic selections from the memory's determined yet vain creativity.

Mediatating on what I had thought I tolerated, I came to a better understanding of the poem as well as the student. This is what we should more commonly expect to happen in our teaching, in spite of generation gaps and protest. Books are not impersonal and fixed but created by peculiarly complex and open imaginations; in the meeting of the reader with the book, we often have a selection made by simplicity from complexity. Therefore two heads are better than one; and just as many occasions make for richness, so too do a collection of responses by different people. If the teacher tries hard not to fix, impose, and assume 'the right meaning', the conflict of responses may disappear and be replaced by the collaboration of response. Such collaboration will produce that especially joyous sensation of finding out something about teaching and about literature.

I once read W.H. Auden's 'Lay Your Sleeping Head' with a group of students. Not deliberately, but in an almost spontaneous reaction to a student who wondered 'if they were married' or perhaps kept on saying 'she', I said that it was almost certainly a poem about homosexual love. I got a very violent reaction from one student, who angrily said I had spoilt the poem for him and that he wished very much I hadn't told him. We did not go on to an extra-literary discussion of sexuality or tolerance, but the violent human reaction, the third voice of the student, was clearly of very great extra-literary interest, and probably led, not in explicit and on-the-spot discussion, but in the ongoing thinking that is often more creative and valuable than what happens in the class, to a rethinking of rejection and tolerance. The strong and unexpected response took me into further reflections about the nature of the poem, and eventually to further reflections about homosexual and heterosexual love-poetry, homosexual and heterosexual love. The teacher's tolerant, liberal, bland voice, the student's intolerant, candid, angry voice and the poet's veiled, troubled, masterly voice joined in a unique occasion. Untied, the thread led off in different directions. The occasion was alive. Poem, student, teacher, were all changed.

Some teachers have the gift of inspiring students to talk first about life and then look at the books in the context of talk about life-outside-literature, but for most people it seems to work better the other way round, so that the book on the table, the thing out there and common to us all, can focus, provoke and safely impersonalize the discussion. This is not, of course, to say that the discussion will never get on to generalities or specific personal experience. I can remember many such movements, friendly and illuminating. There was the moment when a discussion of religious feeling in *Anna of the Five Towns* led both teacher and some students to begin by verifying details from their experience – such details as the feeling of shame and envy and superiority that you can feel if you are an unresponding member of a revivalist meeting. The discussion went from Bennett to our own lives and back to Bennett again. The result was not only a fine implicit tribute to his realism, without overt analysis or judgement, but also good talk in which his voice was one of many voices.

On many occasions – probably most – the personal experience is not made explicit: we may sense it in the quality of a voice's feeling, a smile, a frown, or a stroke of insight or rejection. The balance of the subject/object response will vary not only according to the nature and relations of teacher and student but also, evidently, according to the institution. In a paper[2] written for the seminar on 'Response to Literature', for the Dartmouth Conference of 1966, Wallace Douglas (of Northwestern University) and I formulated this subject/object response this way:

We often suppose, encouraged by schematic literary criticism and the demands of examinations, that formulation should be explicit, broad, and objectified. As teachers we should remember how long it takes even to respond to poems of our own choice, how often we are quite naturally numb to parts of wholes as we encounter literature and not expect too much from the students. First encounters in the classroom should deliberately hold back formulation, should back away from everything that isn't tentative and partial. We need to encourage, very warmly, verifications from personal experience, not frown on the 'That's me' identification with a character.

People who need to use the concept of 'discipline' in talking about response will be uneasy about the freedom of 'That's me', but it can perhaps be accommodated even to a literary respect for the work of art. 'That's me' has two components, and our aim is to move dynamically from the 'me' of personal identification to the 'that' of the poem or the object in the poem. The discipline lies in the attentiveness to the 'that', and it should be made plain that there is no real dichotomy here, but a natural movement from subject to object and back again. The 'That's me' may well reveal a very partial and too selective selection from the work, but the teacher will get nowhere in the attempt to make the work meaningful as experience if he does not begin with the 'me'. And this identifying is often more interesting than it looks. A middle-aged schoolmaster who said 'I am Bobadil' was not just being confessional, for he proceeded to look around and say that everyone else was too. The discussion of the 'that' was a discussion of the humanness of Jonson which moved miles away from autobiographical chat. But the particularized responses should be primary. There will be movement round the many people in the class, and a restrained and thoughtful sharing of personal, incomplete, and implicit response which can lead back to the particular work, and to repeated sensitive readings. The reference to life is not purely illustrative but confirms the affective experience of literature, and is of course its foundation.

The teacher should aim at the teacher's, not the scholar's best, dropping the possessiveness we all seem to feel so readily for works of literature. The teacher reporting the 'low level' exclamatory response, or 'the autobiographical bit', or the 'extreme' selection betrays an unholy preference for poems rather than persons. If the implicit or partial or wrong response is stamped on by these literature lovers, there will be little chance that the student can be taken back from the 'me' to the 'that' in an extended exploration of the work's properties.

The extreme assurance of this extract shows the heady air of educational conferences. I hasten to add that the model suggested – there will be movement round the many people in the class . . . and so on – describes a collective act of response I have hardly ever experienced sustainedly since the Dartmouth Conference. In most undergraduate teaching in university there is very great difficulty in combining the 'that' and the 'me' of literary response.

One class where I did feel a coming together of the 'that' and the 'me' was a graduate seminar in Northwestern University, on the topic of 'Feeling in Fiction'. The students were fairly mature, probably especially willing to co-operate with a visitor, at work on a human topic, and unbound – for that class – by formal examinations. I had chosen a topic that I hoped would let me teach against the environment without the burden of having to unteach before I could teach. It was also a topic on which I had done a little but not too much thinking, so that I was able and eager to learn with the students. My texts were all chosen with an eye to openness. Some of them were novels I knew well, but had only thought about very vaguely in connection with this subject (*The Mill on the Floss* and *Henry Esmond*); some were novels I knew well but had not thought about at all in connection with the subject (*Persuasion, Sons and Lovers*); and two were novels I didn't know at all well (*To the Lighthouse* and *Anna of the Five Towns*). The students knew *The Mill on the Floss* and *Persuasion*, a few of them knew *Sons and Lovers*, but *Esmond, Anna* and *To the Lighthouse* they mostly came to for the first time. 'Nothing on symbols and structure' said someone, only half pleased. And that was pleasantly true. But the conditions in which we were learning were unrepresentative and rare.

In attacking the impersonality and sterotyping of literary criticism, I have another reason for separating analytic criticism from teaching. One of the advantages of being a critic as well as a teacher is that you are in a position to attack what is part of your own life. Those of us who have moved from a taste for symbolic and structural analysis to a better appreciation of the particularities of feeling and character, can know the process of over-systematized study. Only those who have done formal analysis can know its unholy charm. It is easy to be superior about its hold on uncertain students who have been trained not to trust their own response. It is easy to say scathingly that structural analysis is easy to teach, and can be taught to anyone who can read, write and count. The teaching of literary sensibility, judgement and intellectual comprehension is a very much more difficult matter. But it is unfair to the fascination of formal analysis to stress its accessibility: it is also absorbing. Spot the symbol and catch the image-chain is a lovely game. And to go back to what I said earlier, we are all caught up in the academic environment where someone has at some time played or heard of someone else playing this game so that very often we have to teach it in order to unteach it. There are the trained products of examinations, over-sophisticated sixth-form teaching and proliferating teaching aids all around us. If I want to say that a certain passage makes a particular impact, as well as being important in its relation to the total structure, theme and symbolism, I can hardly ever just talk about the particularity. In order to do so, I usually have to take up and put down formal analysis. The environment has made us familiar with such analysis, and a simpler, more humanly sensitive but in some ways more 'superficial' response is very hard to encourage. Add the fact that in examinations at all levels the questions tend to require the impersonal 'learnt' and 'rehearsed' analysis or judgement, and it will be seen that teaching against the academic environment is not easy even for those eager to throw off their very own chains. 'What's wrong with image and symbol, then?' asks a puzzled colleague setting an exam paper. 'Where does form come in?' asks a teacher to whom I have been preaching the doctrine of taking the work by the minute and on the surface.

Of course there are good, bad and middling ways of teaching formal analysis. The analysis of image and symbol tends to be particularly dry and stereotyped because cut off from life. A discussion of Dickens's food-symbolism in *Great Expectations* may be used, as it customarily is in formal analysis, to describe the 'organic form' of the novel, with reference to the aesthetic relationship of the parts to the whole. But this symbolism can also be thought about more humanely. The problems of generosity, need, hunger, hospitality, good manners, showing-off, aggression, snobbishness, gracefulness, false and good ceremony can be used to relate the symbolic meals to the moral and social significance of meals in life outside literature. Thus 'formal' analysis can be life-directed.

To take a larger instance: if the values of order shown in fiction are related not only to abstract notions of aesthetic order but to the impulse to shape, tell, record, plan and fantasize in all our fiction-making, a connection will be made which can valuably connect the experience of life with that of literature, and clarify the human particulars in relation to the individual reader. Books are not objects of disciplined study, not absolutely dead things, but are pieces of living. Their rhythms are related to the rhythms of our passions and perceptions, their symbols are like ours, their fictions made of the same stuff as our dreams, memories and anticipations.

The most influential English critic of our time, F.R. Leavis, certainly cannot be accused of the segregation of form from life that is typical of much New Criticism. Leavis indeed used to attack the claims of the classicists in much the same terms as those some of us use to attack the narrowness and impersonality of English studies. He has always emphasized the transfer of the value of a critical training from literary study to living. I repeat what I said and quoted in the talk I gave to the NATE conference in York, Easter 1968. This began with an extract from *Education and the University* (1943), which I described as 'the most forceful and lucid statement I know of the critic's belief that literary criticism, analytical and judicial, should be the purpose and centre of an English school'. Then followed this passage, which starts with Leavis:

> He says: 'The essential discipline of an English school is the literary-critical; it is a true discipline, only in an English school if anywhere will it be fostered, and it is irreplaceable. It trains, in a way no other discipline can, intelligence and sensibility together, cultivating a sensitiveness and precision of response and a delicate integrity of intelligence – intelligence that integrates as well as analyses and must have pertinacity and staying power as well as delicacy.' Leavis makes it very plain that his belief in the importance and centrality of what he calls the literary critical discipline has a moral base and impulse. He is not, as an English teacher and judicial critic, arguing for any kind of literary parthenogenesis. He doesn't want the kind of education in and through English that is going to produce more and more literary scholars and literary critics. On the contrary, he sees this training in sensibility, intelligence and judgement, as a training for life, and he says, a little later on, that the judgement that we, as teachers of English, should be concerned to train, is inseparable from that 'profoundest sense of relative value which determines or should determine, the important choices of actual life'. He is saying that the teacher of English in universities should be concerned with the literary critical discipline *and* that this is an education for living.
>
> In looking back at this book, there are some things I am very impressed by. I am very impressed by his concern for relationships between English Studies and other studies. I am impressed by his emphasis on what he sees as a humane discipline in a society which he says has a technocratic drift. I am impressed by a good deal that he has to say about the nature of the sensibility that one wants to train, and about the delicacy, the integrity, and tact that are involved in the act or art of teaching. There are some things, however, that impress me less. One of the things that most depresses me is the way he seems to pass over the problem of the student.[3]

Leavis's students are often impressive because of the quality of their caring both about literature and about teaching. They are not, however, in so far as one can generalize about a group of disciples, impressively open-minded as judges. Leavis's celebratedly tentative, 'It is so, is it not?' has two dangers. The excellent teacher can over-teach, can persuade us to accept rather than to question, tease, test, and possibly reject. Further, behind the tentative rhetoric lies an admirable, well-reasoned but fixed book of judgements. We know the Great Tradition, and like all books of judgement it is a personal structure. It is a reasoned anthology, to be sure, but shaped by the pressures of a particular life in a particular time and place.

He is an excellent teacher, and accordingly his book of judgement speaks eloquently for more than the personal structure. It is neither bizarre nor idiosyncratic but as representative of its time and place and – especially – of his academic environment and his Englishness – as Johnson's book of judgement is of his environment and temper. Teachers of very different experience and values, like David Holbrook or John Dixon, have plainly been very influenced by Leavis's predilection for the affirmative and constructive voice. Of course, events have moved swiftly in the last decade, and we are already finding that some dents have been made in the Great Tradition. But the Schools Council pamphlet *Humanities for the Young School Leaver: An Approach Through English* and the now classic anthology and aid, *Reflections*, for all their social conscience, breadth and anti-élitism, share Leavis's criterion of moral affirmation and life-enhancing quality as well as his optimism about transfer from literature to living.

Our present students make it difficult for us to hand over the canon, and though their criterion of 'relevance' is one it is easy to feel superior to, it proffers a useful corrective to the sense of High Value. The High Value, even for Leavis, has tended to have a certain national prestige, no doubt in the face of the dread 'Americanization' of value. But many students who do not share the faith in Englishness or European civilization can come up and challenge the very life-affirmation for its smugness, complacency and lack of eloquence. We have to make room for Swift, without apology and with pride, for the late bad writing but marvellous good faith of Mark Twain, for Sylvia Plath and Hubert Selby.

Such sacrifices will hurt some of us more than others. It is still possible to make literary judgements: the weaknesses of James Baldwin, like those of Twain's *The Mysterious Stranger* or George Eliot's *Daniel Deronda*, are explicable in human terms. It is hard for the artist to pare his fingernails and be like God in some moments of history. Questions are coming up from the students. It is getting harder to stay behind the rostrum and teach without learning. We do not have to go in for relevance and give up all other value, for the quest for relevance has the advantage of providing not so much good answers as good topics for debate. There is the question of the degree of relevance: of course there has to be some, but once more the subject/object relation of the 'that's me' comes in. We identify, but not wholly. Tom Jones's defects and merits are not wholly ours, but his divisions and debates are psychologically recognizable. Jane Austen's world is socially very different from ours but the very differences highlight the shared residue. This was made plain in a recent response I met in an American student writing about relevance. Many students use the criterion of relevance as a quick substitute for reasoned rejection of Jane Austen, but this one pointed to the characters' lack of freedom to choose their environment and constrasted it with her own sense that she was free to choose her society. The comment led in two directions, like all the best 'That's me' insights: to a discussion of Jane Austen's sense of environmental closure and then to a sense of her interest in changing environments, shown perhaps most impressively in *Mansfield Park*; and also to a questioning of the student's supposed freedom of social choice.

The demand for relevance does indeed force the teacher to concern himself with judgement. It is my belief that the training of judgement, like the pursuit of happiness or salvation, is best attained implicitly and indirectly. Constant exercises in comparison combining analysis with judgement, seem often to produce in the student a premature judicial itch, a nervous unrest, which may inhibit the relaxed searching of wise passiveness. I was once asked to comment, more or less unprepared, on some passages from fiction, and began with Mrs Gaskell's account of Esther's death from the end of *Mary Barton*. My examiner, in this private experiment, set me this passage in the expectation that I would reject it, especially as it was placed with some more powerful and particularized Dickens and Hardy. I picked out, very much at random, details that struck me, and began by praising certain aspects of Mrs Gaskell's dramatic handling of pathos. I did eventually come to some statement of disapproval, though modified by the suggestion that Mrs Gaskell could do better and Dickens could do as badly. In several ways I disappointed my examiner. The truth was that I am not very interested in the explicit evaluative comparisons of literature and even when faced with several instances of different quality will tend to look at them as distinct rather than competitively related. But students brought up to analyse comparatively and judicially will probably react in the opposite way, and start off at a suspicious distance from their texts. Judgement is tricky, is a matter to be earned, as Longinus says, by considerable intellectual experience, but the mature judgement can only too easily impose itself on the immature response. Which would we rather have – a genuinely personal affection for Lawrence Durrell or an imitated respect for the Great Tradition? Let us accept the shifting of taste, and let us show our faith in the Great Tradition by teaching as much as possible of the literature we admire, without worrying too much about canons and with attention to variety rather than moral unity. Let us admit that good taste and proper judgement have to be worked out slowly and painfully and personally, and that it is each man for himself. We are less likely to alienate, corrupt and inhibit judgement if we refrain from direct inculcation of value.

Easier said than done. Trying to ensure both my own freshness of response and judgement, I asked some first-year students to choose some poems for analysis. One man chose 'The Black Country' by D.J. Enright. To begin with, we were all taken up by the act of comprehension, then of appreciation and some not over-systematic analysis. I soon began to feel a strong distaste for the tendentiousness of the poet's use of argument, and was longing to say to the students: 'Stop thinking about his marvellous sense of colour and his structure: how is he pushing his attitude to life, his dislike of system?' There were pedagogic arguments for interfering *and* for sitting back. I decided to sit back, since the class was in any case one where I nudged rather than shoved. But it nagged at me: this was not simply a matter of disliking a doctrine, but the poet was doing precisely what he was criticizing, he was using poetry to twist truths, telling us that the Black Country (lovely old Black Country) was now all changed for the worse, and made uniform. The poetic lie was told by setting up a value for extremes, for black and white, and a distaste for grey – a subtle manipulation of aesthetic colour prejudice – paying no attention to the other connotations of black, or to the other aspects of social change. In the end, I dropped a hint, but not a very strong one. A typical liberal teacher's compromise. Had I violently rejected the poem I would have been rightly pushing on the side of life-values against purely formal concerns: but I should also have been imposing my judgement on the students. They had, after all, only had about half-an-hour on the poem. Moreover, it had been offered as someone's treasure. Next time they would feel less free, start to give me what I might want. I was probably right not to push. But it was a typical teaching problem, and typically unsolved. The dissenting voices are loud here, and perhaps they are right.

I want to end with an imaginary example, from *The Tempest*. It is an example chosen for two reasons: it is a moment of strong feeling, where you want your students to recognize the strong feeling; and I am looking at it for the first time, as I cannot be in instances I have already looked at in class.

In Act V, Scene I, Prospero, after lying to Alonso about the 'loss' of Miranda – it is actually a quibble not a lie, the product of Shakespeare's and Prospero's cunning – shows Miranda and Ferdinand playing at chess:

Miranda: Sweet lord, you play me false.
Ferdinand: No, my dearest love,
            I would not for the world.
Miranda: Yet, for a score of kingdoms you should wrangle,
            And I would call it fair play.

Like all scenes that are deeply eloquent of feeling and striking pieces of craftsmanship, this tiny passage raises the issue of priorities. What might we want our students to say about this exchange? Although this is a marvellous compressed and resonant passage, speaking out many of the central themes of the play – struggle, reconciliation, kingship, forgiveness, control, treachery, love, order, art, acting – I would not care if my students saw this thematic complex or not. But if they missed the particularity of passion, the rendering of this moment of love, I would be sorry. What matters about the game of chess is not its relation to the structure of idea and symbolism in the play as a whole, but its perfect rendering in four lines, framed and heightened in the action of the game, of the light and shade of this love, this relation. The four lines speak for the playfulness of love, its exaggeration, its teasing, its confident laughter at the idea of falsity, its capacity for forgiveness, its knowledge and admission of its own tolerance. They speak, if you like, straight from the heart of passion, passion that we all immediately recognize, in its affectionateness, its praise, its intimacy, its relaxation, its power, its gentleness. They also speak for these two people. The game allows them to play and to control: the game of chess is just right for innocent, chaste and ceremonial lovers who have promised to wait for marriage. Its elegance and intricacy is right for their status, role and intelligence. Its smallness is right for their self-contained relation. Its symbolism brings out both that smallness and the size of the world outside; its play reminds the audience of the serious version of struggle, reconciliation, and kings-and-queens that is making their destinies. Its courage is right for their youth, and especially for Miranda's sheltered innocence. The game of chess stands to the real world as her 'brave new world' stands to Prospero's larger experience. If you like, this response to feeling involves some literary criticism, and looks at the total effects of the dialogue and situation. But it is primarily concerned with ends, not means. With the end of human feeling. And – I suggest – this kind of comment on the immediate, the particular, the moment – will draw on the varied experience of the students. Different people will speak of different aspects of the feeling: one will be impressed by its tenderness, one by its wildness, one by its formal ritual, and so on. All our knowledge of playing and loving and being young will bear on the passage. If a discussion brought out this kind of response, I would be assured that everyone in the classroom was alive, including Shakespeare.

Notes

1. 'The teaching of English: life, literature and literary criticism', *English in Education*, vol. 2, no. 2, 1968.
2. *Response to literature,*1968, ed. James Squire, Urbana, Illinois, National Council of Teachers of English.
3. 'The teaching of English: life, literature and literary criticism'.

13   Modes of Response: Some Interactions between Reader and Literature*

Mike Torbe (Curriculum Development Officer, Coventry Education Authority)

I have always found the teaching of literature the most difficult of businesses. For many years I taught *about* literature, and shied away from the central questions I was posing myself all the time: what sort of sense are my pupils making of this piece of literature? How am I helping them to approach nearer to that essential centre of the work that first made me feel I wanted to place it before them? Like most English teachers of my generation, I found the conventional modes of literary criticism unsatisfactory. What was available to me when I started teaching and for years afterwards did not seem to help me in my search for something dimly seen: classroom discussions, literary critical essays, out-of-class chats with enthusiastic pupils, visits to theatres and museums – none of this seemed to help in assisting pupils towards the feeling centre of the work. When recently I read Barbara Hardy's article on 'Teaching literature in the university',[1] I felt a strong flow of recognition:

> There are three sets of human particulars in a teaching situation: the particularity of the work and the author, the particularity of the teacher, and the particularity of the student . . . . Too often there is only one voice in the lecture and even the seminar and the tutorial – that of the teacher. More commonly there are two, the voice of the teacher and the voice of the author, but the teacher may . . . drown the author's voice.

What was missing from my teaching, I came to see, was any recognition of the interaction between the voice of the author and the reader, which did not necessarily, or even usefully, involve the teacher. The teacher's role, which I had seen as being to mediate between literature and reader, could in fact be obstructive and harmful to the pupil's active engagement with a text. I needed to find some kind of teaching structure that would remove the teacher from the centre, and focus pupils simultaneously on their reading, and on their response to the reading. It was because of these concerns that I designed the course I will describe.

Because of recent reorganizations, the English Department in this Primary College of Education had devised a unit-based course, with compulsory and optional elements. My course was a second-year, five-week option course, three hours a week, with all three hours blocked on one morning. I decided we would concentrate on Twain and Hemingway,

---

*Abridged, by permission, from *English in Education*, vol. 8, no. 2, summer 1974.

especially *Huckleberry Finn*, *Farewell to Arms*, and *The Snows of Kilimanjaro*. The structure of the course included powerful constraints; apart from my choice of particular authors, and particular books of theirs, I drew the following limits:

1. The whole group (fourteen opted for the course) must work in subgroups of three or four.
2. The sub-group would, during the first week, make a tape-recording of itself talking about whichever of the books it had chosen to explore.
3. The sub-group *must* listen to this tape of the discussion.
4. Each individual must keep a personal logbook in which she was to jot down both what happened in the course and also what she thought and felt about what she was doing and reading.
5. The sub-group had to decide on a final piece of work, the only criterion for which was that it must *not* be a conventional literary critical essay. This product could be either individual in design and execution, or group-based.

Later, at the group's suggestion, we added another requirement – that we all meet together for the last hour or so of the morning.

My own role was left vague. I was around during the morning for consultation, and I tried to spend a session each morning with whichever group happened to be around, particularly when they were listening to their discussion on tape, because I felt (rightly, it turned out) that most of them would have difficulty in listening to their tapes with any real understanding and would need help in attending to what was actually there, rather than to what their predispositions led them to expect to be there. On two occasions, I had long sessions with individuals at their request. In the whole group discussions I tried to mediate between the work the different groups were doing – because working apart, they lost contact with each other – and to suggest ideas for general consideration.

I was concerned not only with literary response but also with the fact that these students were teachers in training, and it seemed important to me to consider literary response as an example of one kind of learning. In the College of Education it is possible to teach and learn and simultaneously to make the process of that teaching and learning the subject of inquiry, so that student-teachers can analyse the learning process to illuminate their future behaviour as teachers. Thus, I felt it necessary to explore the whole question of *languaging* – the choosing of forms and modes of language appropriate to what one is doing rather than those modes of language expected by academic custom or by conventionalized thinking about writing. Douglas Barnes suggests in 'Classroom contexts for language and learning'[2] that most teachers 'see language in terms of performance instead of in terms of learning'. The fact that the written work students in this college do is mainly in essay form supports Barnes's contention. An essay is, of its very nature, not the process but the product of learning, where the writer has to structure and organize what he previously learnt: thus most students and perhaps most school pupils too are being asked to learn and organize simultaneously. Simply, this is not possible. One organizes for public utterance what one has already learnt. In this context 'learning' involves the whole question of the image one has of oneself as a learner, and of oneself in relation to others; and one learns in this sense most successfully, it seems, in what James Britton calls 'expressive language':

> Expressive language is language close to the speaker: what engages his attention is freely verbalised, and as he presents his view of things, his loaded commentary upon the world, he also presents himself. Thus it is above all in expressive speech that we get to know one another, each offering his unique identity, and (at our best) offering and accepting both what is common and what differentiates us.
>
> Secondly it is in expressive speech that we are likely to rehearse the growing points of our formulation and analysis of experience (Britton, 1971).

There are several modes, private and public, appropriate for any learning situation, and for the learning to become meaningful the learner must decide for himself which mode to employ, why that and not another, and what demands this mode makes upon its user. The logbook was intended to offer a situation in which the student could use expressive language rather than the formal transactional modes she was used to being asked for in college. The kinds of response possible in this mode differ greatly from those possible in conventional modes.

Another problem for the students in encountering these modes was to define their audience. We discussed together whether the logbooks should be made public to the rest of the group: the decision, because of the way each individual had chosen to define the audience for their writing, was that they should not share their logs, because they had identified me as the reader, not each other, nor an impersonal marker-of-essays. Once they had made this decision, the logbooks, for many of the group, took on a particular intensity, in which the explorations of the group work and the literature became a searching out of new dimensions of response, which emerged with a growing coherence and confidence from the vagueness and aimlessness of the early entries in the logs. With their permission, I quote some entries from logs, to show what I mean.

Alethea is 20. Her first entries, like so many of the logs, are tentative and rather conscious of the situation:

> Monday June 5th. Read couple of chapters in the evening, had to put the book aside through lack of interest and concentration. Began to seem unreal.

I mentioned above that I expected students to have some difficulty with listening to the tape of the discussion. Alethea comments:

> Not too bothered by the tape recorder however found it difficult to speak about the book. Points were brought out but not further developed.

Three days later, the group listened to the tape:

> Listened to the tape. Better than I thought it would be. We had mentioned some good points but not discussed them deeply, we tended to skip the surface. For my part I think I lack understanding of the book and am having to explore different aspects.

This is a radical change for Alethea; before the *book* was seen as being the barrier: now she sees the barrier as being within herself, and needing an active effort on her part to overcome it.

A week after making the tape:

Listened to the tape with Mr Torbe. Listening to it brought up many points we had not previously thought of. What makes us say the things we do? It became obvious in one point how in trying to help Sue with a particular point she was making I cut off all line of thought – mine and Sue's. I couldn't carry on the idea as it wasn't mine, Sue wasn't thinking what I had thought. What would happen in a teaching situation? Became obvious how we drifted from the book as art form to the book as part of real life. We saw the characters as real people. Many points had just been passed over on the tape could now be considered.

I have just discovered how much easier I am finding it to talk in lectures. It has taken me two years to overcome it.

That something important happened to the way Alethea evaluates her reading, and therefore, perhaps, to the actual quality of her reading, is suggested by a later entry about *The Old Man and the Sea*, very different in its openness from the simplistic comments of the early entries in the log:

Haven't as yet managed to sort out my ideas. I suppose I don't really know what it is about. An old man battling with a fish, to overcome it. What has he to show for his trouble? He risked his life to overcome it with merely the skeleton to show for it. Everyone could see the result but nobody could know what he went through. He was alone except for the boy, who cared for him. What meaning is behind this story, prompting its writing?

At the end of the course, trying to evaluate what happened to her reading of *Huckleberry Finn*, she concludes:

I am gaining a slow liking for the book. The slowness of movement in the book reflects itself in my slowness of understanding. I am now determined to look further into it, a progression from my first disregarding of it.

Sue's comments throughout her log are longer and more relaxed and personal than many of the others. It was as though she found this mode offered a way of handling thoughts and feelings that had been denied to her in the conventional modes she was used to. I am not certain why this should be so: but part of the reason is that she finds the logbook writing afforded a relief from the feeling she is familiar with when she usually writes – that her thoughts are on public display, with all their inadequacies paraded to be mocked and belittled. In her log she moves steadily towards deeper understanding of the book, and of the process of literary response. Her entry for the day on which we listened to the tape:

We did not have the discussion after all but talked about our tape instead. I really believed that there was not much on the tape that was really relevant but as parts were pointed out I could really see their significance. The main thing that came out of the discussion was that, although we had all said that we hadn't liked the book much as we talked about it the more we realised (when hearing it) that the more we liked the book. How strange! I really wish that I could have a discussion after every book I read because I am sure it would iron out a few points and I would understand it more. One reads a book, enjoys it, puts it down and then usually forgets about it even though there are parts of the book that could be stretched and talked about further. I don't think it would do me much good writing about my thoughts on paper because my thoughts do not develop as much as when I'm talking and discussing them. Also when I write things down I feel that they are no longer part of me because the words, i.e. my thoughts, are now staring me in the face and therefore they are no longer part of me – they are no longer private – they have been made public for everyone to see and comment upon. Whereas when one is speaking, these ideas and thoughts are still yours even though they are being spoken – they still belong to me and are part of me because they are being spoken directly by me. This is very hard to explain. When writing it down – I really must talk about it. Other people have no difficulty in writing down their thoughts, but I do because they come out all disjointed and with not much order or sense to them – I think I'll have to take a course on writing down one's thoughts.

Sue's self-deprecation shows that it is possible for an intelligent girl to reach the second year of higher education without ever having been shown that this problem is not uniquely hers, but is common to all writers – 'trying to learn to use words . . .' She has been led by her experience of writing to feel that it must be of necessity structured and public, instead of being helped to discover that it may be a powerful learning mechanism. When the pressure of public display is removed, as it was in the logbook, what she writes shows a constant exploration of the new thoughts that come to her. It was this early, relatively unstructured stage of formulation that she had needed. The importance of this stage is immense: Vicki's log throughout shows thoughts at the point of formulation. Freed from the need of satisfying anyone but herself, she is able to speculate in ways that would have been impossible in the formal essays, in a language that is inconsequential, mazy, and implicit:

> How can some people teach the rest of the group anything? How do you point out to people what they have learnt? I suppose they could pick them up & say you wouldn't have said that before or you didn't have any ideas at all on that before. I think the trouble is that a lot of people have learnt an attitude towards the teacher & so don't want to know what they have learnt as it would not be in context with their attitude to the teacher. Its no good saying this is what I have learnt as they'll pick out lots of silly reasons to say why you have learnt & give lots of silly reasons to say why they didn't want to. The fact is they just don't want to face what they have learnt & some perhaps haven't learnt at all.

Liz Hatton, on the other hand, engages in a different kind of formulation, facing in her log powerful emotions, and coming to terms with them by writing about them:

> Read *Farewell to Arms* in the train going home. Finished it. I thought I was going to faint at the end – it made me feel really bad. I have never felt so disturbed by a book before. I am still suffering from shock. The trouble with being such an

optimist, or perhaps with reading too many second rate novels, is that I couldn't believe it was going to end with her death. It was too hurtful. Her death meant the end of everything . . . . It's awful writing this – it isn't making much sense because everything I write is subjective – I suppose the experience of the book is too near to be anything else. I was full of a sense of injustice.

Not all the writing in the logs is tentative or in process of being formulated. Pauline Marriott asks herself what she has learned from the course, and answers her own questions impressively:

I thought [when I started college] that English meant studying authors' lives and their work. I know now that it means much more than that. English is everything, it is our response to everything we read, it is the relationship between the way we feel and what we read and what we write . . .
What happens when I read a story? Just a few thoughts:
(a) I involve myself in a series of happenings and incidents.
(b) I'm not conscious of looking at words.
(c) A story adds a new facet to my experience.
(d) A story is always there to be looked at again.
(e) I never forget completely a story that means something to me at the time I read it.

It would, then, be wrong to suppose that the logbooks can only produce one kind of writing: they were used in different ways by different individuals. Margaret Pemberton, writing a sequence of poems about Time, generated by her thinking about the River in *Huck Finn*, found it unnecessary to do more than chart dates; Jane called hers 'Portrait of a self-engrossed adolescent'; while Liz Hatton was concerned with refining for herself a theory of art. 'All cases are unique, and very similar to others': what is unique to each log is the individual response of that person to the total situation of the course. There was no demand for some kind of conformist reaction confined by a known structure; and thus the similarity of the fourteen logs is in the sense of their release into the freedom of felt and expressed response.

It is more difficult to talk of the taped discussions, because of their length. I want to concentrate on one tape only, and suggest general trends which apply to the others, and perhaps to any discussion of literature among adults. Kath, Jane, Vicki and Liz discussed *The Snows of Kilimanjaro*. The transcript of the tape runs to thirty-six pages, and the tape lasts over an hour: the first thing to note, then, is that the discussion was found profitable enough by the participants for them to want to expend this much time on it. Why? There were, I think, two factors: one is the warm, strongly supportive feeling in this self-chosen group, which enabled a high degree of tentativeness and hesitancy to exist without demanding resolution; and the other is that this atmosphere encouraged the group to explore certain areas of their response to the story that they might otherwise have held back from, and by so doing to attain to simultaneous insights about the literature and about themselves as people. Thus the response to the story, both individual and shared; each person's honest appraisal of herself, supported by the group; and the group's interrelationship: all enrich and deepen the discussion. It is the intimacy and shared experiences of the discussion that lead the group to wish to extend it.

Here is an example of this sharing and mutual support going on. Liz has asked a question about the women in the story:

Liz: But is this, is this his wife, the one who's in the story now?
Kath: I don't know, I shouldn't think so.
Liz: I couldn't quite work that out, you know, who was who.
Jane: It sounds as though it's something she might do, which is sort of his way of describing *all* women, isn't it?
[*General agreement.*]
Jane: He doesn't use, there's nothing special about his sort of, the words he uses about his wife as to other women.
Liz: Mmm.
Kath: He doesn't make that clear at all, does he?
[*Pause.*]
Jane: Perhaps it *is* sort of true in a way, though, because I think we do see people who we love – our children, our, you know, adults who we do love – as um images of ourselves. They're sort of a bit hung on to us, aren't they? We only see them from this point of view of loving them.
?: Mmm.
Jane: And like people want things for their children, they don't want them for their children, they want them for *them*. And –
Liz: They want to see their children sort of in a certain way, don't they?
Jane: Yes. Yeh, because they're starting out from this position only in viewing their children and just as we view –
Liz: Do you think this is what's wrong with relationships, then, that people *do* this?
[*General agreement.*]
Vick: Well, you can't do it any other way, can you?
Jane: You can't no, really.
Vick: Cos um you can't see other people from any other eyes but your own.
Liz: No you can't but there's a difference between seeing them only in relation to you and seeing them as a sort of a whole person. I think you can see 'em as a whole person if you try hard enough. I think it's very hard to sort of to not think of yourself when you are looking at 'em, but I think perhaps you can do it.
Jane: Yeh.
Vick: But you've got to put *yourself* in their position then and live and try and live their lives.
Liz: Sorry? I didn't hear.
Vick: You've got to put yourself into, make yourself become them, then, and see how they live and how they look at the world and how they react to different people.
Liz: Mmm.

Kath: It's very difficult, um, this business of children, I find. Er, you have ideas and theories on life and things, theories that you've proved for yourself to be true. And er it's marvellous for other people, it might, okay, be all right for yourself, but um it's only up to a point that probably you can accept it fully for your children.
?: Yeh.
Kath: You have to start, um, thinking very very deeply and, um, and hard about whether, you know, this *is* right for your children. I don't – I have to fight this one constantly . . .

At this point, Kath's tentative contribution, following her lengthy silence, suggests this is a subject of some importance to her. Indeed, it becomes clear later that she is thinking of her relationship with her own children. (This extract is on pages 11–12 of the transcript; on page 27 Kath returns to the matter.) The rest of the group give support in two ways at this point – by allowing Kath to talk her way through a difficult and complex preoccupation, and by trying to reformulate the problem in such ways as to give a different, more generalized, perspective on it, without in any way being hostile to Kath's formulations. Thus:

Liz: I think probably that the hardest part about being a parent must be realizing that your children have *got* to make their own mistakes and battle through it on their own, cos really . . .
[*Two talk at once.*]
Kath: This is futile, this business of um – only I know it has to happen – I I was exactly the same. It's so damn futile though, when if only people would benefit from other people's, er . . .
[*Several talk at once.*]
Kath: No, I know this. I know this. I – I – I've always said the same thing.
Liz: There's nothing real unless you've experienced it yourself.
Kath: Quite.
Liz: People can tell you till they're blue in the face, but unless you know yourself it doesn't . . .
Vick: The more you find out from other people, you can find out if you're going, people will tell you something, and you do it and you make mistakes, then you realize that other people *are* telling the truth and then you learn from them.
Kath: But it's a – it's a great pity, in a way, that people have to get hurt and kicked in the teeth and battered around, um, but on the other hand, if you don't have these things happen to you, then you're not really a, a . . .
General: person.
Jane: No.
Kath: I suppose the more kicked in the teeth and battered around you get [*laughter*] the more of a person you are.
Liz: Character building's the phrase isn't it?
Kath: Character building. Yes, I suppose so.

112

Vick: Some people have to cut themselves off.

Jane: Like he has. I think *he's* cut himself off. He doesn't seem to feel does he? He doesn't have the sort of irrational, emotional behaviour.

And the group has achieved a new insight into the piece of literature which is serving as the catalyst and focus of their discussion. The weaving in and out of the story, the seeing of the interrelationship between life and art, is the dominant feature of the discussion. Thus, there is a long stretch on the transcript where the discussion has apparently moved completely away from Hemingway, and is debating very personal morality, and the standpoints of the four towards violence; but that it is ultimately derived from the literature is clear, because the examples chosen are bullfighting, boxing and warfare. The conversation ranges over these into very intimate comments about personal behaviour, out into the question of integrity and personal honesty and love affairs. Then suddenly, right at the end of the tape, the group returns to the *Snows of Kilimanjaro* with an unexpected insight of real power:

Liz: Probably because you've got a picture of how you would die even though you've no idea about death, you know, you sort of envisage what your death will be like and it's always perhaps a little bit romantic, a romantic view.

Jane: Perhaps that's the illusion. But I think he *does* have an illusion about it.

?: Yeh. Mm.

Jane: I think that's his own illusion in it, about his death.

Liz: And that's why, that's why it's the mountain, because it's searching for us, you know, like the leopard, it sounds so noble that he was up, found on the moun – er what was it? 'Close to the western summit there is the dried and frozen carcase of a leopard. No one has explained what the leopard was seeking at that altitude.' You know it's as if, as if nobody will know what he was seeking, isn't it?

Jane: Yeh, it is yeh, and this petty squabbling and irritability between them is – he doesn't want that, it's too honest for him, isn't it? He wants something more, that is his illusion.

It is only because of the nature of the discussion that has preceded this moment that such responses can be made.

The taped discussion raised for us all two important matters. The first is a common   something more, that is his illusion.

It is only because of the nature of the discussion that has preceded this s me to my original concern with literary response. What happens in a discussion like this is different from what happens in the usual teacher-controlled discussion; the stress here falls not on the individual response, with a certain competitiveness with one's peers to see who can reach nearest the 'correct' response; it is a shared, supportive discussion which returns us to a pre-Romantic notion of a sharing community who work together, rather than the inspired isolate, trusting in his talents to set him apart. The group concept that a discussion can generate is of potentially greater strength than any individual's concept, and the satisfaction of working with a group, the exhilaration of feeling that one sees all sides simultaneously, is a rich reward. The sharing that goes on in these tapes does not stop at a simple relationship-bond, but means much more than that, as Vicki commented:

> Our group's discussion brought the four of us together and made us form a group relationship – it was a good one in which we eventually formed a trust in each other to admit honest personal opinions and attitudes. In our discussion we abstracted from the book ideas and feelings which seemed significant to our own lives. Our own experiences helped us to understand what was going on in the story, whilst the story illuminated our own experience a little more. In this way our understanding of different concepts could be deepened and widened. Similarly, if something did not have much significance to one person, it was given a relevance by the experience of the discussion and the relationship of the listener and the person who was offering to share their experience and the relevance of it with them. We used the other people to bring us close to the meaning of the story and we used the story to bring us closer to the people in the group.

This work supports all the evidence of the *Children as Readers* project: that readers can reach the heart of a piece of literature without the presence of a teacher, and may go further in honest, perceptive response when the teacher is absent. But it is also likely that the ways in which readers are expected or allowed to *express* their response, actually alter the nature of the response itself. As Stratta, Dixon, and Wilkinson say in *Patterns of Language* (Stratta, Dixon and Wilkinson, 1973), 'Response is inseparable from the words in which the response takes place.' These students had to find ways of both coping with their responses, and learning to *value* them, to be secure and confident in their shared opinions, instead of diffident and vulnerable as they had often been before: it was through the tentativeness and hesitant early formulations of what was only indistinctly felt, in talk and in writing, that they worked through to the confidence of opinion and evaluation.

Vicki wrote afterwards: 'The main thing is that it isn't finished . . . I felt during the course as though something important had been shared. Things are always better when they are shared.'

Notes

1. In *English in Education*, vol. 7, no. 1, spring 1973 (Chapter 12 in this collection).
2. In *Educational Review*, vol. 23, no. 3, June 1971.

References

Britton, J. (1971) 'What's the use?' *Educational Review*, vol. 23, no. 3, June.
Stratta, L., Dixon, J. and Wilkinson, A. (1973) *Patterns of Language*, London, Heinemann Educational Books.

Part V

Curriculum: 'I know Where I'm Going'

There is only one subject-matter for education, and that is life in all its manifestations (Whitehead, *The Aims of Education*, p. 10).

A community is a powerful force for effective learning (Bruner, 'The process of education revisited' p. 21).

A party of explorers travelling through rough country is fortunate indeed if their leader is able to maintain, over decreasing distances, a view of their destination. He can't foresee the *route*, of course, since the intervening terrain is unexplored and full of obstacles; but having a clear sense of ultimate direction gives him a basis from which to calculate the odds and try to distinguish necessary detours from the unnecessary ones.

I doubt if curriculum planning can be any more precise, any less problematic, than that. A teacher with a firm sense of direction must at the same time make a study of the terrain before he can see the next move; and by terrain I mean above all the individual abilities, interests, intentions and expectations of the people he teaches. These are the constraints upon their learning and without taking them into account no course can be planned for the group or anybody in it.

Which implies – and this is where my analogy breaks down – that there will in fact be alternative routes to the one destination, and different students will pursue different routes. However, it is precisely at this point that the view of the destination, the sense of direction, becomes of paramount importance. Originating with the teacher (and constituting the basis of his leadership), it is increasingly taken up by others in the group, and is modified, diversified, amplified in the course of the interaction. Lines of activity, routes to the common destination, will now be both chosen by individual students and ratified by the teacher, not for their resemblance to a previously devised 'master-plan', but by their promise of movement in the right direction.

Garth Boomer and his Australian colleagues are clearly in the lead in exploring the altered conception of 'curriculum' implied in the notion of a negotiated programme. Fascinating questions arise: how much choice can be utilized without loss of direction and without robbing a co-operative learning situation of its drive? How do we distinguish a non-negotiable requirement from a pressure that teachers and students alike should resist?

The major choices to be offered to students will continue to be of concern to English teachers. Time in school is precious: how best should it be spent?

115

While such decisions are not non-negotiable, first responsibility rests squarely on teachers' shoulders. In the chapters that follow, Ian Pringle and Dorothy Heathcote put forward the claims of two activities – language study and dramatic improvisation – to a place in the English curriculum: each of them speaks from expert knowledge and with disarming honesty.

14   Negotiating the Curriculum*

Garth Boomer (Principal Education Officer, South Australia)

Introduction

It is becoming fashionable for schools in Australia to produce language policies *across the curriculum*. Because I am now convinced that such policies will be ineffectual unless they are accompanied by changes to the school's administrative structure, its curriculum and its educational philosophy, I want to explore an issue that goes behind language to the eternal triangle of education: the *teacher*, the *child* and the *curriculum*.

This exploration owes a considerable debt to Professor James Britton, who offered valuable encouragement and advice in the early years of the work of the various 'language and learning' teams in Australia. Britton supported our growing belief that the more profitable question to put to whole school staffs is not 'How can we develop the child's language?' but 'How do children (and for that matter, we) learn?'

The first question quite often threatens those teachers who consider themselves unqualified to teach language, and it can also lead to petty bickering about the perennial bogey surface-features of spelling, punctuation and 'proper' presentation. If language across the curriculum is associated with the English faculty, Sampson's 'Every teacher is a teacher of English' (Sampson, 1921) becomes a misleading focus.

But put the second question, and all teachers, lecturers and directors-general are, or should be, equal. This is a question to which we all should have personal, articulate and perpetually speculative responses.

Allied to the question of 'How do children learn?' are further teasers, such as 'Under which conditions do children learn most effectively?', 'What is learning?' and 'Do we all learn in the same way?'

On learning theory

Since 1975 the Language Across the Curriculum project team in South Australia, and more recently the Curriculum and Learning Unit that grew out of it, have been asking teachers questions like this, as well as looking into official, departmental curriculum statements to see if any of these

*Reprinted, by permission, from *Negotiating the Curriculum*, ed. Garth Boomer, Sydney, Ashton Scholastic, 1982.

address themselves directly to what may loosely be called learning theory. Few departmental statements address learning theory. Certainly *teaching* theory abounds, either implicity or explicitly, and it may be argued that, however tenuously, teaching theory must be based on some notion of how people learn. However, our team in South Australia concluded, on the basis of widespread inquiry, that few teachers can articulate what they assume about learning.

By having a learning theory I do not mean being able to précis Piaget, Skinner and Bruner. I mean being able to state one's own best-educated understanding as to how people come to internalize new information or to perform new operations. It can be argued that we come into the world *theorizing*. Certainly Year 1 children can very easily be encouraged to talk about how they learnt to talk. Teachers likewise can examine the learning theory implicit in their classroom practice.

So I come closer to the topic of negotiating the curriculum through classroom practice. Imagine education-department curriculum guides, with no explicit learning theory, being taken by teachers with no explicit learning theory and turned into lessons for children who are not told the learning theory. Some of the best of these children then graduate to become teachers. And so on. Isn't it about time that we all tried to articulate what is surely there behind every curriculum unit, every assignment, every examination?

If we can tell ourselves our present theory, we can also tell it to our students in terms that they can understand, so that they can try it out to see if it works in helping them to learn. From our joint evaluation we can then modify the theory, and try again. So, collaboratively, teachers and students may build learning theories, if by 'theory' we mean a kind of working hypothesis.

But learning theory cannot be disconnected from the criteria used to select what is to be learnt and when (i.e. our theory about the *curriculum content*: the subject offerings and the subject sequencing). These, in turn, are framed by a theory about society or culture.

Professor Basil Bernstein talked about the framing and sequencing of curriculum (at the National Language Development conference in Canberra, January 1978). He spoke of the way in which we often attribute divine universality to what may be simply culture-specific subject offerings and lock-step teaching sequences. When I look back on many years of work in schools, I think that education is an almost self-perpetuating chain of subjections. The education system is subject to the ingrained educational myths of society (deified into theories in the universities); the teachers are subject to the myths of the system (reified into curriculum guides, textbooks, standardized tests and public examinations); and the children are subject to teachers who choreograph all the myths in subjects, each educational genre with its own ritual, language, sequences and decor and each with its own value (e.g. classical physics is worth more than popular art, which is worth more than punk rock, sex education).

The aim of this chapter is to suggest tentatively how this chain may be broken by articulating the mythologies or theories at all levels and then taking a constructively irreverent stance towards them. I have already suggested that teachers and children may collaboratively build learning theories. I now extend this to include curriculum theories and theories about society – and I mean this quite seriously *from Year 1 to Year 12*.

Summarizing, I have so far questioned language as a *way in* to whole-school teacher development, and I have suggested learning as a more profitable topic. Learning is, or should be, inseparable from curriculum theory, but curriculum theory is shaped by the mythologies of a specific culture and based on *teaching*, handing down and initiating children into valued ways of looking at the world. Teachers who become their own learning theorists also need to become their own curriculum theorists.

Experiments by the Curriculum and Learning Unit in South Australia have shown interesting consequences when teachers, each having reflected on something recently learnt, together build up a learning theory, after which they are asked a simple question: 'How would you then fare as a learner in your own class?' They are generally forced to conclude that schools are institutions of teaching, not of learning.

On power

Before focusing specifically on the curriculum, it is necessary to reflect a little on power. It was not the brief of the Language Across the Curriculum project to inquire into the politics of education, but the project officers now believe that no discussion of language and learning can afford to ignore the structure of systems and schools.

We sat for hours reflecting upon teachers' problems, our own problems and data gathered in classrooms. Inevitably, we kept returning to the question of power relationships: inside the classroom, within schools, within the system and in society itself. Perhaps initially we inclined too hastily to apportion blame to teachers; we would now want to question the very bases of our society.

With our interest in learning, we set out to gain insights into how teachers perceive knowledge and how they think wisdom is achieved. With exceptions, of course, we found that a kind of pharmaceutical metaphor is widely applicable. Teachers define the knowledge to be dealt with, prepare the medication, and dispense the knowledge according to the prescribed dosage.

Knowledge is perceived as transmittable, and the learner's mind as a passive receptacle. The assumption is that teachers *have* the knowledge and that children *have not*, the 'have nots' being dependent on the 'haves'.

Now, even when teachers profess humanism, democracy, respect for the learner and horror at the mere thought of manipulative behaviour, we have come to have doubts – not about the teachers' sincerity, but about their ability to perceive the power vested in them, simply because they are *adults* and control the dispensation of knowledge.

Indeed, we are beginning to wonder whether the outright autocrat is not less dangerous than some self-deluding humanists. At least the former may make the rules of the power game explicit. We looked closely at so-called 'child-centred' progressive teaching techniques, where teachers purport to take a largely facilitative role. Here, teachers who still retain the significant, ultimate powers often pretend to divest themselves of power by giving limited decision-making opportunities to the children. For example, children may be free to choose one of several options without having the option to reject the options.

Moreover, many attractive learning packages in schools demand little creative, individual, teacher and learner contributions.

A crucial question arises: 'Are schools dedicated to the promotion of the child's power to learn, and ultimately to learn independently of instruction and guidance?' I am sure that administrators and teachers throughout Australia would answer with an unequivocal 'yes'. Why is it, then, that we find dependent learning rather than inquiry and experiment? Why is it that we find so few questions from children? Why is it that *fact* is so often revered above *principle*? What is the reality?

On constraints

The teachers with whom we have worked in South Australia have impressed us greatly with their concern to help children to learn and with their self-critical approach to the craft of teaching. Many devote themselves to education with awesome energy, but we are left with the feeling that, in isolation, these teachers have little power to affect the many feudal structures long embedded in both schools and the system. Sadly, we have talked to many good teachers who are frustrated and often plagued with guilt because they are falling short of their ideals, when the real cause often lies not in themselves but in a subtle combination of various manifestations of external control. These may include a fragmented timetable, disguised streaming of children and teachers, external examinations, large classes, or a limited choice of commerically produced resources all with an implicit, behavourist learning theory. The more we have speculated about the nature of schools, the more we have come to believe that a massive deep-seated inertia, not of the school's wishing, persists – despite cosmetic changes from closed to open space, from 40 minute lessons to hour modules, from English to general studies. It is devilishly difficult to effect change, yet we feel that radical structural changes are needed to produce a school context in which language can flow powerfully between teachers and students in the pursuit of action knowledge.

For example, where individual teachers wish to change the emphasis from teacher as examiner to teacher as collaborative evaluator with the students, they act in a broad context quite inimical to their intentions:

students socialized for years into seeing the teacher as judge, a school system geared to external reward for effort, and a society based on competition. Depending on their own personal charisma, teachers may begin to succeed in winning the confidence of some students, who may then feel aggravated by their other teachers; but the more usual result is that such teachers are devalued as soft or even slightly crazy. It is therefore very difficult for teachers to share their power with students, because society and schools are not based on such a philosophy.

It is my belief that *there are some existing strategies that can be improved.* For instance, our reflections on power have led us to question our South Australian team's strategy of working with *individual* teachers in the hope that good things will ripple out. There may be some rippling, but the steady hands of custom and ritual soon calm the waters.

To summarize again, I accept that there is an inevitable inequality between teacher and child and that teachers have wide powers. In turn, I see individual teachers as relatively powerless themselves within the governing frames of society and the education system, so they are often reduced to the status of intermediaries, translating society's values and initiating children into these values. Where administrators of the system, with respect to teachers, or teachers, with respect to children, purport to hand over powers, I believe that the harmful effects of their power may be increased, because the subjects of this power are likely to be more *mystified* about the actual sources of control.

On demystification

Now, our specific concern in the South Australian team is to promote more open communication, more talk to exchange and seek information, and more questioning to relieve mystification. This follows from one of our basic assumptions: that learning is vitally connected with the language resources that can be brought to serve it.

A more equitable distribution of power (or at least a more healthy exercise of power), which we know can be used either benevolently to let in or maliciously to exclude, will not come while those *in* power monopolize the talking space (i.e. the language), thereby keeping other people in relative ignorance.

So, what should be done? I believe that there are three important areas of action:

1. Strategies should be applied at *all levels* of the system and society. That is, politicians, parents, administrators, teachers and children all need to be brought into *discussions about how we learn*, if we are to raise the quality of thinking and learning in schools and society.
2. There will always be inequalities of power in both schools and society, and the harmful effects of power will be offset only *if those in power make*

quite explicit the values, assumptions and criteria on which they base their actions. In this way others will have a better chance to defend themselves, more opportunity to question and more chance of negotiation, at least where the power figure is not totally despotic.

3. Significant change will come only *through collaboration at all levels*. Individual action is usually contained and rendered ineffectual when it begins to threaten the established order.

This does not mean that individual teachers should delay action until they can find support from their colleagues. At least, teachers can talk to their students openly about why they do what they do, about how they think people learn and about the societal consequences of various behaviours.

I have found perhaps the most exciting and challenging strategy offered in the book *Language, Truth and Politics* by Trevor Pateman (1975). Pateman says that we should ourselves be able to do, and then in turn be able to teach children how to do, the following:

(a) question an unreasonable assertion;
(b) say that we don't understand if we don't understand;
(c) pause to think;
(d) say that we don't know if we don't know.

This should be accompanied by a good deal of thinking aloud in front of students, so that they can have open access to the teacher's thinking powers.

On motivation versus negotiation

Motivated learning

Now, Model A in Figure 14.1 represents the traditional curriculum model in which, after reflecting on past experience and the content to be taught, teacher A, within the practical constraints of school and society, intends to teach a certain program.

Before teaching can proceed the students must be motivated in some way. If the topic is 'Weather and Climate', this may be achieved by a trip to the local weather station, or by a lesson in which the coolers are turned off to draw attention to the topic in hand. The powerful motivator thus *by indirections finds direction out*, and the children, to varying degrees, come to intend roughly in the same direction as the teacher. Throughout the planned curriculum unit there is tension between the teacher's goal and the children's intent, but most students eventually receive marks or grades for written work, which tell them how close they have come to the teacher's intentions. Sometimes the mark is externally decided.

As Model A in Figure 14.1 shows, even at best the children's learnings only approximate to the teacher's goals, so the curriculum may touch only a little of each child's key and associated interests. This leaves a good deal of what has been learnt unexamined and unevaluated, because the teacher, or external examiner, tests only what is set on the curriculum. Of course, the overlapping shown in the model may not occur at all, and the child is failed or subjected to remediation, which requires more intense motivation. In either case the child appears to have learnt much less than is actually the case.

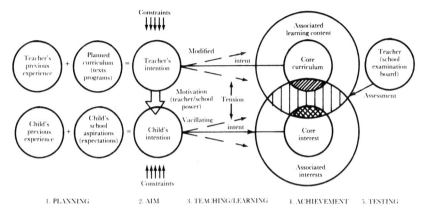

Figure 14.1   Model A: motivation

Irrespective of the teaching style of the teacher, there will be great wastage if this model is applied.

Negotiated learning

Armed with a Pateman-like outlook on open communication, a personal learning theory and an awareness of the harmful effects of inexplicit power, a teacher may develop strategies for negotiating the curriculum as represented in Model B, in Figure 14.2.

Here, teacher B reflects in the same way as teacher A to find worthwhile curriculum content and strategies based on past experience, coming to fairly non-negotiable conclusions about the basic content of the unit. If the unit is 'Weather and Climate', the teacher finds some core input that should illustrate the key *principles* and *concepts* to be learnt. At this stage the teacher talks openly to children about the topic to be covered, why it is to be included, why it is important and what constraints prevail (e.g. it may be a set topic in H.S.C. geography; it may have been made obligatory by the faculty head; it may have to be finished in three weeks). The talk centres on what the children already know, how the teacher thinks the new information may be learnt, how the necessary tasks are to be shared and what constraints the children have (e.g. 'We've got an enormous amount of reading in English this week').

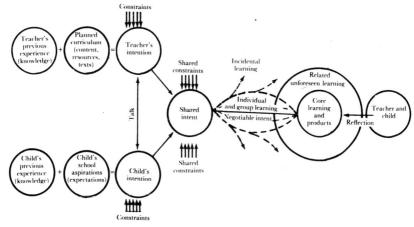

Constraints

1. PLANNING AND NEGOTIATION 2. AIM 3. COLLABORATIVE EXPLORATION 4. ACHIEVEMENTS 5. EVALUATION

Figure 14.2 Model B: negotiation

The next step is for teacher and children to plan the unit, the activities, the goals, the assignments and the negotiable options. (Compare with Model A, where this programming takes place *without children present, before* the sequence begins.) Collaboratively, a fairly tightly structured unit of work is prepared, in which the class, the groups, each child and the teacher all contract to make contributions. The unit takes into account unforeseen learning related to the topic and incidental learning along the way. The unit is, however, tightly constrained but open to negotiation at all points by either the teacher or children. *While the topic and central content are prescribed, specific outcomes cannot be set down in advance.* The broad aim that children will come to deeper understandings of certain key principles and concepts *can* be set down. Indeed, specific objectives would effectively sterilize such an approach, because they would lead the teacher and children to creep down a narrow, direct path, guide book in hand rather than to explore boldly the broad territory of the topic. The teacher's main role in a negotiated curriculum is to give information and teach only when it is needed.

When the products of learning have been written, made, modelled, painted or dramatized, the teacher and children carry out the crucial process of *reflection*. This is when the class shares its valuing – when there is comparison, respect for quality and rejection of inferior work by those who did it (class, group or individual).

On quality

I think that Model A is a recipe for standards where many will fail; Model B, if adopted, will lead to dynamic exploration and rigorous pursuit of quality by all who contract to be in it. Model A relates to both traditional, whole-class teachers and modern, individualized-transmission teachers; Model B relates to clear-thinking, self-aware teachers willing to make a wager on the learning power and resources of children.

These teachers do exist, and they do not just survive in our schools. They even generate more of their kind, because their philosophy of collaboration is applied to colleagues as well as to children and because what they do is seen to be effective. They are hard-headed, articulate theorizers about practice, not plagued by guilt at what they cannot do, nor defenceless against attackers, armed as they are with both their theory and the obvious quality of their practice. They have learnt the futility of trying to stand alone, and they know how to compromise without capitulating.

They are not prey to educational fads (e.g. the latest spate of language exercise texts). Their greatest allies are their students, and the parents of their students who are brought into the collaboration. They even get excellent examination results.

Conclusion

If teachers set out to teach according to a planned curriculum, without first engaging the interest of the students, the quality of learning will suffer. Student interest involves student investment and personal commitment.

Negotiating the curriculum means deliberately planning to invite students to contribute to, and to modify, the educational program, so that they will have a real investment both in the learning journey and in the outcomes. Negotiation also means making explicit, and then confronting, the constraints of the learning context and the non-negotiable requirements that apply.

Once teachers act upon the belief that students should share with them a commitment to the curriculum, negotiation will follow naturally, whether the set curriculum is traditional or progressive, and whether the classroom is architecturally open or closed.

References

Pateman, T. (1975) *Language, Truth and Politics*, Nottingham, Stroud & Pateman.
Sampson, G. (1921) *English for the English*, London, Cambridge University Press.

15 The Case for Restoring Grammar*

Ian Pringle (*Department of Linguistics, Carleton University, Ottawa*)

The more things change, the more they stay the same. A fashion becomes old, and then disappears, and then it returns as the latest fashion: almost before we have recovered from the costs of the fad for the 1930s, we find that the arbiters of fashion and the purveyors of 'pop' culture are busy making us feel nostalgic for the 1950s. Education also has its fads, its changes of fashion, its recurrent concerns, and not always so trivial, or so blatantly commericial. A recent study of education in Ontario in the first half of the nineteenth century shows very strikingly the extent to which recent concerns in education here repeat or parallel those of one hundred and fifty years ago (Wilson, 1974). Complaints then included the low salaries paid to teachers, the large number of Americans teaching in Ontario, the menacing dominance of American textbooks in Ontario schools and, most strikingly, a call for the restoration of grammar to its proper place in the curriculum.

Among the traditional core subjects of the school curriculum, grammar has always been most subject to swings of fashion. We are just emerging from a period in which it has been unfashionable. In the nature of things, it should be becoming fashionable once again. Certainly there is increasing discontent about what is called the illiteracy of our high school graduates: letters to editors grumble about the growing corruption of the language; politicians and businessmen assert that 'permissive' theories have led to a society of young men and women who cannot add, write, spell, or even make themselves understood; while universities create new remedial programs in expository writing, and grumble that the high schools are not doing their job.

Some of this, of course, is mere tradition, and some of it due merely to the pendulum effect of changing fashions. But beyond mere matters of tradition or fashion, these rumblings are evidence of a fairly strong feeling in some influential quarters that formal grammar teaching should be resumed in Ontario schools. Such pressure is naturally of considerable concern to teachers at a time when local and provincial politicians, for reasons that (one might suggest) are not always primarily concerned with education, are willing to stir up, play on, even create, popular dissatisfaction with education or teachers. Moreover, the rumblings are reinforced from a very different direction in that many of those concerned with English as a discipline feel that the enormous advances in linguistics in the last forty

* Reprinted, by permission, from *The English Quarterly*, vol. IX, no. 3, Fall 1976.

years should be reflected in the language arts and English curricula.

But before we give in and agree to start busily teaching grammar, it might be just as well to stop and ask why. Why should grammar be taught? What is it supposed to do? Looking at some of the grammar and composition texts that have been used in Ontario schools in the last fifty years or so, one finds statements of goals that most teachers will readily agree with: 'Knowledge of the mechanics of the language and the functions of words in the sentence, and sentences in the paragraph,' according to Winter and Smith in *Learning to Write* (1961), 'will further the student's ability to write with clarity and precision'. Bassett and Rutledge, in the preface to *Form and Content* (1959), claim to have designed the sections on usage and grammar in order to maintain 'precision and correctness'.

As early as 1920, the anonymous author of *Composition and Grammar for Public Schools* was claiming that the chief purpose of the study of grammar in Ontario schools (primary schools) was 'to acquire such a knowledge of the functions, forms and relations of words as will enable pupils to speak and write the language with a greater measure of clearness and propriety than they might otherwise attain'.

No one would want to attack or even question such aims. Whatever else we want our students to acquire in the course of their education, it is surely reasonable to want them to be able to speak and write, when necessary, with more clarity, precision and correctness than they would otherwise attain. Moreover, when the complaints about the failures of modern education are not merely traditional or merely political, they are often due to precisely the fact that schools do not seem to be doing enough to achieve these goals.

What is not recognized, but must be insisted on, is that there is no evidence at all that the kind of grammar that has been taught in Ontario is of any help at all in attaining such goals. On the contrary, there is evidence that in most cases the teaching of formal grammar is actually a hindrance. The number of carefully controlled studies of the effectiveness of teaching grammar is not overwhelmingly large, but all of them point to exactly the same conclusion.

Perhaps the study that most deserves our attention is one of the earliest ones. In 1947 W.J. Macauley published in the *British Journal of Educational Psychology* the results of his investigation into grammar teaching in Scottish schools. This study is important for three reasons. In the first place, it is thoroughly scholarly and objective, and not mere assertion by a university linguist who is perhaps more enthusiastic about his discipline than enlightened about its usefulness to teachers. Secondly, it is important simply because the system investigated is the Scottish system, which, since the eighteenth century, had prided itelf on the thoroughness and intensity of its grammar teaching. Thirdly, it is important to us because in its attitudes to grammar, as in many of its strong points, the Scottish system exercised a marked influence on the Ontario system of the nineteenth and early twentieth centuries.

Macauley's study showed that the ability of pupils to identify parts of speech was low after four years of primary-school grammar teaching, dropped in the first year of secondary-school grammar teaching, and began to approach competence only in the last three years of high school, and then only in advanced or enriched classes, and then only if the students were also learning a second language. In this small, elite group, a little fewer than half the students were able to identify parts of speech correctly more than 50 per cent of the time. Macauley went on to claim that the conceptual difficulties of school grammar are such that it cannot be grasped with any real understanding by pupils under the age of 15; he thus explained the parrot nature of much of the learning and the absence of any transfer into students' writing. In addition, he rejected the idea that grammatical knowledge is necessary for grammatically correct writing. In his own words, 'our figures show conclusively that the assumptions on which our courses in grammar for primary and junior secondary schools are founded are unwarranted by the facts and indeed false' (Macauley, 1947). A similar study by F. Cawley of grammar teaching in English schools confirmed Macauley's results (Cawley, 1958). Nora Robinson, another English researcher, concluded after studying second- and fourth-form pupils in four English grammar schools, that there was an insignificant relationship between grammatical knowledge and competence in writing. As a matter of fact, she found that the *lowest* of her correlations was between grammatical knowledge and accuracy in writing (Robinson, 1960). After reviewing a number of similar studies, three American researchers concluded:

> In view of the widespread agreement of research studies based upon many types of students and teachers, the conclusion can be stated in strong and unqualified terms: the teaching of formal grammar has a negligible or, because it usually displaces the same instruction and practice in actual composition, even a harmful effect on the improvement of writing (Braddock *et al.*, 1963).

Similar studies have continued to accumulate since the American survey.[1] All the evidence shows that teaching grammatical rules in school has no beneficial effect on students' actual performance in speech or writing, and that fact, however unpalatable some people may find it, must be accepted.

Since it is so clearly established, it raises two questions. The first is, why does grammar not do the things it is supposed to do? The second is, since there is no reason to believe that grammar teaching was ever more efficacious than at the time of the various studies I have mentioned, why do so many people believe in it with such fervour?

So far as the first question is concerned, the answer is clear enough. What has been taught as grammar in Ontario schools, as well as everywhere else in the English-speaking world, has usually consisted of two parts: an analysis of the parts of speech and the kinds of structures of which they may be part, up to the level of the sentence and a list of rules about what is called correct usage. An enormous number of linguists, particularly American structuralists, have shown that there are fatal inadequacies in both parts.

The point has been made so clearly and so often that it should not be necessary to repeat any part of the demonstration. Unfortunately, it does have to be repeated: even in such a recent textbook as Heather Hooper's *Starting Points in Language*, the traditional definition of a sentence is given: 'A sentence is a word or group of words that tell a complete thought.'[2] It is very easy to show that this definition, which occurs with only minor changes of wording in 95 per cent of the dozens and dozens of Ontario language, English and grammar texts that I have examined, does not define. For example, there are all sorts of structures that can reasonably be said to express a complete thought that are not sentences. Much of the effort of the New Criticism was devoted to showing that single poems by writers such as John Donne express a complex, but single thought; but while it is often the case that they can be said to express a single thought, it is not normal for them to be a single sentence, and most of them are not. The same point could be made even more emphatically about the fashionable cinquain. A well-constructed paragraph should express a complete thought. A cogently argued essay often expresses basically a complete thought. On the other hand, there are groups of words that are certainly sentences and yet do not express a complete thought. *This is one.* It follows that even if it is true that teaching students to identify sentences helps them to avoid such mistakes as comma splices and sentence fragments (an assumption that has never been proved), teaching the traditional definition of a sentence will not help them to avoid those errors, because it will not help to identify sentences. The definition does not define.

In various ways, nearly all the other definitions of traditional grammar can be shown (and have been shown) to be just as inadequate, and therefore just as useless. As for that part of school grammar that focuses on so-called good usage, it is probably true that some of these rules are valid as descriptions of what is often found in formal written English, a style for which we have rather rigorous expectations.[3] However, that is not how most of them have been taught; they have usually been taught – unsuccessfully – as absolute laws which must be obeyed at all times and in all circumstances. It is clear that none of these rules has such a status, and some of them have no validity at all. They have been attacked from all points of view in innumerable studies.

What is the basis of such rules? The answer that has always been implied or stated in Ontario textbooks is that they are based on common, national, reputable usage. But this is not the case. Clearly they are not based on common usage; if all the 'correct' usages were already common, it would not be necessary to teach them. But neither are they based on national usage. For example, everyone has been taught at some stage that it is bad usage to end a sentence with a preposition (unless you have nothing else to end it with). But it has always been the practice in English, as in all the other Germanic languages, to end sentences with those particles called prepositions, and thus to do so is and always has been national usage, not only in Canada but in every other English-speaking country, as also in all the other countries where Germanic languages are spoken. But they are not based on reputable usage, either: all the great historical dictionaries and historical grammars of English are full of examples of sentences by such writers as Shakespeare, Milton, Swift, and even Jane Austen, which break these so-called rules, and it is just as easy to find examples of 'infractions' in the works of such modern Canadian writers as Morley Callaghan, Mordecai Richler, Margaret Laurence, and even Robert Fulford.

If the rules are not based on common, reputable usage, then what are they based on? The answer is, on grammar books. All the traditional rules governing so-called correct usage can be traced back through various Ontario school grammars of the twentieth and nineteenth centuries to their immediate sources in British school grammars of the nineteenth century, and the rulings in those grammars can be traced back in turn to their sources, amateur grammars written usually in the eighteenth century, invariably by men who had no particular qualifications for writing grammars. The traditional definitions are older still. The definition of the sentence quoted above from Heather Hooper is an attenuated descendant of the defintion given by Bishop Robert Lowth in his *Short Introduction to English Grammar*, first published in 1762: 'A Sentence is an Assemblage of Words, expressed in proper Form, and ranged in proper Order, and concurring to make a Complete Sense.' In this area, however, the tradition is much older: indirectly, Bishop Lowth's definition is ultimately a descendant of a definition first formulated over 2,000 years ago by the Greek grammarian Dionysios Thrax, who defined a sentence as 'a combination of words, either in prose or verse, making complete sense'. It was not a satisfactory defintion when he formulated it, it remained unsatisfactory when Bishop Lowth adapted it in 1762, it is unsatisfactory now, and it will still be unsatisfactory tomorrow.

In any other area of inquiry, the amount of unacknowledged copying that has taken place in traditional school grammar would be called plagiarism. Apparently, however, you are no more guility of plagiarism in copying someone else's definition of a sentence or ruling on ending sentences with prepositions than you would be in copying one of the Ten Commandments from the Bible. Traditional school grammar is like a religion in that it has a long, authoritarian tradition behind it to back it up, with a number of revealed texts that everyone can copy and no one can question. Apparently in our grammars, as in the Ten Commandments, what we are dealing with is Revealed Truth. And this may have something to do with the faith that people continue to evince in grammar, despite all its defects and inadequacies. Probably those parents and editorialists and letter-writers who are calling for the restoration of grammar are thinking back to their own experience of grammar in school. If their experience was typical, they can remember something that was apparently pointless, and somewhat painful; presumably they therefore conclude that it must have had enormous moral value from which modern youth would benefit.

In other ways, too, such grammar becomes a kind of faith. For one thing, the claims that it makes cannot be tested by those who are not willing to accept them. The religion of the Vikings claimed that those who devoted themselves to the heroic ideal and died a hero's death on the battlefield would be carried off to Valhalla by a Valkyrie. If you want to find out whether or not that claim is true, then you devote yourself to the heroic ideals and die a hero's death on the battlefield. Then, if it is true, you have your reward. But otherwise there is no way to have this reward. Those of us who are not willing to accept the Viking's belief can never know whether it is true or not. Similarly, if you accept the claim that certain unnatural usages are always good grammar, then you will be rewarded by that warm inner feeling of triumph that is enjoyed by those who cheerfully distort syntax in order *pointedly* to avoid splitting infinitives, or the satisfaction that comes from placing *only* only immediately before what it modifies, or the delight of never ending sentences with prepositions (except when there is nothing else to end them with). Those who are not willing to accept the claim that such things constitute good grammar will never know these rewards.

In one further respect, such grammar is most of all like some kind of religion. Nearly every one professes to believe in it, but hardly anyone actually practises it.

If traditional school grammar consists largely of myths, what place should it have in our English and language arts curricula? Surely it should have none at all, just as the phlogiston theory of combustion, long since shown to be erroneous, has no place in our chemistry and physics classes. Like the phlogiston theory of combustion, traditional grammar does not account for the facts. It does not even take account of the facts. It is hardly surprising that teaching materials based on such an analysis of English cannot be shown to have been beneficial. In most cases, traditional grammar has been harmful.

It is true that when it was taught, some students managed to get a feeling for their language, for how it works and how it can be used. There is every reason to believe that they would have done so even if they had not studied grammar. Others were turned into *only*-snoopers or *hopefully*-haters or split-infinitive sleuths. These are the ones who now write letters to the editor complaining about the flood of corruption; probably they sleep with their copies of the gospel according to Fowler by their bedsides.

For a larger number of students, learning traditional school grammar had the effect of creating an almost pathological fear of English teachers. In addition, grammar made many students inhibited about writing, which was a much more serious weakness. It is for this reason that many teachers were happy to give up grammar when the pupil-centred approach made it unfashionable, and it is certainly true that, as a result, many high school graduates are less inhibited about writing than was formerly the case.

Although it is impossible to prove it, there may have been a still more serious effect. One of the dreams of the nineteenth-century educational reformers was that by making education universal and compulsory, they would make the treasures of the English literary heritage available to the mass of people rather than the very few who had been able to enjoy them until that time. After more than a century of compulsory, universal education, it is clear that even if most people are literate, their literary tastes are so limited that there has been no cultural enrichment at all. The proportion of people who read classic works of literature with real understanding and enjoyment remains as small as it ever was. It is certainly conceivable that this failure is due to the boredom and resentment that the grammar component spread over the whole of the English curriculum.

It remains to be seen whether the adoption of Leavisite ideals recommended by such people as David Holbrook and Ian Robinson will change this situation. But there is every reason to believe that the restoration of traditional grammar will jeopardize the attempt to change it. The theory of English teaching that has evolved since 1950 tries to involve all children, whatever their intelligence, age, sex, background, or career prospects, in work that will get them absorbed emotionally and imaginatively in what David Shayer has defined as 'an educational experience which will touch them at the deepest levels of awareness and be of permanent benefit to them' (Shayer, 1972). At the very heart of this theory lies 'a specific creative methodology of the intensive, imaginative writing kind which embodies the key values of the whole theory'. It is precisely this methodology of intensive, imaginative writing that is most vulnerable to the blight of traditional school grammar. The gains for English teaching in giving it up far outweigh any disadvantages.

However, there has been one real loss, the loss of a particular skill that many graduates of the old system had: the ability to write in that special register of written English which is formal expository prose. It is because so many people come out of our high schools without any mastery of this particular medium of English that the universities, the business world, and some parents complain so much.

In part this is perhaps due to an inadequate understanding of the new methodology: according to David Shayer, there is 'evidence that suggests that where the "new" English is not properly understood, the skills of spelling, punctuation, sentence structure and style generally are not only being put second to actual writing, but are being ignored almost to the point of disappearing completely . . . . To leave children to circle endlessly in a colourful abundance of their own unchecked spontaneity is to leave them stewing in their own unformed linguistic juices to nobody's advantage' (Shayer, 1972, p. 186). To a larger extent, however, the problem is due to a real dilemma that arises from the recognition of the inadequacies of school grammar and the dangers of teaching it. It is impossible to talk about the conventions expected in formal written English without having some kind of grammatical terminology with which to label the things you want to talk about. How can you talk about the problems of subject-verb agreement if you have no terms for subject, verb and agreement?

And so the wheel threatens to come full circle. Any syllabus in language

132

that includes among its goals the aim of making students as competent as possible in that style of English that is most different from the styles of which English-speaking children normally have a native command, must contain some kind of description, some set of definitions, some technique of analysis. It must contain some grammar.

If this is why grammar has to be taught, however, then the grammar that is taught will have to be different. For_this reason, teachers should support the demands so often made by university linguists that the language and English curricula should contain a language component drawing on linguistics and aimed at making students consciously aware of the characteristics and possibilities of their native language by inductive methodologies.

Unfortunately there are, so far as I know, no teaching materials that really provide the kind of grammar instruction that is needed. It is true that recent years have seen the appearance of a number of good, inductive, language-centred English texts. In most cases, however, whatever the other merits of the texts, the grammar component remains as attenuated and trivial, and in some cases as mindlessly traditional, as in any composition text written in the 1940s. As for the structuralist texts developed for school use in the late 1950s and early 1960s, most teachers disliked them because of what seemed to be unnecessary complications and because their *laissez-faire* attitude to problems of usage simply did not serve the teachers' purposes. Nowadays most linguists would object to them on theoretical grounds. The various attempts to teach some kind of transformational grammar have not only not improved students' competence (any more than traditional grammar did), but have burdened pupils and teachers with an extremely complicated apparatus of description, replete with arrows and with terminology that only computers can pronounce, while providing no more than minimal insight into the workings of the language, and none at all into problematic areas like regional, social and stylistic variation in English, which is the aspect of language use where lack of awareness is most likely to lead to complaints by universities, businessmen and concerned parents. Moreover, it is likely that the conceptual difficulties of both structural and transformational analysis place them at least as far beyond the reach of most school children as traditional grammar was.

However, one of the prerequisites is now available: for the first time in many decades, a comprehensive, up-to-date, reliable grammar of English is available.[4] The analysis of English in *Grammar of Contemporary English* can provide the base on which the language curriculum can be built.

Unlike some of my colleagues, I do not think that the language component is the first priority of the English curriculum. In English teaching, as in everything else, there is always a danger that matters that are good in themselves but only of partial importance may get treated as though they were of central importance, and allowed to dominate the subject. If asked to give my own notion of priorities, I think I would place three components ahead of grammar. I think all students should be helped to develop some literary sensitivity, and given some idea of the richness that is in books. Secondly, in this age of Watergate and William Davis, I think we should help our students to see through the lies and distortions of politics, advertising and journalism. Thirdly, I agree that those who complete the syllabus should be able to write well. But, fourthly I also think that all students should acquire some conscious knowledge of what their language is and how it works. All of these requirements – except, possibly, the first – involve teaching about language, and thus involve using the kind of grammar that I have in mind. The new grammar should not be the largest part of the English syllabus, but it should be central in it.[5]

Notes

1. See especially W.B. Elley, I.H. Barham, H. Lamb and M. Wyllie, 'The role of grammar in a secondary school English curriculum', *New Zealand Journal of Educational Research*, vol. 10, no. 1, May 1975, pp. 26–42.
2. H. Hooper, *Starting Points in Language*, 1971, p. 230. Ms Hooper tells me that this definition was included because the publisher's editor insisted on it, despite her wishes. If the editor's insistence was due to his own ignorance, it would be reprehensible enough. But suppose it was due to a cynical realism about the ignorance of those who choose and buy such books?
3. One of the many linguistic tasks that need to be undertaken in Canada is an extensive survey of usage which will find out which of these traditional rules are in fact valid in Canada. Which ones are still applied? Who uses them, in what kind of speech or writing, under what circumstances? Until the answers to such questions are ascertained and published, one of the essential tools for teaching cannot be provided. In the meantime, however, there is nothing to stop English teachers and their pupils from conducting their own surveys of Canadian practices in matters of disputed usage.
4. This is the *Grammar of Contemporary English* by R. Quirk, S. Greenbaum, G. Leech and J. Svartvik, London, Longman, 1972. It draws on, and draws together, the results of decades of research by hundreds of linguists. Many teachers will prefer the abbreviation by R. Quirk and S. Greenbaum, *A University Grammar of English*, also published by Longman. It must be emphasized, however, that both grammars are reference works; neither is totally suitable for use as a class text.
5. Professor Britton kindly allows me to add, ten years after this paper was first written, that although I still believe it would be useful to teach an empirically valid grammar, I am much less confident than I used to be that it would be justifiable to do so, given the cognitive difficulty of grammar as a subject and, as a result, the amount of time that would have to be devoted to it if it were taught in sufficient detail to be useful. In addition, the whole question of the level at which such teaching would be appropriate and feasible still awaits research.

References

Braddock, R., Lloyd-Jones, R. and Schoer, L. (1963) *Research in Written Composition*, Champaign, Ill., NCTE, pp. 37–8.

Cawley, F. (1958) 'The difficulty of English grammar for pupils of secondary school age' (abstract of a University of Manchester M.Ed. thesis), *British Journal of Educational Psychology*, vol. 18, pp. 174–6.

Macauley, W.J. (1947) 'The difficulty of grammar', *British Journal of Educational Psychology*, vol. 17, pp. 153–62.

Robinson, N. (1960) 'The relation between knowledge of English grammar and ability in English composition' (abstract of a University of Manchester M.Ed. thesis), *British Journal of Educational Psychology*, vol. 30, pp. 184–6.

Shayer, D. (1972) *The Teaching of English in Schools, 1900–1970*, London and Boston, Routledge & Kegan Paul, p. 139.

Wilson, D. (1974) 'The teacher in early Ontario', in *Aspects of Nineteenth Century Ontario*, ed. F.H. Armstrong, H.A. Stevenson and J.D. Wilson, Toronto.

16 Improvisation*

Dorothy Heathcote (Institute of Education, University of Newcastle)

Drama is becoming 'respectable' in our schools. Many timetables now take cognizance of this activity and the word is being introduced into our staff rooms and conferences, but to many teachers it still remains a great mystery better left alone, and not the least mysterious facet of it is the activity called 'improvisation'. Why should this be? One reason lies in the fact that there are as many definitions of it as there are practitioners. So let us try to define it simply and clearly. Throughout this chapter I am assuming certain attitudes in the reader and define them as follows:

1. He respects children and what they bring to the learning situation.
2. He is prepared to accept and use what they offer in class situations.
3. He sees himself as a member of a team – older, more experienced, as a rule, able to keep the team together, work them to capacity, forwarding their projects efficiently, using their strengths and helping them to know and overcome their weaknesses, stretching their potential all the time and keeping their 'sights' true for the task in hand.

How the reader interprets these factors will naturally affect his interpretation of what follows.

Improvisation in my view means 'discovering by trial, error and testing; using available materials with respect for their nature, and being guided by this appreciation of their potential'. The *end-product* of improvisation is the *experience* of it. Any artist in any field will tell you this. What, then, is improvisation in drama? Kenneth Tynan's definition of drama will help here. In *Declaration* he states, 'Good Drama for me is made up of the thoughts, the words and the gestures that are wrung from human beings, on their way to, or in, or emerging from, a state of desperation'. Obviously, then, dramatic improvisation is concerned with what we discover for ourselves and the group when we place ourselves in a human situation containing some element of desperation. Very simply it means putting yourself into other people's shoes and, by using personal experience to help you to understand their point of view, you may discover more than you knew when you started. What this 'more' is depends upon the purpose of the exercise in the first place, i.e. what the motivation was. More of this later.

We use this system of discovery, naturally, all the time – it seems inborn

* Reprinted, by permission, from *English in Education*, vol. 1, no. 3, autumn 1967.

in us, as natural as breathing – in our first playing, in our reading for pleasure where we share the lives of others, thus stretching our experience; when we seek to understand another person as in friendship and caring; in the world offered by cinema, TV, radio and the theatre. This of course is always a *personal* role-playing, *personally* motivated, whereas the class is a group which requires motivating at specified times during the school day. The mystery has arisen partly because of this, and because the real issues have been clouded by theatre and 'showing' issues, both laudable in themselves and to be desired in their place.

It can now be seen, I hope, that improvisation is not a subject area (though it *may* be so sometimes), it is really a tool for the teacher, to be used flexibly at times when 'personal identity' role-playing is the most efficient way of crystallizing what the teacher wishes to make clear. It is available to teachers of science as well as of the arts, though it will *possibly* be employed by the former in a somewhat more limited form. 'Possibly' – because we have not yet done sufficient research into matters like this, but wherever understanding of human behaviour, feelings, hopes and attitudes is required it will function speedily and efficiently. It must be understood at this stage that I am not writing of the improvisation used by children in their own play, or of the improvisation used in class when the teacher takes up the position of onlooker in order to enable children to have child-drama opportunities. I am concerned, here, solely with the use of improvisation to aid a learning/teaching situation, and many child-drama elements will be present in a well-conducted one – it cannot really succeed if they are not. An example used recently with a fourth form in a secondary school will serve to illustrate what I mean. The main purpose of the work was to try to break down the verbal shyness of the form (remember this all the time as you read on!). So the teacher began with the question, 'If we had a million pounds to spend for the good of humanity, on what would we spend it?' The debate ranged over Oxfam, 'the pill' for India, research into cultivation of deserts, Cheshire Homes, geriatric and maternity wards, and for a time remained polite and uninspired. But as soon as the class were asked to explain Oxfam and, in this case, the use of a modern highly efficient plough, to the teacher, who became an Indian peasant anxious only to work the land of his ancestors in the way his father before him had done, then the real and deeper issues were thrown in their faces. Once the deep issues were raised, the class worked in a different dimension of communication and no longer could it remain at a polite level, it became a series of personal committals, highly demanding and equally satisfying. This class of children were astonished at their ability to become involved in the problems of an Indian farmer and even more astonished at their ability to *express* their involvement. Because the teacher's aim was to help the children to enjoy verbal communication via argument, role-playing, debate and discussion, he did not allow the situation to be developed as a *play*; he kept the verbal challenge as the first priority. How the various officials portrayed character, etc. he did not interfere with; timing and all the theatrical aspects were not his concern, only their means of achieving *verbal* understanding did he press – though of course he realized that many other facets of this situation were available to him should he wish to press them, for as soon as we place a man in his environment, with his prejudices, attitudes and hopes, the world is our oyster in study terms. This is why dramatic improvisation is of such value to us, and yet so confusing, for selectivity must be used and this is a great difficulty for many teachers.

Can this be made easier? A class is a series of individuals who bring not only their individual points of view but their individual experiences, visions and interpretations to the situation. This often causes a teacher to fail when he first tries this way of working. Let us see if there is a recipe for built-in success. In my experience these factors *must* be present for improvisation to succeed:

1. A genuine desire by the teacher to bring relevant class experience and information to the fore and be made available to all the group. (This, of course, can be uncomfortable for the teacher, for some of this he may find hard to accept, e.g. moral attitudes he does not approve of, expressed in terms he finds disagreeable.) This cannot happen unless there is a good working atmosphere promoted by permissiveness and mutual respect between teacher and class.

2. The core of entry to the situation must be tailored to fit the experiences and attitudes the class will *generally* hold. For example, a group of rather tough youths recently were challenged to examine their moral code regarding work. The situation started in a pub, this being acceptable to them; it ended (if it will ever be ended – for who knows what reflections will continue in their minds after the initial class experience is over?) after two hours, in their examining *how* they were different because one tramp had braved the bright lights of the pub and caused them to measure *their* world of day-to-day work and events against his. The teacher in this case was interested to press for 'moral code at work' to be examined, but many more issues could have been taken up. I consider it to be the teacher's task to ease the way into the situation for the class. This means a sensitive examination of and willingness to understand what will be the 'kicks' for the class. If a 'pint of bitter' start does it, then it's worth using. There *must* be withdrawal of moral judgement on the part of the teacher but this does not mean that he may not take a moral stand for himself on any issue – but he cannot set it up as the 'right' one. There are none that are 'right' for all people in all circumstances.

3. The teacher must understand the way in which dramatic improvisation functions. As pictures need pigment and surface, drama uses the six elements of stillness, movement; silence, sound; darkness, light in *every possible* combination and gradation. These six elements are the only means of communication in this medium. I will try to clarify this by example. Let us take a situation often used by teachers in primary schools – the capture of Persephone and the ultimate agreement reached between the earth mother

and Pluto. Persephone is often playing with her friends when the god of the underworld takes her to his kingdom. Here we may have the *sounds* of children's voices at play, their *movements* at play. Suddenly this may be frozen into *silence and stillness* as the god emerges with *sounds* unlike those previously heard and with *movements* unlike those previously seen. They (Pluto and Persephone) may then depart with *movement* of a quite different intensity and accompanied not by *sound*, but *silence*. The friends may then depart in *movement* totally unlike their first play and the place be left in complete emptiness and *silence* or there may be the *sound* of Persephone's weeping. Likewise all these situations will be richer if *light changes* occur as well, and musical sound may be used effectively too. This theme is capable of being explored by a hundred different combinations of the above, depending on: (i) what the children feel at their stage of development to be 'true', and (ii) the purpose the teacher has in mind in choosing (or allowing the children to choose) this theme. The theatre with all its resources can *only* employ these six elements and drama must do exactly the same. Of course, in the classroom, teachers often lack the resources of light and darkness and musical sound but the children are adept at imagining or 'making do' and an unlit lantern used by a child 'creates' darkness. Try it if you don't believe me, but you must *believe* the children if you do try it!

4. The teacher must be prepared to enter the children's world once they begin to work in the medium. It is easy to 'believe' if you encourage in yourself two attitudes:
(a) a 'willing suspension of disbelief', and
(b) a 'serious' approach to their work. I do not mean here an absence of humour of course. Drama and gaiety go hand in hand as do drama and tears. The latter situation is often easier for the tentative teacher.

5. The teacher must know the *basic* purpose of the exercise and in the development of the situation keep this to the fore. He must continually be selective as he helps the work along. There may be many different possibilities for development within the improvisation situation. For example:
(a) children showing what they know factually about, say, a period in history so that the teacher can learn where to clarify or develop in this field;
(b) children revealing how they function in small groups. Who are the natural leaders?
(c) children revealing ability to concentrate;
(d) children being challenged *to listen* to each other;
(e) children's response to verbal ideas, and so on. These are but a very few of the vast field open to the teacher via this medium. I have no space in this chapter to clarify this more fully.

6. The things to be taught must be discovered via human beings *in action* – that is, 'living through' the situation (the Greek meaning of drama). If this kind of discovery cannot be made, then improvisation is the wrong medium, and the teacher should look about for a more efficient way of bringing understanding to the class.

When these elements of permissiveness, belief, sympathetic entrance to the theme, guidance to teaching point, understanding of the medium and the things it can and cannot achieve, are present, then improvisation will succeed in the task of stimulating personal discovery for children and teacher alike. You may feel none the wiser for having read this. All I can suggest to you is that you try it with your classes for just five minutes the first time; openly discuss with them your difficulties as far as you are able to clarify them and gain their co-operation to help this method of work to succeed by discussion and trial and error. No written help can give you as much as that given to you by experience gained with your classes. Remember to keep in the forefront of your mind this maxim. *Drama is* not *stories retold in action.* Drama is *human beings confronted by situations which change them because of what they must face in dealing with those challenges.* An 'open-ended' situation is easier for the teacher who feels himself to be a novice than a story where the beginning and end are pre-known.

Part VI

'Commission 7' or the Politics of Language and Learning

Can it be we are not free? It might be worth looking into. Samuel Beckett, *Molloy*, p. 38.

When 500 US, Canadian and British delegates attended the international English conference in York in 1971, they had twenty-four hours to settle into a strenuous programme of work in one of six commissions before a conference newsletter appeared on the breakfast table asking 'What are we doing here?' Prepared by three NATE members, the broadsheet claimed that there was considerable agreement as to what English teachers believed and tried to practise, but that their views conflicted with those of the wider society: hence, 'English can make small local gains without impinging in any way on the society which produces the inequalities which the English teacher is trying to abolish'. How far, they asked rhetorically, should the conference be concerned with such matters?

Responses were immediate, heated and diverse – enough to justify calling an open session to discuss the issue. About 300 delegates turned up, and after long and animated discussion a seventh commission was set up to pursue the issue. About fifty people left their original commission to join the new one. Before the week was out, Commission 7, realizing the enormity of its undertaking, issued a simple statement: 'In order to explore the effects of social, economic, educational and other pressures upon the quality of teaching and learning in English, we have formed Commission 7, a commission whose work, to which we pledge ourselves, should in our belief be a continuing concern of the sponsoring Associations'.

And so, for a time, it was. At the conference closing session a resolution was passed approving in principle that our Associations should 'take steps to offer more active and direct support to teachers who, pursuing the kind of teaching we have fostered, find themselves frustrated or at risk in the existing systems and structures of education'.

In the years following, Mina Shaughnessy of the City College of New York produced a Commission 7 newsletter; and NATE held its one and only Extraordinary General Meeting – to consider the future of the Association in the light of criticism from members in two camps, the radical and the pragmatic. Commission 7 had an effect on NATE, shifting the emphasis of its annual conference towards the practical and the political.

I document this because it provides a history for the concerns expressed here by Margaret Gill in Australia (Chapter 17), Jack Shallcrass in New

Zealand (Chapter 19) and Peter Medway in England (Chapter 18); and because I should like to keep the spirit of Commission 7's resolve alive in the Federation.

17 Preparation for Newspeak: The English Teacher's Responsibility?*

Margaret Gill (Victoria College of Advanced Education (Rusden Campus))

I want to begin by raising some questions about the imperatives lurking in the title of this Chapter, and to foreshadow the importance of the question mark at the end of the title. *Preparation.* For what exactly? *The Teacher's Responsibility.* Who says? I want to examine the notion of 'preparation' as it applies to what English teachers do when they teach English. Secondly, I want to state what I think English teachers demonstrate they are responsible for, and illustrate this with some examples drawn from classroom practice.

'Preparation'

At the Queensland English Conference two years ago, I examined the ways in which different pressure groups in society tell schools (and teachers) what they 'ought' to do – often from the most questionable motives. It seemed to me then – and now – cause for both admiration and concern, that schools tend to listen with sensitivity to these multiple voices, and to respond to the pressures they impose. Neil Postman, in his recent book *Teaching as a Conserving Activity*,[1] puts this point well. Although he is describing the American scene, it is relevant here:

> Americans have not hesitated to use their public schools as instruments to solve the myriad and intractable social and political problems their other institutions have been unable to handle. Historically the schools have taken on such goals as de-ethnicizing the immigrant population, preparing youth for entry into the job market, and training children to become avid consumers and bank-using, insurance-minded, money-saving citizens. Within our own lifetime, we have seen the schools go into the sex-education business, the drug-education business, the driver-education business, the brother-hood business, the psychological counseling business, the free-lunch business, the baby-sitting business, the racial integration business, the social equality business, the motivation business, and lately, the business of *ethnicizing* the population, after having failed to de-ethnicize it. . . . Schools have assumed the burden of solving extremely important problems, but they are simply not equipped to achieve the solutions. If you heap upon the school all of the problems that the family, the church, the political system, and the economy cannot solve, the school becomes a kind of well-financed garbage dump, from which very little can be expected except the unsweet odor of failure.

*Abridged, by permission, from the proceedings of the 1982 National Conference of the Australian Association for the Teaching of English.

143

Has this conference run the risk of adding another item to Postman's inventory? The brief for one commission begins with the following statement: 'Teachers of English/Language Arts have a responsibility to anticipate the language needs of children after they leave school.' There are problems in looking at the English teacher's role in these terms. Firstly, it is not at all clear what is meant, nor is it clear how teachers should go about the task. What should preparation for these future 'language needs' consist of?

The danger in defining English teaching in terms of preparation for something else is that it may legitimate a bad pedagogy. It can stop teachers from paying close attention to what the teacher and learner are actually learning, or needing to learn, right now. It can force teachers to take their eyes off the quality of the immediate learning experiences they offer children. To use Donald Graves's term, it takes teachers off their 'turf' and away from their essential expertise. That expertise always acknowledges, often implicitly, that quality learning in the present is the best foundation for the unforeseeable life and language demands of the future.

When we stop to look at this kind of preparation approach in action it can be seen to produce some very odd English teaching. At the beginning of schooling it is responsible for the Preparation-for-Learning-to-Read school of thought that prepares young learners for reading by *not* letting them read. And so we have 'Pre-reading' activities where the child produces sound-symbol noises, or fills in letter shapes, or draws base lines. All this is a substitute for real book experience. It is little wonder we end up with remedial pre-readers, who then have to be prepared for pre-reading.

At the other end of the school curriculum, the preparation approach may map too easily on to a 'neoclassical' education tradition, as Gerry Tickell has described it: 'I know this is boring, but you may need it in the exam.' Too often this approach traps teachers into defining the content of English as memorizable lumps of 'knowledge', which may become a substitute for the active organizing of ideas, or the active savouring of literary experiences, right here and now, in *this* classroom, in *this* lesson.

In between these two oversimplified extremes there is the preparation approach which prepares students for real language uses later on, via curious forms of rehearsal: 'Learn this word list, convert these adverbs into adjectives, fill the right words in these spaces . . . because it will prepare you for real writing later on.' Or it prepares students for greater efficiency in reading, by providing gutted extracts from fiction, and then invites the reader to answer questions that actually throw into reverse the powerful, predictive involvement with language that characterizes the reading process.[2]

Teaching has to be founded in the learner's experience. Not just his or her future language experience, but the whole range of present experiences, since it is these that contribute to the child's growth, development, mastery of language, autonomy as a learner and, therefore, his or her potential as a future learner.

A second danger in defining English in terms of 'preparation' is that it is often accompanied by verbs like 'ought'. This changes the tense of teaching away from what teachers actually do, and often appears to imply a deficit view of English teaching. Again, it takes teachers off their 'turf' and puts them unnecessarily on the defensive. In Victoria recently, as part of the review of the present Higher School Certificate English course, teachers were sent a questionnaire asking them what the compulsory elements of the syllabus *ought* to be. The replies were confused. In a subsequent interview programme we asked teachers: 'What do you find are the strengths of the present course? What are the problems?' The replies were consistent, coherent, reflective, expert. Teachers were talking from the professional base-line, which is the classroom, a point to return to later.

The final danger inherent in English-as-Preparation is the way the term has sometimes been used in relation to transition education programmes. There is a political rhetoric that says that schools should prepare young school leavers for the workforce; that increasing youth unemployment makes such preparation programmes imperative if the young school leaver is to have any chance on the job market; that schools are failing the young. This sort of rhetoric needs to be looked at carefully. Richard Sweet's studies (Sweet, 1980) of the labour market relative to youth unemployment and employment are revealing. For example, in May 1964, when the total unemployment rate was 1.4 per cent of the workforce, teenage unemployment represented 35 per cent of that total. By May 1979, when total unemployment had quadrupled to 6.2 per cent of the workforce, teenage unemployment was 33.4 per cent of the total. The proportion of youth unemployment is virtually unchanged (in fact, it is slightly less) yet the current political slogans emphasize *youth* unemployment, and place the blame on schools, thus diverting attention away from underlying, long-term structural changes in the economy.

Many schools have responded sensitively and quickly to such pressures by developing transition courses that emphasize job-related skills, such as 'business maths', 'receptionist and telephonist skills', 'office skills'. Yet if we look at the areas where jobs are disappearing most dramatically (book-keeping, general clerical and office work, telephonist work, junior typists, junior postal workers) they are precisely the areas that are likely to utilize these particular skills. Teachers need to go on the offensive when they answer the question 'Preparation for what?'

Responsibility

I want to turn to the other key word in my topic and ask the question ' 'What *is* the English teacher's responsibility?' In answering that question I believe we can make sense of the term 'preparation'.

The following summary is built on what English teachers actually *do*, and is followed by a series of examples drawn from the classroom that illustrate what is meant. It is worth noting that these examples, like all good practice, turn out to be based on powerful theoretical understandings, though it is the case that English teachers tend not to talk about their teaching in such terms. It is also worth noting that the summary has a very basic look about it, and perhaps that is not a bad thing in a climate that has destroyed a very useful word. The summary can be improved on; the terms are not entirely satisfactory, but the key areas are there. Here it is:

English teachers help children achieve mastery – or give them successful experiences (for my argument both mean the same thing) – in the following areas:

Authorship: to discover their own 'authentic' voice in writing, in order to organize, reflect on, celebrate personal feeling and experience; analyse, criticize, synthesize knowledge and information; explain or defend a point of view (this of course assumes mastery of basic literacy skills, which, by secondary level, is a shared responsibility for all teachers).

Readership: to achieve the attentive, active and satisfying engagement between reader and text that is a mark of the successful reader (whether literature, 'content' materials, or other messages in print).

Sociocultural awareness: to explore and understand the ways in which language carries (and also masks and distorts) the messages and values that tell us about our (multi) culture and society, and where we belong in it.

Authorship

'Discovering their own "authentic" voice in writing' runs the risk of sounding like the latest buzz phrase about writing. What does it mean? Firstly, we know immediately when it is absent. The following piece of writing does not need to have its context explained:

Why I Should Not Talk in Class

There is no reason why I should talk in class especially when the teacher is trying to explain something. The only time to talk is when answering a question or explaining something. It is very rude to disturb a teacher, and you would get the same feeling if someone disturbed you while you were trying to explain something, so show respect for other people. Another thing is that other people are trying to learn, and if you don't want to learn then keep quiet and give the others a chance. Those who want to learn should not suffer because of your stupidity and rudeness, so whenever a teacher is saying something, give way for them and the students.

The messages carried by this piece of writing are clear:

(a) writing is a medium for punishment;
(b) learning equals passive listening;
(c) the child's own spoken language is devalued and has no place in the classroom;
(d) in school, writing can be used as the vehicle for inauthentic, phoney or abject messages;
(e) in this child's classroom, power resides with the teacher.

In the language of 'cultural capital', this writing represents a debased and devalued currency.

The next example illustrates the beginnings of a quality that *could* be called authorship. The classroom context here, as always, is crucial – otherwise we may retrospectively attribute to the child's writing the intentions or qualities we want to see in it: it proves what we want it to prove.

Craig, the author of the following piece of writing, could be described as a reluctant learner. A student teacher inherited Craig in her Year 8 English class. He controlled the back row, arms folded, moulded plastic chair permanently balanced on two legs. The supervising teacher reassured the student teacher: 'Don't worry about Craig, he hasn't written anything all year.'

The student was working with the class on a theme about school. They had read poems like 'Bird in the Classroom'; discussed extracts from Laurie Lee and Edward Blishen; made their own architect's plan of the perfect school. In this class they were asked to write about their most vivid school memory. Craig resisted expertly. The student teacher encouraged:

'Why not?'

'I hate school.'

'Well write about that.'

And he did – with the proviso that it was not to be read to the class:

I hate school – and to tell the truth I am hated here. Hate isn't strong enough. I loathe, despise and detest school – and that's on my good days. All the time I am counting the days till I can leave.

I suppose that's why I never get on with anyone here, because I hate it and everything to do with it so much.

I am horrible in the morning. I can't face anyone – anyone at all until I've had at least 2 cups of coffee inside me (yuck, I hate coffee). I wish I could wake up more quickly, but I just can't. Some people are just made like that, I suppose. I only wish I wasn't one of them.

I hate girls who chew gum. It's fine for little kids but not for girls. How do you think it looks to see a lovely girl and all of a sudden this horrible pink bubble oozes out of her mouth. Disgusting . . .

The trouble is, I like chewing it myself. But not bubble gum. That's the limit.

I have a sneaking passion for love poems. I could do plenty. I could – sometimes do – read them all day long. They make me feel good inside. I wish I could write a love poem.

When Craig had finished writing he changed his mind. He allowed his writing to be read to the class. He was pleased when the student teacher asked to read it to her English Method group. He owned it. As a piece of writing it may have begun as a manifesto against school, but it ends as a manifesto for Craig. The *'enfant terrible'* voice has, one suspects, been deliberately amplified. In other words, the phrase 'authentic voice' means something more complex than simple confessional writing. It involves a sense of authorial control and, finally, satisfaction with a finished product that 'says it how I wanted to say it'.

My next example is taken from a collection of writings by the South-East

Asian students of Richmond Girls' High School in Victoria. Valerie Falk, their ESL teacher, defines her role more broadly than that of simply helping the girls become proficient in English as quickly as possible. She works from the sound principle that 'everyone has a story', and the book is a collection of thirty-five personal narratives, some written in English and edited, others written in home languages, such as Mandarin or Vietnamese, and translated. But in all of them the sense of authorship is clearly established, even before these children have mastered a new language. Ngoc Huong begins her story:

> If you have not lived in a poor country you don't know how terrible hunger is. If you have not been a refugee, you don't know how dreadful decampment is. I feel that our life is a stage and everyone in the world is following the dictates of God to come down to this stage and play a different role. Unfortunately, God gave our Vietnamese poeple a very miserable role to play, a role of ruined families and exile. Our Vietnamese people can only accept this sorrowful fate of grief and calamity without complaint. As for myself, I think that I have been very lucky for although I am a refugee and have had a distressing journey, I did not die on the sea nor was I killed by pirates. Compared with the experiences of my friends, my journey was commonplace. However, to me it was unforgettable. From this trip I awoke from the dream of childhood and could understand the meaning of growing up. There-fore, it is strongly impressed on my memory – and now let me tell you about it.

'. . . and now let me tell you about it . . .'. The authentic voice of the story-teller. In the introduction to the students' anthology, Valerie Falk writes:

> We do not, I think, need to ask whether [these students] are right to have come. They have come in the same way that others came during the last 20 years.
> They are a part of our society and we need to hear their story. Everyone has a story, and I am sure that all members of our society should tell their own story. We need to tell each other about ourselves for if we don't – how can we ever get to know each other? Books have been written about the English, the Irish, the Scottish, Italian, Greek, Turkish and many other people telling their stories, so now here is one about the people of South-East Asia.

Authorship, finally, extends beyond the achievements and satisfactions of the individual author; it enriches the community to which the author belongs.

Readership

Recent studies of reading begin to ask, and answer, interesting questions about the reading process: How do readers actively engage with a text? How do they attribute meaning to a text? How do they interact with a text to make it 'their own'? We know that successful readers show an ability and willingness to reflect on whatever they are reading, and to interrogate the text, so that the reading process is more accurately described as the active encounter of one mind and one imagination with another. We also know that successful readers have had many experiences of the satisfactions and pleasures of reading. Good classroom teaching supports both these observations and explains what I imply by the term 'readership'.

In this example a competent reader is caught in the act of engaging with a text. It tells us a lot about how good readers read. The Year 9 class were asked to listen to and read a poem, and to write down 'whatever was going on in your head'. The poem chosen was deliberately difficult: the uneasy, mental breakdown world of Philip Larkin's 'Going':

> There is an evening coming in
> Across the fields, one never seen before,
> That lights no lamps.
>
> Silken it seems at a distance, yet
> When it is drawn up over the knees and breast
> It brings no comfort.
>
> Where has the tree gone, that locked
> Earth to sky? What is under my hands,
> That I cannot feel?
>
> What loads my hands down?

One student, perhaps with greater aptness than he realized, simply wrote: 'I think the man who wrote this poem needs help'. Another student wrote the following:

(1) First of all, why is this poem called 'Going'? When I read the poem through several times, I get the impression that the poet is uneasy about something. The 'evening coming in' seems strange – it is unique – not seen before, but why does he choose that it 'lights no lamps'? Perhaps it is simply that the
(5) evening is having no effect on earthly objects and has a light of its own. But what is this evening? 'It brings no comfort', although 'at a distance' it is silken. It is supposed to bring security, perhaps, or warmth. Still – what is the evening, that doesn't bring comfort (Why should it?) and 'lights no lamps'? Why this, especially? The poet feels lost, and I think he is feeling the
(10) approach of something new – perhaps a stage of life. Perhaps he is dying, or expecting a dramatic change. All the order and security, tree, earth and sky, has gone and something is near yet he 'cannot feel' it. And then, something is above his hands which loads them down. This poem bewilders me because it is simple and complicated at the same time. I think he portrays his feeling of
(15) bewilderment at something ahead of him, unknown and frightening, and the evening is like a trumpet blast, heralding this thing's approach. It is hard to say if I like this poem. Do you have to understand a poem to like it? Or just interpret it? I think it is called 'Going' because the poet is going from the order of the tree, earth and sky, to something which he cannot understand,
(20) only senses. 'That lights no lamps', it 'brings no comfort' these puzzle me. These things are very important – light and comfort. What, indeed, 'loads [his] hands down'? Foreboding? the burden of his future? Everything seems to be breaking up.

The pattern of her thinking is interesting. There is an ebb and flow between question and answer. All the questions are directed towards grappling with the central meaning of the poem. Not all the questions are answered to her own satisfaction, although there is a sense of confidence in the questioning: a belief that asking questions is a good way to go about understanding the poem.

Her first question (line 1) appears to be abandoned, but is answered confidently and without warning in line 18. Some questions are repeated. The meaning of 'That lights no lamps' continues to puzzle her (lines 4–5, 8–9, 20) and is returned to with progressively sharper responses. After the question and answer sequences she moves outward to broader reflections on the nature of her own responses (lines 9–10, 13–14, 16–17, 20). After her final, and apt, sentence, she commented that she had said everything she could. When asked whether she was satisfied with the answers to her own questions she said no: 'but I think that's how the poem is'.

Perhaps one way of helping children achieve 'readership' in the sense in which I am using the term, is to legitimate this kind of activity in the classroom, so that a difficult text is not seen by the child as a tricky code to be deciphered but, as in this example, the active encounter of one mind and one imagination with another.

Sociocultural awareness

This is the last, and vaguest-sounding, of the list of English teacher responsibilities. There are any number of curriculum starting points. One might be a 'socially critical' curriculum model. Another might be a curriculum that attempts to apply the insights of Bolinger's *Language: The Loaded Weapon* (Bolinger, 1980) to the students' language environment. I want to claim Bolinger for English teachers when he writes:

> to make language serve the flow of messages in society as it should, we must be free to talk about language itself. We must build the fabled fire in the wooden stove and use language to expose language. Our courts, bureaus, businesses, and advertisers must be held accountable not only for what they do but for what they say and the way they say it. Language is no one's personal domain, and there should be no diffidence towards invading it, no embarrassment at pointing out an abuse of the passive or an underlying structure of presuppositions or a semantic net that has been spread to catch some poor fish. It should be as natural to comment on the linguistic probity of public figures as to comment on their financial probity – in both cases they are manipulating symbolic systems that are the property of everyone.

I believe English teachers already take for granted the importance of Bolinger's statement in the work they do in studying the media with their classes. For example, a real field-day for 'using language to expose language' was provided by the British media reporting the Falklands 'crisis'.

There was the reversion to cosy schoolboy bully-talk by the crew of the

Invincible: 'We'll bloody their noses'. Even responsible newspapers dehumanized Argentinian solders by labelling them 'Argies', in exactly the way that the North Vietnamese became 'Gooks' – but in a different way from the attribution of 'the Hun' to German soldiers. (*Why* is the latter different? How do we identify the difference?)

The best example, as is so often the case, came from television. It loses substantially without the voices, but emphasis on the underlined words helps convey the values (one conference member insisted a Monty Python tape had been substituted to brighten the lecture!). From *Nationwide*, an extract from a BBC interview with several elderly ex-war-lords, May 1982:

> Interviewer: How do you assess Rear-Admiral Woodward's turn-around from seeing the – the task as being a walkover, and then seeing it as a long and bloody battle? Why has he changed his mind, and which of those two statements ought we to be believing?
>
> Lt Col. X: Well, the *first* one, because, in the *first* one the Admiral was talking to the soldier. He was in the atmosphere of his *own* task-force, and he was talking to the *soldiers*, to the *marines* and *parachute regiment*, and *sailors* and *airmen*. And he spoke as all commanders speak to their men. And all he said was absolutely gospel *true*. I mean, anyone who's done *any* campaigning at all would know that what he was saying was the way that senior officers *do* talk to their troops: 'It's a pushover' – (it's not a pushover, he didn't use that phrase): 'We've done *frightfully* well'. And all he said was *true*.
>
> Then, of course, when you start interpreting that in the – in the *suburbs* of *Hampstead*, and amongst the *media*, and everything, my golly! He's said all the wrong things! So they sent him out a new dictionary and he has to use *other* phrases. [*Laughter*].
>
> He's got to use phrases that are acceptable *politically*. But *behind* it all, the Admiral is a fighting admiral. He's got a *fighting force*. The *British/Regular/Services* are not, sort of, a bunch of *choir* boys going out to sing these chaps off the Pampas. They're going out to put in a *military operation*, and, if it doesn't work, or if the Argentinians get very *stupid* and try and fight us the *hard* way, there will be a lot of very *dead* Argentinians.

Year 12 students who listened to this tape were able to recognize that, according to Lt Col. X, there are different kinds of 'truth' – and that, OBVIOUSLY, EVERYONE knows that. They could guess that Hampstead is probably where the 'liberal-leftie-trendies' live. In the concluding flourish they could *almost*, but not quite, feel sorry for an old man playing war games.

Good teaching in this area tends to go beyond examination and dissection of samples of Newspeak. It tends to lead to social involvement; to students who begin to react to the message-makers with organized action. The Year 11 students at Sunshine North Technical School prepared and presented a submission to the Australian Broadcasting Tribunal hearing of Channel Seven's application for a licence renewal. Their study of television had led them to identify four main problem areas in Channel Seven's programming: the excessive number of quiz shows, the lack of Australian drama, the lack and poor programming of teenage series, and the percentage of repeat programmes. Their critique is perhaps presented at a fairly low level of consumer self-interest, but at least it represents an important beginning. It establishes the importance of action as a necessary part of knowing how our increasing visual culture works – and is controlled, as the students began to discover when their submission was dismissed, because, in the words of the QC representing Channel Seven, 'it represented a very small interest'. The students replied:

> We are the television generation. We grew up with television and we have the right to express our opinions and ideas concerning the future programmes on Channel Seven. . . . We're only young and growing, but we'll be watching TV for the next forty years and people don't think of that. We should be taken notice of and listened to.

The 'active voice' is an essential element in the development of sociocultural awareness.

And finally, to return to a broader theme: English teachers need the opportunity to nurture their own sociocultural awareness in the face of the new technocracy. They need opportunity, such as this conference has provided, to begin to understand the new technology, and to estimate its implications and possibilities, rather than retreat in 'Luddite-flight' from the microchip. They need, in Reinecke's term (Reinecke, 1982), to become informed 'technosceptics'.

If the vision of the new technocracy, as glimpsed in Reinecke's book, is anything like a true picture of the future, than it isn't just the *English* teacher who has responsibility; it is a responsibility shared by every voting citizen of the developed countries of the world.

Notes

1. Postman, N. *Teaching as a Conserving Activity*, New York, Delacorle Press, 1979, pp. 109–10.
2. For my favourite example, see R.K. Sadler, T.A.S. Hayllar and C.J. Powell, *Language Four: An English Course for Secondary Schools*, Melbourne, Macmillan, 1978, pp. 1–3 and p. 4, question 1.

References

Bolinger, D. (1980) *Language the Loaded Weapon*, Longman, p. 186.
Sweet, R. (1980) 'A labour market perspective on transition programs', paper presented at a Conference of Tasmanian School Vice-Principals, July.
Reinecke, I. (1982) *Micro Invaders*, Harmondsworth, Penguin.

18 The Bible and the Vernacular: The Significance of Language Across the Curriculum*

Peter Medway (Knowles Hill Comprehensive School, Devon)

One would not expect an educational movement like 'language across the curriculum' to be flourishing at a time when immediate survival is a problem, but if things get easier will it once again be vigorously pursued? Should it be even if they don't? How do those who have taken responsibility for promoting it (advisers, teacher–educators, some heads) now feel about it? Are they badly frustrated or rather relieved not to be in a position any longer to press the cause? For those who are determined to battle on, it is hard to find strength and courage in what has already been achieved since there is so little quotable evidence on this. *Aspects of Secondary Education* (DES, 1979) reported little progress towards whole school language policies, but then few people understand what those would be anyway. It may well be that large numbers of school departments have taken steps to improve the language experience of children in their lessons, and that even more individual teachers are teaching better than they would have been if all the language publications and courses and discussions had not taken place in the last ten or twelve years. It would be impossible to measure such diffuse but important effects; and it would be easy now to believe that little has happened. My own impression is that there are places where children's experience in some subjects has been significantly improved because conscious consideration has been given to language, but also that widespread resistance has been met.

Whatever the truth may be about progress so far, I consider it important to keep the issue alive. In examining briefly what seem to me to be the underlying implications of 'language across the curriculum', I hope to suggest how much is at stake and to indicate at the same time why the task will continue to be a hard one.

As far as I know, no history of that strand of educational thinking and reform that came to be called 'language across the curriculum' has yet been written. This is my own understanding of its origins. In the 1950s and 1960s, a group of English teachers, in schools and in teacher education, broadened their interests beyond 'subject English' to embrace language as a general human function; they took particular note of the work of Piaget and, when it was published in English, of Vygotsky, on the connections between language and thought. Turning back to our education system, they consciously noticed, perhaps for the first time, the nature of language

---

* Reprinted, by permission, from *English in Education*, vol. 15, no. 1, spring 1981.

in schools and were struck by the way it regularly worked *against* the avowed teaching and learning purposes of the institution. Pupils were confronted with texts and utterances the comprehension of which called for linguistic experience they did not possess, and tight constraints on the occasions when and the manner in which pupils could talk and write prevented language from being used to assist the thinking on which learning depended. Nor was there any consistency or rationality in the different range of language demands imposed by different subjects, teachers and 'orders' of the school.

The teachers involved in this concern with language worked or had worked for the most part in grammar schools. Moving into comprehensive schools, many of them encountered bright but non-academic working-class children who failed in school and yet whose verbal resourcefulness and fertility were an inescapable fact and an object of admiration and delight to their teachers.[1] The failure of this group could in no way be ascribed to slowness or dullness, or to any general deficiency in language; rather the problem seemed to be a discontinuity between two sorts of language, theirs and the school's.

The development of this consciousness in teachers was given a great impetus by the arrival of cheap tape-recorders. English teachers, and increasingly others too, joined linguists and dialectologists, collectors of folk song and oral history, and the makers of 'radio ballads', in finding it worthwhile to record the spontaneously produced speech of ordinary people – in this case, their pupils. We (because from this point I can speak partly from my own recollections) were able by repeated playbacks to reconfirm for ourselves our sense of the range and vitality of working-class speech, but what was newly exciting was to discover what it was intellectually capable of. We were surprised and delighted at what ordinary kids could do. Given the chance and the encouragement to talk together in ways that came naturally to them, they were able to express and to understand ideas we had considered beyond them. And in the tapes we could observe, in ways Piaget and Vygotsky had alerted us to, the thought developing as the language flowed.

A similar examination of expressive writing showed that it too could help children to get into a relationship with and to make sense of the knowledge, experiences and ideas they encountered. And if pupils were allowed to express their understanding in more personal or more poetic forms than the traditional essay and formal answer, a quite different picture of their understanding often emerged.

The tapes and pieces of writing collected in the late 1960s and early 1970s by practising teachers and teachers in training, study groups and funded research teams, gave us the confidence to back children's own everyday language as a major means towards their educational development. From the insights we had gained, two main items in the 'language across the curriculum' platform wrote themselves: more opportunity for talk in small groups, and the encouragement of alternative forms of writing which went beyond the setting down of purportedly true statements in a public language. Other important ones were evaluation of the total language experience provided by a school and, as a major element in the latter, attention to the appropriacy of the language of instruction and of textbooks. The arguments seemed, and were, rational and reasonable: *this* sort of language gives pupils a greater opportunity to learn than does *that* sort. But in fact it has turned out that much more than language is involved, and that is why this set of ideas has not swept the board. In discussion of language policy, attitudes on wider issues – educational, social and political – are readily brought into play. For what is being proposed is no simple technical change in 'teaching method'; it is not a matter of substituting language type B where before we had language type A, in the same slot and without alterations to anything else. True, there are some straightforward bits of rationalizing and checking out that have needed to be done, and some schools have been quick to attend to these, describing the arrangements as their 'language policy': agreeing common conventions for marking, concerted attacks on prevalent spelling mistakes, readability tests on worksheets. But the central propositions are less easily agreed on and may involve shifting deeply rooted assumptions and interests.

The case of 'the expressive' exemplifies how pursuing a language idea can get one into deep water. Out of that general interest in language that certain English teachers developed emerged a theory of the functions of language (Britton, 1971; Britton *et al.*, 1975). Three functions were defined, one of them being the expressive function. Language adapted to fulfilling this function is characterized by a number of features: communication (of information and ideas) inextricably mixed with expression (of self and affect); assumption of the listener's/reader's interest in the speaker/writer as a person; absence of a felt need for strict accuracy or for tight logic or coherence; responsiveness to the changing directions and emphases of thought. Thus 'the expressive' entered the scene inoffensively enough as part of a scientific attempt at a coherent classification of types of language. Then the close association of expressive language with the ongoing thought process was pointed out as a feature with obvious relevance to education, where the promotion of certain sorts of thought was a central concern. Examples suggested that when pupils are able to engage with a topic by handling it in expressive language, they are helped to make sense of it. Thus there was a clear case for promoting expressive talk and writing in the classroom.

If we may judge by our impressions of prevailing practice today, the case has not been generally conceded. We can only speculate why not; but we can see how the notion of promoting the expressive has implications that would make its acceptance difficult in some quarters. First we may note that the category of the expressive cuts across the strongly established 'folk' categories of 'factual' and 'creative', in that in expressive language *cognitive* advances may be made within a matrix of openly expressed *affective* involvement. Thus the simple dichotomy can no longer be maintained by means of which the 'creative' mode, at which it is acknowledged that ordinary working-class children may be good, can be dismissed as having relevance only to English and the airy-fairy side of the curriculum, while a different and rarer ability is required for the disciplines. For that expressive mode of relating to realities and ideas, one that appears to be the common property of most children and which English teachers have been so successful in channelling into writing, is also potentially the means of coming to grips with history and science. It is the early vehicle of analysis and explanation as much as of 'response'. We can see how the suggestion that *many* people have 'got what it takes', and that quite common abilities may be the means of access to the mysteries, could be hard to swallow for those who have sweated through specialized and rarefied procedures to arrive at their mastery.

But a more important point may be that the call for pupils to be actively engaging with material through expressive talk and writing is not one that teachers can easily meet. When the requirement was for little more than oral and written statements of facts, teachers knew that generally speaking they could guarantee to deliver. But expressive pupil language – a personal and revealing language of wondering, questioning, tentative formulation and risk-taking comment – is not available to order. It *may* occur when two conditions are met – when the speaker or writer is interested in the subject, and feels at ease with his or her audience. Clearly, these conditions are much harder to meet than those necessary for what has usually passed as acceptable 'work', and they are not entirely within the teacher's power to bring about. It takes two to make the necessary relationship of trust and security. Thus acceptance of the need for expressive language implies a shift to a more equal distribution of power between teacher and taught, and places new demands on the teacher.

In this way a point about language turns out to have implications for relationships, the role of the teacher and the status of the pupil as controller of his or her own learning. Moreover, 'language across the curriculum' is also implicitly a critique of the curriculum. When the London Writing Research team found that the transactional or would-be transactional writing that constituted the bulk of school writing often afforded no evidence of qualities of mind which showed clearly in the (expressive or poetic) writing done by the same pupils in English, this was in effect a finding not only about the writing opportunities afforded but about the sort of knowledge presented, which offered little to be intelligent about. The implied question was, what is the value of an education that allows so little scope for important intellectual processes – reasoning, hypothesizing, using evidence, drawing conclusions and so on? In fact, a criterion for the curriculum is suggested: if a particular content does not lend itself to being 'handled' in the expressive language of ordinary pupils in such a way that it yields rewarding insights, what business has it in a curriculum that is supposed to be open to all?

And that is the underlying thrust of the 'language across the curriculum' movement – *to make education a reality for the majority*. For although its most extensive promotion had to await the publication of the Bullock Report in 1975, its spirit is unmistakably of the late 1960s (which is one reason it is having a hard time of it now): the programme is democratic and optimistic in its assertion of the possibility of educational achievement by the majority of children and in its appeal for traditional rigidities and conventions to be relaxed; it is 'ecological' in its respect for existing working-class culture and language and its objection to their displacement by imposed and schematic formats for learning. It expresses two essential contentions about language in education: that language has been an *unnecessary* barrier to many children – the disciplines can be presented with fewer difficult terms and structures and in a language closer to that of the pupils; and that when people apply to the content of the disciplines processes of exploring and interpreting akin to those they already use on their life experiences, they are capable of understanding more than schools have traditionally supposed. Its position is reminiscent of those earlier demands that the Bible be printed in English, not Latin, and that people be allowed to discuss it and interpret it for themselves. We are responding as if our pupils had been saying, 'Talk to us in language we can understand, and give us the chance to use the resources and skills we already possess to make sense of the things you are showing and telling us.' The 'linguistic deprivation' to be taken seriously is the one for which we ourselves have been responsible, since denial of the opportunity to talk and write in personal modes is a reduction in the chance to learn. It is in effect a human rights issue.

The effect of success for the 'language across the curriculum' programme will be that the dice are less heavily loaded against the bright working-class children whose striking linguistic competence, debarred from contributing to their own educational progress, provoked so much of the initial activity. The game will be set up in such a way that native wit, so widely distributed through the population, will count for as much as that special kind of generalized motivation which enables some pupils to persist indefinitely in performing ritualized operations on materials which they may find of little personal significance. The drive is towards an education that builds on mental and linguistic processes which are available at some level to all of us, and not on special and uncommon predispositions and abilities. That, for me, is the reason why we should continue to press this language case – as it is also the reason why it will be powerfully opposed.

Note

[1] I am grateful to Professor Harold Rosen for pointing this out to me.

References

Britton, J.N. (1971) 'What's the use?', *Educational Review*, vol. 23, no. 3.
Britton, J.N. *et al.* (1975) *The Development of Writing Abilities (11–18)* (Schools Council Research Studies), London, Macmillan Education.

19   The Politics of English Teaching: A Broad View: Have Vision and Do What Is Possible*

Jack Shallcrass (Reader in Education, Victoria University of Wellington, New Zealand)

I'd like to share some of the doubts and hopes I have about teaching after forty-two years of practice. It would be splendid to talk about certainties in our job but they are rare. We're not alone in this – it's a general condition. All our institutions and values are in question. Public confidence in our systems – health, education, administration, economics, politics, etc. – is low and declining. The institutions are out of phase with the time.

In writing about the nature of scientific revolutions, Thomas Kuhn said that we get a paradigm shift when anomalies become embarrassingly numerous. Though he was looking at scientific thought, his insight applies equally to social and political thought. We may be on the edge of a paradigm shift.

As teachers we're in this up to our ears because we're part of a system that transmits and conserves the culture. Further, our work is public and our failures are obvious. Let me give you an extreme example from another society.

Barbiana is a small rural community in North Italy. It's a desperately poor peasant community. The children of Barbiana went to school in a large neighbouring village. At the age of 11 they sat national examinations designed to select those who were worthy of more education. The failures had to leave school. Inevitably it was the poor and underprivileged who failed. The class of 1964 all failed and returned to their families in Barbiana to work in the fields like generations before them.

Well, they would have done if Don Lorenzo Milani had not come to Barbiana. He was a priest who was banished to Barbiana as a political. He believed that Christians should be identifiable by their actions, that they should be with the poor and the dispossessed. It is not unknown even in New Zealand for politicians to be upset by such priests.

When Don Lorenzo learned of the children's failure at school he offered to teach them. They accepted.

'It will take two years,' he said. 'We'll work for six days a week. You will learn to read so that you can find out; to write clearly and simply so that people can understand you; and to ask questions. With these skills you can do anything.'

At the end of two years he gave the children, now 13–14 years old, two tasks. First they must pass on their knowledge to others for it is a precious

* P.R. Smart Memorial Address, NZATE Conference, Christchurch, 1982.

158

and holy thing to be shared. To use knowledge for power and advantage over others is ignoble. Thus did Don Lorenzo speak and even today there are self-sustaining groups through Tuscany teaching that curriculum. Just before he died Don Lorenzo set his second task which was for the children to write a book exposing the injustices of the Italian education system.

So they began. They read, thought, talked, questioned and wrote. After they had written a piece they took out the words that did not add to the meaning. Then they gave it to people who could read but not particularly well. If they understood, it was right; if not, it was written again.

To add to the impact they included statistics in unusually dramatic forms. Their maths was rudimentary but, since they knew how to ask questions, they could find the best way of presenting their material. For this work they won the most prestigious prize of the Italian Physical Society.

Please remember that by now these children were about fourth- or fifth-form age and rejects of the system.

Their book was published and has since been translated into many languages and sold hundreds of thousands of copies. It is called *Letter to a Teacher*[1] and begins:

Dear Miss,
   You won't remember me or my name. You have failed so many of us. On the other hand I have often had thoughts about you and the other teachers, and about the institution which you call 'school' and about the children you fail. You fail us right into the fields and factories and there you forget us.

Don Lorenzo's great achievement was to turn defeated children into independent, self-reliant young adults. They had also learned that they could help change society because they had power – not to impose, but to negotiate. The school could have given them the same skills and confidence but it was in the business of selection, of which failure is a necessary by-product. Unlike the schools, Don Lorenzo achieved both excellence and equity.

I chose this story because it encapsulates many of our political, social and educational problems and because it suggests some solutions. It also has much of significance for teachers of English, not least because it comes close to the essence of the New English curriculum. Don Lorenzo'a curriculum might not be well received in our scholarship schools but it makes sense in those schools that live beyond the fringe of privilege.

This theme is developed profoundly by Paulo Freire in *Pedogogy of the Oppressed* (Freire, 1970). For him education is the means by which people become aware of themselves within a culture. Awareness of self and awareness of the culture are both necessary for the process to be significant to the learner.

Freire grew up in poverty-stricken north-east Brazil. He became involved in adult literacy programmes in which he worked with the very poor. By trial and error he devised methods that succeeded dramatically. In essence he looked for key words and phrases that reached deep into the experience of the learners – words like oppression, landlord, hunger. He taught the words in ways that related to the learners' lives. The words were useful tools but the learning was also a political education. With skills and with insight came a sense of power and purpose – a true liberation. Education that does not liberate in this way only serves to increase oppression because it gives skills without insight or power. To Freire power is not power *over* others but power *with* them. There is no general gain in having the oppressors and oppressed change roles. What is needed is universal liberation.

When the children of Barbiana were at the village school they learned that they were insignificant and powerless. Don Lorenzo offered them the chance to liberate themselves. It was a negotiated, reciprocal relationship.

Freire discusses schools as supermarkets that dispense knowledge as a commodity. He refers also to the banking concept of education in which knowledge is *deposited* in the learner. In both cases all learners are oppressed because they are treated as objects within an imposed set of relationships.

While Freire was reaching these conclusions with adults in Brazil, Sylvia Ashton-Warner was doing the same with 5-year-old Maoris in New Zealand. Freire was gaoled as a subversive by the military junta in 1964 and then exiled; Ashton-Warner[2] was simply ignored and went into self-exile. Their message was, and is, dangerous for all who enjoy power over others.

Teachers belong in this group because they exercise power over children who have no choice but to attend school. There's an uncomfortable coercive element at the base of our work. This is true of all we do, not least in the curriculum over which clients have no control. In a sense, they are colonized.

English teachers are peculiarly subject to this kind of imperialism because, as members of the dominant class, they impose their own dialect on children. Since education is concerned with selection through standard-ized procedures, children who use other dialects are at a disadvantage. If they want to gain advantage from the system they must learn the dominant dialect. The Romans used Latin to colonize Europe; we use Remuera English[3], to colonize South Auckland, so far without too much success. In the long run that may be a matter for rejoicing.

Linguists such as Labov (1973) argue that no dialect is inherently superior to any other within a broad language group. However, a child speaking 'black' English in New York or Maori English in New Zealand is left high and dry by the school system. Conversely, a child who shares the teachers' dialect is already halfway to winning.

There are teachers who fight this tendency with some success but they know how powerful is the enemy.

Ivan Illich (1979) has explored the way in which court languages were used to extend the power of the centre over the periphery. He claims that this has diminished the status of the *vernacular* for reasons that are political rather than linguistic.

He develops the argument that a dominant dialect is used to extend the influence of existing power blocs in society in ways that make their language a commodity. He contrasts the vernacular ('born into'), which is the reverse of commodity ('from the market'). If we thought of language *usefulness* rather than language ornamentation we might give more attention to variants of the vernacular in our schools.

Many of you would have been astonished at what Dorothy Heathcote achieved with children in her drama through negotiation. Teachers in Ponsonby denied the evidence of their eyes and ears. 'They're not doing what I see or saying what I hear.' Part of the Heathcote success is that she listens to all language codes and negotiates equally.

The issue is important to us educationally but it is also of great importance politically. As minority groups become aware of their oppression they will demand recognition of their unique characteristics in language and custom. In extreme cases they will reject us as agents of oppression. However, if we recognize and use other dialects as equals, the nice, well-educated people who belong to the powerful groups will punish us. Equity and social justice are noble concepts so long as you don't put them to work. In dynamic times we run the risk of pleasing no one and becoming irrelevant. Whatever we do has political connotations that demand awareness, choices and commitment.

This was underlined last year during a visit of Yehezkel Dror who is chief adviser to the OECD (Organisation for Economic Co-operation and Development) on social planning. He said that all the economic indications were for a steady slide into *long-term* economic depression. The Keynesian remedy of priming the pump wasn't working and there was no likelihood of the stimulus of a major but limited war because of the danger of nuclear weapons. He thinks that there are grounds for believing that industrial culture is faltering and maybe dying. Its values and assumptions no longer accord with observable reality. Certainly there are forces at work that we can't explain and can't control.

The system has worked well for a couple of hundred years thanks to regular growth in productivity. We've developed complex and generally effective ways of sharing the surpluses – indeed, it is one of the great national pastimes. In the process we have come to expect *more* year by year and generation by generation.

The difficulty is that there have been no surpluses since the mid-1970s but that hasn't stopped us behaving as though there were. Most of us continue to do very well but someone has to pay. In New Zealand it's people with brown skins and women who carry the burden of the decline. They make up the bulk of the growing army of official and unrecognized unemployed. Thanks to feminism and to Maori nationalism, there's a growing awareness of this discrimination. Willy-nilly we're part of it; sooner or later we'll have to decide where we stand – another choice.

In a surplus economy there's been a pay-off for educational success – a job. There's no guarantee of that any more. The reward system is failing, and, with it, much of the appeal of what we have to offer.

161

At the same time the failures ask why we didn't give them useful skills and attitudes – the Barbiana ethos perhaps? Dror says there are only two political options open. We live with a value system of rising expectations but with an economic system that can't satisfy them. Either we will voluntarily accept less or powerful central governments will coerce us into doing so.

The alternative to a coercive society is a negotiated society; we are directed or we participate.

Though the elements of both are established here, a prudent gambler would have to bet on the coercive model – at least in the immediate future. Read *Smiths Dream*.[4]

If we keep moving towards a coercive state the schools will be required to follow suit. They'll become more competitive, there will be more examining, obedience and conformity will be rewarded, the hierarchies of power will be intensified, behaviour-shaping psychologies will be the norm, and there will be less lay participation. It will be a culture of absolutes and certainties.

If we move towards a negotiated society schools would become less competitive, there would be more concern for individual growth, power would be more widely shared, psychology would be eclectic and there would be more lay participation. It would be a culture of probabilities without absolutes. Everything would be negotiable.

I'm sure you will recognize that the foundations for both possibilities are in place in New Zealand.

Also, you will recognize the frantic efforts of the power groups to rush back to the truths of the past – back to private enterprise, back to basics, back to fundamentalism . . . back to more of what lies at the heart of the sickness. Naturally they don't mention the real purpose, which is the protection of privilege and greed.

Yehezkel Dror says that we now face an embarrassing number of anomalies in our systems and change must follow. We can either retreat from liberalism into authoritarianism or seek a new consensus.

No one escapes the choice, whether they're aware of it or not. The outcome will be the cumulative effect of our individual behaviours.

What we do carries the value and the message.

In the long term we are likely to be nudged towards the open, participative model by natural laws. Our present political–economic model takes no serious account of long-term costs in relation to short-term gains. Some of the results are top-soil loss, ecological imbalance, build-up of carbon dioxide in the atmosphere, groundwater loss, extinction of species, advance of deserts and pollution, to name a few.

They are the consequence of the single-minded pursuit of surpluses through growth without regard for cost. An iron-law of the universe is that there's no free lunch – everything costs. It is known as the Entropy Law or, strictly, as the Second Law of Thermodynamics. And what has that to do with English? Stay with me.

The Entropy Law (Rifkin, 1980) states that energy and matter can be changed only in one direction, from usable to unusable, from available to unavailable. Entropy is the measure of the extent to which energy in any sub-system or in the universe itself has been made unavailable. Whenever order is created, it is at the expense of greater disorder elsewhere. All systems run down but they don't need to do it as fast as ours is doing. Industrial culture is exploitative for immediate ends without regard for the future. This is the cancer at its core. It is what Hazel Henderson calls 'flat earth economics'.[5] We don't inherit the earth, we borrow it from our children.

If we move to a centralized coercive state it will be to protect the people who get the most out of exploitation. Since this would raise, or at least maintain, the entropy count, it could be only a pause on the way to a post-industrial culture which would be marked by appropriate technologies, recycling, renewable resource management, sustained yield economies, decentralized political systems, participative decision-making and holistic health and education. Such a model must come.

There's a strong and growing literature that is pressing for a new model.[6] Industrial culture belongs to an age that was sired by Newton and that inherited his mechanistic and reductionist world-view. Reason was the measure of all things and it was by the fruits of reason that humans would conquer nature. It was a world of certainties and absolutes. And it is collapsing around us.

As always in these circumstances, new models and philosophies appear. Remember Kuhn and his paradigm shifts? A new paradigm is on the way. It is already affecting science and is sending shock waves into economics, medicine, education and elsewhere. Quantum physics began the erosion of the mechanistic world-view. There are more random processes and more uncertainties than the Newtonian world thought possible. Even the dream of objectivity is in disarray. In place of reductionist thought came holistic views which sought truth in the overall functioning of interlocking systems. Nature was suddenly more complex and less predictable as were humans and their social systems. This requires minds that see larger rather than small, that synthesize rather than analyse, that call on compassion, intuition and imagination as well as intellect. In fact, just the kind of synthesis and understanding that good English teachers have in mind. You're up and running without knowing the forces that are with you.

It doesn't stop there either. Teilhard de Chardin,[7] a distinguished palaeontologist and Catholic theologian, teaches that evolution, the basic force of the universe, has produced humans out of its random functioning. Because we have such complex central nervous systems humans have the ability and the responsibility of turning evolution from a random into a moral and ethical process. That's our fate. Life was easier when some other Being had the responsibility; now there's no cop-out – what happens is the result of what we think, believe and do. The significance for education is profound as de Chardin, Freire and others are quick to point out.

Like the Newtonian world that spawned it, our education is about reductionism and quantification. When the next paradigm shift matures, we may find it taking on the qualities of the uncertain, varied world of quantum physics.

Support for this view comes from Systems Theory, particularly from the Law of Requisite Variety that states: 'Take any connected system, whether in electronics or people, and the element with the widest range of variability in its behaviour will be in control; it will always have one more response that can make the difference'. In essense, variability and versatility are supreme survival values.

There will be hard lessons for institutions like ours to learn. Most of them, and not least education, are well adapted to what is. They need to attend to anthropology's Law of the Retarding Lead which can be summarized as 'nothing fails like success'. Why change a winning formula? The best adapted institutions and societies have the greatest difficulty in dealing with change because, being so well adapted, they have a big stake in the *status quo*.

So the change agents will be those schools, teachers, pupils and parents who are on the edge of the system and have little or nothing to lose. If you want new pathways look to the outsiders, the oppressed, the losers and to those who identify with them for they have the best reasons for change. These will include schools in depressed areas, Maori activists, feminist groups, the co-operatives, the unemployed workers' unions, environmental groups, the Coalition for Open Government among others.

If you despair, think of the children of Barbiana who found independence and purpose in doing simple things well; think of Freire and his education for liberation; think of Dorothy Heathcote and the use of drama as negotiation; think of colleagues who are feeling their way towards new paradigms; think of being in the same stream as modern scientific philosophers; think of de Chardin.

Teachers of English span all these and more, with all the opportunities entailed. We can't do it alone or quickly but we should be clear on where we stand and why. For that we need generous visions and the ability to do daily what is possible.

Notes

1. The Children of Barbiana, *Letter to a Teacher*, Harmondsworth, Penguin, 1970.
2. S. Ashton-Warner, *Spinster*, London, Secker & Warburg, 1960, especially pp. 178–97; *I Passed This Way*, A.H. & A.W. Reed, 1979.
3. Remuera is the upper-class residential area of Auckland.
4. C.K. Stead, *Smith's Dream*, Auckland, Longman Paul, 1973, relates the fated attempts of a man to withstand the totalitarian regime created by a leader who takes over the country in a time of financial crisis.
5. See H. Henderson, *Creating Alternative Futures*, New York, Berkley Windhover, 1978; and *The Politics of the Solar Age*, New York, Anchor Doubleday, 1981.
6. I. Illich (1979), pp. 31–75.

7. See P.T. de Chardin, *The Phenomenon of Man*, Fontana Religious Books, London, Collins, 1965.

References

Freire, P. (1970) *Pedagogy of the Oppressed*, New York, Seabury.
Illich, I. (1979) 'Vernacular values and education', *Harvard Education Review*, vol. 81, no. 1, pp. 31–75.
Labov, W. (1973) 'The logic of non-standard English', in N. Keddie (ed.), *Tinker, Tailor*, Harmondsworth, Penguin.
Rifkin, J. (1980) *Entropy*, New York, Viking.

Part VII

Problems and Opportunities

Ah! Don't say that you agree with me. When people agree with me, I always feel
that I must be wrong.
Oscar Wilde, 'The Writer as Artist', in *Poems and Essays*, p. 335.

When I first sketched out a proposal for this book I suggested that its focus
might be on 'ideas in action'. I was in fact inspired by a piece of writing that
has been part of my precious collection for many years. It was written by a
Canadian teacher for a course I taught in the University of British Columbia in
1965. Having discovered Susanne Langer's distinction between discursive
and presentational symbolism (in *Feeling and Form*), he wrote: 'Is it not
possible that many of the problems which face English teachers have arisen
because they have been caught in the iron grip of discursive language, and
have been unable to appreciate that the ineffable knowledge which they are
trying to pass on lies in the "symbolic transformation of experience into a
presentational form".' Teaching English to Eskimo children (whose native
tongue is not English), he decided to try to encourage writing from personal
experience by relating it to a kind of speech familiar to them in their homes –
a ritual or formal kind of speech he describes as 'conversation-to-exclude-
all-others'.

But it would be difficult to find a clearer example of putting ideas to work
than we have in the 'liberatory' curriculum described in the first chapter in Part
VII. The authors leave us in no doubt as to what those ideas were: Vygotsky's
theory of inner speech and its relation to thought on the one hand and writing
on the other; and Paulo Freire's pedagogy aimed at releasing the oppressed
from 'the fear of freedom'. It is the power of ideas, when we put them into
action, that enables us to see our special problems as also special opportunites.

Our various multicultural environments present us with a range of problems and a sheaf of opportunities – and there is probably no aspect of the
educational scene that more sharply distinguishes the one perspective from
the other.

I can't help wondering whether Bernard Gadd (Chapter 21) would regard
commitment to prepare Bahamian students, as Nan Elsasser did (Chapter 20),
for the conventional English Department test as a flagrant case of cultural
assimilation, or whether – with his compatriot, Jack Shallcrass – he might
justify it as an example of facing the impossible by tackling what is possible?
This is, in any case, not an area in which there are going to be easy answers.
Without doubt the most important contribution to our thinking on such

matters has come in recent years from the application of anthropological approaches to educational problems. I am delighted to have Shirley Brice Heath sounding the closing note to this collection (Chapter 22), and I can think of no more appropriate note to close on than one that celebrates talk in the classroom.

20 'Strangers No More': A Liberatory Literacy Curriculum*

Kyle Fiore (The University of New Mexico)
and *Nan Elsasser (The College of the Virgin Islands)*

College of the Bahamas
November 17, 1979

Dear Kyle, Pat and Larry,

I think our basic writing curriculum works! After ten weeks of discussing reading and writing about the generative theme of marriage, students have actually begun to use their newly won knowledge and skills for their own purposes. Last night we were reviewing for the final – a test designed, administered and graded by the College English Department – when Louise, one of my students, broke in to say that no test could measure what she had learned over the semester! Another student nodded in agreement. She said, 'We've learned about marriage, men and women. We've learned to write. We've learned about ourselves.' Perfect Freirian synthesis! As if that weren't reward enough for one night, Eurena suggested that the class – all women – summarize and publish their knowledge. Then everyone jumped in. Our review of dashes and semicolons was forgotten as the class designed its first publication. It's hard to believe that in September these women had difficulty thinking in terms of a paragraph – now they want a manifesto! I'll keep you posted.

Love, Nan

Nan Elsasser's letter elated us. That semester she had been experimenting with a remedial English program we had designed[1] in the spring of 1978. We had first come together just after Christmas, drawn to each other by the desire to share our classroom frustrations, our successes, our gripes, over a common pitcher of beer. Trading stories with one another, we discovered we were four teachers in search of a curriculum. Standard English textbooks and traditional curricula did not fit our students at the University of Albuquerque and the University of New Mexico. Chicanos, Blacks, Anglos and native Americans, they had enrolled in our courses to gain writing skills that would help them succeed in college and carve a place for themselves in society. Once they arrived, however, our students found themselves strangers in a strange world. A wide gulf stretched between the classroom curriculum and their own knowledge gained in the barrios of Albuquerque and the rural towns and pueblos of New Mexico. Confronted by a course that negated their culture, many failed to master the skills they sought. Others succeeded by developing a second skin. Leaving their own customs,

* Abridged, by permission, from *College English*, vol. 44, no. 2, February 1982.

habits, and skills behind, they participated in school and in the world by adapting themselves to fit the existing order. Their acquisition of literacy left them not in control of their social context, but controlled by it. We were troubled. We wanted our students to be able to bring their culture, their knowledge, into the classroom. We wanted them to understand and master the intricacies of the writing process. And we wanted them to be able to use writing as a means of intervening in their own social environment. Sparked by our common concerns, we decided to create a curriculum that would meet our goals. As we cast about for theories and pedagogies, we discovered the work of Lev Vygotsky and Paulo Freire. These scholars intrigued us because they believe writing involves both cognitive skills and social learnings. Their approaches parallel and complement each other. Vygotsky explores students' internal learning processes. Freire emphasizes the impact of external social reality.

Vygotsky's work clarifies the complex process of writing.[2] He postulates that learning to write involves the mastery of cognitive skills and the development of new social understandings. According to Vygotsky, we categorize and synthesize our lives through inner speech, the language of thought. In inner speech, a single word or phrase is embroidered with variegated threads of ideas, experiences and emotions. The multi-levelled, personal nature of inner speech is illustrated by a woman student's response to a word association exercise: *sex*: home, time, never, rough, sleep.

Vygotsky explains that to transform the inner speech symbols to written text, this woman must consciously step outside the shorthand of her thoughts and mentally enter the social context she shares with her reader. Only from this common perspective can she begin to unfold the mystery of her thoughts to create written prose.

Focusing on the learner's environment, Freire discusses the social and political aspects of writing. A designer of liberatory or revolutionary literacy programs, Freire maintains that the goal of a literacy program is to help students become critically conscious of the connection between their own lives and the larger society and to empower them to use literacy as a means of changing their own environment. Like Vygotsky, Freire believes the transformation of thought to text requires the conscious consideration of one's social context. Often, Freire says, students unaware of the connections between their own lives and society personalize their problems. To encourage students to understand the impact of society on their lives, Freire proposes students and teachers talk about generative themes drawn from the students' everyday world. Investigating issues such as work or family life from an individual and a socio-historical perspective, students bring their own knowledge into the classroom and broaden their sense of social context.

For example, one woman beaten by her husband may think she has simply made a bad choice and must bear her lot with dignity. Another woman may think her husband would stop if she could live up to his expectations. When they talk with each other and other women, these two discover that brutality is a social phenomenon; it is widespread in the community. As they read, they learn that many aspects of their problem are rooted in the social realm and can best be attacked by pressing for legal changes, battered women's shelters, more responsive attitudes on the part of the police. Through continued discussion, these women realize how they can use literacy to win those changes by swearing out complaints in court, sending petitions to public officials, or writing newspaper articles and letters to the editor.

We decided to base our curriculum on Vygotsky's theory and Freire's pedagogy. Vygotsky's theory of inner speech would enable students to understand the writing process. Freire's pedagogy would encourage them to bring their culture and personal knowledge into the classroom, help them understand the connections between their own lives and society, and empower them to use writing to control their environment.

As advanced literacy teachers in traditional universities, we realized we could not use a pure Freirian approach. Designed for teachers in revolutionary settings, Freire's basic literacy programs do not consider the time constraint of semesters or the academic pressure of preparing students to meet English department standards. However, we thought it would be possible to combine Freire's goal of increasing students' critical consciousness with the teaching of advanced literacy skills. As Freire wrote in *Pedagogy in Process* (Freire, 1978), 'The best way to accomplish those things that are impossible today is to do today whatever is possible.'

That spring we met every Saturday at each other's houses. Spurred on by coffee and raised glazed doughnuts, we talked about the advanced literacy techniques we were using and explored ways to link those techniques with Vygotsky's and Freire's work. We designed word association exercises to Vygotsky's theory of inner speech. We charted ways to fit rhetorical forms in a Freirian investigation. We finished in May. That same month Nan Elsasser won a Fulbright to teach advanced literacy at the College of the Bahamas. She would be the first to try our curriculum. The next fall Elsasser kept us abreast of her experiment by mail. In the pages that follow we summarized her letters and combined them with copies of student papers to create a first-person account of our curriculum in process.

The College of the Bahamas: an experiment in possibilities

Arriving in the Bahamas before the semester begins, I have a few days to learn about the college.

Located on the island of New Providence, the College of the Bahamas is a two-year community offering daytime and evening classes. Over 90 per cent of the students at the college are black Bahamians. Many work by day, attend school by night.

The language skills class I am to teach is the first in a series of four English courses offered by the college prep program. All of these courses are taught along traditional lines. To practise grammar, students change tenses, add punctuation, or fill in blank spaces in assigned sentences. To demonstrate reading ability they answer multiple-choice or true–false questions on short paragraphs. A colleague tells me the year before 45 to 60 per cent of the students failed to meet English department standards. She also shows me a College of the Bahamas study demonstrating no significant correlation between grades in English and grades in other academic subjects. Her revelations strengthen my determination to try out our curriculum.

I get to class early on the first night, worried my students' traditional expectations will make them leary of a new approach. Checking my roster, I discover all my students are women (later, I learn women make up two-thirds of the college's student body). I start class by introducing myself and describing the problems I've encountered teaching English traditionally. Telling the women we'll be using an experimental approach, I stress this experiment will succeed only if we can pick topics, discuss material, and evaluate results together. I admit class will lack coherency at times, and one student asks if they will be able to pass the standardized English exam given at the end of the semester. I say I think so, but that she is free to transfer if she wants a more traditional approach. She leaves; but the rest stay.

To establish a sense of common ground, I ask my students about their work and former schooling. Half of them clerk in banks. The others type or run computers. Collectively, these women represent the first generation of Bahamian women to enter the business world and go to college. They have an average of six years of education behind them. Recalling her early school days, one woman speaks of days spent copying poems from a colonial primer. Another recounts the times she stayed at home to care for the younger ones while her mother went to sell her wares at the straw market. They all remember problems with writing.

So they can begin to understand the cause of their problems, we spend the next three weeks investigating the complexities of going from inner speech to finished written product. We begin with a series of word association exercises designed to illustrate Vygotsky's theory. Comparing their responses to trigger words such as *sex, home, work*, the women start to see that even at this most basic level they categorize and store information in various ways. Some students list contrasting affective responses. Others jot down visual images. One woman divides the inner speech word into sub-topics, like an outline: 'job: where you would like to work, type of boss, what specific field'. Contrasting their different ways of organizing and listing thoughts, students gain a strong sense of why they need to elaborate their thoughts in writing. To end the session, we each transform our private lists to public prose.

To continue our study of the transformations involved in writing clear, explicit prose, I look for a topic that will stress the value of personal knowledge, break down the dichotomy between personal and classroom knowledge, and require explicit elaboration. As a newcomer to the island, I ask them to advise me 'What You Need to Know to Live in the Bahamas'. I introduce this assignment by talking about writing as an interaction between process and product, personal and social points of view, concrete and abstract knowledge. A student writing a recipe for conch salad needs concrete knowledge about preparing conch combined with the abstract knowledge of an audience as people with some shared assumptions as well as some lack of common ground.

The women have a number of problems with this assignment, evidencing what Freire calls the inability to step outside immediate contextual realities and incorporate broader points of view. Some students write very brief suggestions. Others write in the first person or list topics of interest, but don't include concrete information. Still others complain they are stymied trying to figure out what I'd like to do. Though she knows I am a stranger to the island, the woman writing me a recipe for conch salad assumes conch is a familiar food. Yet another woman constructs an imaginary audience to help herself focus on the assignment: 'What You Need to Know to Live in the Bahamas. A Young married couple on Vacation. Leisure Activities. Whatever your taste in holiday diversion you'll never be at a loss for something to do in the Bahamas'.

This assignment extends over several sessions. Students write and rewrite their essays. During this time we develop the basic procedure we'll use to investigate a generative theme. First, we discuss the topic at hand (e.g. 'What You Need to Know to Live in the Bahamas'). Then one student volunteers a thesis statement related to the topic. Other women help narrow and sharpen this statement and develop an essay outline. Students use these outlines as guidelines for their rough drafts. I reproduce the drafts, and we read and comment on them. After prolonged discussion, each woman rewrites her draft to meet the questions we've raised.

In moving from the discussion of inner speech to writing about the Bahamas, students take on more and more responsibility for the class. While in writing they are still trapped by their personal perspectives, in discussions they begin to critique and respond to one another's views. Gradually they start to investigate their environment. Before, they passively received knowledge. Now, they pursue it.

Freire states that students caught by their own subjectivity can break through personal walls and move to a collective social perspective through investigating generative themes. Such themes must be selected carefully so that they encourage students to write for a broader, more public audience and empower them to use writing to change their lives. Freire advises teachers searching for themes to involve themselves intimately in their students' culture and minutely observe all the facets of their daily lives, recording 'the way people talk, their style of life, their behaviour at church and work' (Freire, 1970). Analysing these observations with a team of other educators, the teacher will discern meaningful generative themes.

A stranger, unaccompanied by a 'literacy team', I can't follow Freire's advice, and in my ignorance I turn to my students for help. We discuss generative themes, and they each select three issues from their daily lives that they would like to talk, read and write about for the semester. When they bring in their suggestions, I list them on the board. We debate them briefly and they vote, picking marriage for their generative theme. This theme affects their lives economically, socially and emotionally. Ninety per cent of these women have been raised by two parents in traditional Bahamian homes. Seventy-five per cent are now mothers. Two-thirds of these are single parents totally responsible for their children's physical and emotional well-being.

Having chosen their theme, the women break into groups. They discuss the areas of marriage they want to investigate and construct an outline of sub-topics, including *housework, divorce, sexuality*, and *domestic violence*. With these sub-topics in hand, I start to hunt for reading materials. I look for articles that bridge the distance between students' lives and society. We'll use these articles as a basis for dialogues about individual problems, common experiences and the larger social world.

My search of the college library yields nothing on contemporary Bahamian marriage. Writing back to the United States for articles, culling my old *Ms.* magazines, and hounding the local news-stand, I collect a packet that fits our course outline. Initial reading assignments come from popular magazines: an article on wife beating from *New Woman*, one entitled 'Why bad marriages endure' from *Ebony*. As students' reading skills and knowledge increase, we will use more advanced texts, such as *Our Bodies Ourselves* (2nd edn, New York, Simon and Schuster, 1976), and *The Longest War: Sex Differences in Perspective* by Carol Tavris and Carole Offir (New York, Harcourt Brace Jovanovich, 1977). At the end of the semester we will read *Nectar in a Sieve* (New York, New American Library, 1971), a novel by Kamala Markandaya about peasant marriage in India.

For the rest of the semester we spend about one week co-investigating each sub-topic of our marriage theme. I introduce each subject by handing out a related article. To help the women understand new information, I discuss the concepts I think unfamiliar, e.g. the historical concept of Victorian as a set of sexual attitudes. After reading and talking about the articles, we develop a thesis statement following the procedure we devised when writing essays on the Bahamas. When discussing articles and writing critiques students do not follow the traditional liberal arts criteria. Their criticism is not bound by the authors' intent or opinion, nor do they consider all articles equally valid. Rather, they judge the reading by whether or not it connects with their personal perspectives and tells them about marriage as a socioeconomic institution.

During our investigations, students pass through three distinct phases as they hone their abilities to examine, critique and write about marriage. They elaborate their own experience more skilfully, and they perceive stronger links between their own lives and the larger social context. They reach outside their own experience to seek new sources of knowledge. Finally, they become critically conscious of the way society affects their lives, and they begin to use writing as a means of intervening in their own social environment.

In the early weeks many women have trouble discerning the connections between their personal life and their social context. They analyse problems using concrete knowledge drawn from experience. They argue by anecdote. To encourage them to broaden their outlook, I ask for a definition of marriage as a social institution. In response, they describe what marriage should be ('communication'. 'love', 'fidelity'), or they recite personal experiences ('men can come and go as they please, women cannot'; 'men neglect their financial responsibilities'; 'men have sweethearts'; 'men are violent'). Posing questions targeting a social definition of marriage, I elicit broader, abstract responses: 'legal procedure', 'age requirements', 'union between man and woman', 'religious sanctioning of sex'. Looking over this list, they ask me to throw out their earlier, more personal definitions.

Next, they construct lists of the positive and negative aspects of marriage as a social institution. These lists display a mixture of personal experiences, idealistic yearnings and social traits:

Positive	Negative
Safe from rape and break-ins	Sex against our will
Not coming home to an empty house	Security sours relationship
Community approval of the relationship	Loss of freedom

Comparing these lists, the women start to talk about the social aspects of marriage. They conclude that the major benefit of marriage is security and social approval; its major shortcoming, a loss of freedom. Even after our extended dialogue, in their essays on 'The Worst or Best Things about Marriage', women either write empty generalizations or briefly recount their own experience.

I suggest revisions for these essays, reproduce them, and pass them out. Students critique each other's papers, and each woman rewrites her piece. This time a number of students expand their essays through elaboration. However, at this stage no one goes beyond her own experience without writing platitudes, and few maintain a consistent focus throughout the entire paper. The woman writing this third draft has expanded and improved her mechanics and drawn clearer contrasts in her conclusions. She still reverts to an unrelated generality:

Draft III
By Rosetta Finlay

The worst thing about marriage is emotional security. When a couple is married, they tend to become too sure of themselves. One will say, 'All is well I already have whom I want so I don't have to look nice any more; I don't have to say I love you any more; I don't have to show that I care as much; we don't have sex as often and you can go out with the boys while I go out with the girls.'

Marriage shouldn't be taken so much for granted there's always improvement needed in every marriage. Marriage is like a job e.g. – one has a job everything is routine; you have a steady salary; steady hours nine o'clock in the morning to five o'clock in the evening; go to work every day and perform the duties your job position requires.

Marriage is very similar e.g. – one has a steady companion; cook every day; keep the house and laundry clean; have babies and bring them up. Apart from doing the house chores there's the chauffeuse part to be done and the office work.

I personally think that there is a lot more to be done if you want to have a successful marriage. Therefore if more interest is taken in these areas, marriage would be much better than what it is today.

In the sessions that follow, students evidence similar problems with the reading assignment. The article is about battered wives. Although they can read the words, the women have difficulty distinguishing major ideas from details. Where in writing they recounted personal experiences, now in reading they focus on anecdotes. They underline when, where, or how hard Frank hit Marlene, as opposed to the main concept this example illustrates.

To sharpen the contrast between a main idea and an illustration I ask them to list causes of domestic violence on the board. Then we start to talk about the difference between causes and anecdotes. It takes students several sessions to learn to select main points correctly on their own. During these sessions they also begin to gain a better grasp of the connections between their own lives and the forces of society.

I am reminded as I consider my students that teaching and learning are part of a single process. To present something in class is not to teach it. Learning happens when students make cognitive transformations, expanding and reorganizing the knowledge in their cerebral filing systems. Only then can they assimilate and act upon ideas.

By the end of phase one the women have made several such transformations. They have an idea of their own differences and a sense of the common ground they share. Although they still rely on personal experience as a source of knowledge, they are beginning to recognize how the outside society affects their lives. This awareness has improved their writing. They use more detail. They separate ideas and events into paragraphs. They sustain a third-person perspective with greater skill. They clarify generalizations with examples:

A 'Typical' Bahamian Marriage
By Rosetta Finlay

'For richer, for poorer, for better, for worse, in sickness and in health, until death do us part.' God has commanded his children to join in the holy matrimony and obey these rules. Unfortunately, the majority of the Bahamian marriages tend to focus more on the negative, than the positive aspects of marriage. A Typical Bahamian Marriage will begin with both, the male and female being in love with each other, so much in love that the husband will help with the house chores, such as washing the dishes, doing the laundry, taking out the garbage and making breakfast. It will even get to the point where the husband will stay up at night with their first child. Every Sunday the family will go to church and have dinner together. Later in the evening the husband and wife will go to the movies or a special function.

Week days, both the husband and wife will go out to work, usually they both work. After work the wife rushes home to prepare the dinner. The bills are paid by both the husband and wife's salary put together and, if possible, a little is saved. For some period of time, the wife will satisfy her husband's need such as, sharing sex, understanding and the house chores. Then all of a sudden, for an unknown reason the husband changes.

He will start staying out X amount of hours and stop putting his share of monies towards the bills. Comes home and take out his frustration on his wife and children by snapping at children and beating his wife. He does not even want to spend any time at home to help with the house chores or baby sit. He only comes home to change, if he is questioned about money it will end in a fight. Then he will leave home for another day or two.

The wife is now in a situation where she does not have enough money to pay the bills and support the children, no husband to lean on and protect the family. She does not have anywhere to go, because he keeps telling her that she cannot go with out him. Getting a divorce in the Bahamas is completely out of the question. So she will have to 'grin and bear it' until death.

By mid-semester most women have entered phase two. We pause to take stock of our work. Looking back over their gains, women are sparked with pride. They begin seizing more control in class and start to generate their own theories on the writing mechanics. One night we tackle the problem of pronoun agreement. While aware they often switch back and forth in writing from *they* to *you*, *she*/*he*, and *I*, students have little success self-editing for pronouns because we don't know the cause of this problem. Then one woman comments she has no trouble writing general points in the third person. However, she says when she illustrates these points or gives advice, she starts mentally addressing a particular person and slips into a second-person referent. Examining several essays, classmates confirm her observation; as a result, they begin to catch and correct these errors.

Women also start to discover punctuation rules. Although I have not stressed punctuation as such, they observe patterns in the reading, and they hypothesize the rules themselves.

During this phase students also break away from their total dependence on personal experience. They become more confident about gaining knowledge from class dialogues and reading. One night we debate whether or not women 'ask for' rape. Remembering how reading about wife beating changed our stereotypes, one student asks for additional materials on rape. Others second her request. Spurred on by their own curiosity, they assail excerpts from Susan Brownmiller's *Against Our Will* and discuss how her theories and statistics destroy or reinforce their personal myths and beliefs.

Encouraged by their confidence and advancing skills, I begin to introduce the idea of rhetorical forms: cause and effect, definition, comparison and contrast. Rather than concentrating on these forms explicitly, we employ them as a means of pondering, exploring and writing about various facets of marriage.

In phase three students begin to use writing as a means of intervening in their own social environment. A few weeks before the end of the semester the women decide to share the knowledge they have gained about marriage with the world outside classroom by publishing an open 'Letter to Bahamian Men' in the island newspapers. Writing this manifesto takes four weeks. In addition to class time, we meet together on Sunday and put in hours of extra work. We start by writing individual letters. We discuss these letters in class, then outline a collective letter:

A. Introduction
   1. Role of women in Bahamian society
   2. Oppression of women in marriage
B. Women victims of men's inconsiderate actions
C. Men's financial neglect of the family
D. Men's lack of help at home
E. Men's lack of responsibility for their children
F. Men's failure to satisfy women sexually
G. Conclusion: recommendations for Bahamian men

After consulting the concerns each woman mentioned in her first letter, I assign each one a particular topic to develop. I organize the topics into a text, leaving gaps where I think there is a need for further work. From this point on my role is limited to copying, cutting and pasting. Equipped with her own copy, each woman begins to edit her epistle. They go line by line, spending over an hour on each page. Students silent all semester defend their contributions vehemently. They argue over punctuation, style and semantics. They debate whether to separate the list of men's inconsiderate actions with colons, semi-colons or full stops. One woman thinks a reference to *gambling* too colloquial. Another questions the use of *spend v. squander*.

They consider their audience's viewpoint, calculating the effect of their words. They discuss whether to blame the issue of sweethearts on the men or the sweethearts themselves. One student observes that since the letter confronts the wrongs men perpetrate on women, it would be a tactical error to criticize other women. They finally compromise by using the term *extra-marital affairs*. Wanting to state their case clearly yet not run the risk of censorship, they rewrite the paragraph on sex several times. The final letter appears in both Nassau daily papers:

Bahamian Women Deserve a Change

Dear Bahamian Men,

   The social, spiritual and economic growth of Bahamian society depends on men as well as women. For a very long time there has been a downward trend in male support of their wives and children. In the typical Bahamian marriage both the male and the female begin by thinking that they are in love, so much in love that the husband will help with the household chores. The husband will even stay up all night with their first child. Every Sunday the family will go to church and have dinner together. Later in the evening the husband and wife might go to a movie or a special function. Week days both the husband and wife will go to work. After work the wife rushes home to prepare dinner. The bills are paid by putting together both the husband and wife's salaries and, if possible, a little is saved. For some time all will go very well in the home. Then all of a sudden, for some unknown reason, the husband begins to change.

We are a group of women who have all been victim's of men's inconsiderate actions. We would like to focus on the punishment, deprivation, discourtesy, mental anguish and death of the soul for which Bahamian men are responsible: Punishment because some women are beaten by their husband; Deprivation because husbands give wives less and less to survive on each month; Discourtesy because extra-marital affairs disturb the home. Mental anguish is humiliation of the mind, for whose mind can be at ease in such a situation! Death of the soul deteriorates the whole body, for women are made to feel they serve no purpose.

These problems arise when the men begin to neglect their homes. The main problems between men and women in the Bahamas are: child raising, housekeeping, finances, and sex. Men are the root of most of these problems.

In most cases the male salary is more than the females'. Despite this fact, the majority of Bahamian men neglect the financial upkeep of their families in some way or the other. Because of this, the greater part of the financial burden which includes savings, school fees, groceries, utilities, and even mortgages have been left to women. The male finds other things to do with his salary. Some men wait for the women to remind them about their bills. Others expect the women to pay all the bills. How can the female be expected to do all of this with a salary that is less than the males'?

For centuries women have been solely responsible for housework. So men still think that a woman's place is in the home. Men expect women to work all day, come home and cook, wash dishes, clean house, wash clothes, prepare dinner and get the children ready for bed while they sit around and watch. It used to be that women did not work and were solely dependent on their husbands for support. Since women are now working and helping their husbands with most of the financial upkeep, there is no reason why the men can't be a part when it comes to housework. It is both the male's and the female's place to share the responsibilities of the home.

It takes two to produce a child and so it should be two to see to the upbringing of the child. Fathers do not spend sufficient time in the home. The most important stages in a child's life, the most cherished and once in a lifetime moments are when the child says his first word, makes his first step, and claps his hands for the first time. Fathers being around the home when moments like the above mentiond take place are important in children's lives. Here in the Bahamas fathers have failed to be real fathers, and children have been left totally dependent on their mothers. Having children and not supporting them is not a good way to prove one's manhood. A child should have both parents' care and attention. But before men see that their children are well taken care of they prefer to spend money on their own pleasure. Why be responsible for another life coming into the world if men don't care if the children are properly fed, have proper clothing to wear, and get a proper education?

Men tend not to realize the necessity in satisfying their partners when making love. Unfortunately, they are mainly concerned with the fulfilment of their desires. They come home at the most tiresome hours of the night, hop in bed and expect us to respond, without any love or affection. Most Bahamian men don't take the time to caress women's bodies before having sex. Therefore, the instant they get into bed – if they're in the mood – women are expected to perform. However, when women are in the mood, they don't respond. This leaves women dissatisfied and angry.

Our recommendations to Bahamian men in relation to the above are as follows:

a) That men join in family worship at least twice a month.
b) That men stop putting most of the financial burden on women. 75% of the household responsibilities should be handled by men.
c) That men at least buy their children's groceries, pay school fees and buy clothes.
d) That men take their children out for recreation at least once a week.
e) That men do an equal share of the housework.
f) That men do not allow extra-marital affairs to damage or destroy their marriages.
g) That men make more effort to sexually satisfy their wives. Talk about the things that please them. Caress their women until they're ready for sex. Try not to climax until the women are ready.

Men, there is definitely room for improvement in love, affection and communication. Try it.

Sincerely,
English 016-06

Comparing this 'Open Letter to Bahamian Men' with the women's earlier essays on 'Rape and Battered Wives', 'The Worst Things in a Marriage', and life in the Bahamas demonstrates how, through the investigation of a generative theme, students can advance their reading and writing skills, recognize links between their own lives and the larger society, and develop ways of using their newfound writing skills to intervene in their own environment.

At the end of the semester all these women passed the College-administered English exam. Most received 'B' grades on the essay component. Further, they decided to continue meeting throughout the next spring in order to read about women in other countries, broaden their understandings, and write a resource book for Bahamian women.

The success of this pedagogical experiment demonstrates that advanced literacy teachers can modify Freire's pedagogy to fit the needs of their students and the demands of the college. Through this approach students will achieve literacy in the truest, most profound sense: they will understand 'their reality in such a way that they increase their power to transform it'.[3]

Notes

1. The curriculum described in this chapter was developed by Nan Elsasser, Kyle Fiore, Patricia Irvine and Larry Smith.
2. See, especially, *Thought and Language*, Cambridge, Mass., MIT Press, 1962. We would lke to thank Vera John-Steiner for sharing with us her knowledge of and commitment to the theories of L.S. Vygotsky.

180

3. D. de Olivera and R. de Olivera, *Guinea-Bissau Reinventing Education*, Geneva, Institute of Cultural Action, 1976, p. 48.

References

Freire, P. (1970) *Pedagogy of the Oppressed*, New York, Seabury, p. 103.
Freire, P. (1978) *Pedagogy in Process*, New York, Seabury, p. 64.

21 Teaching English in the Multicultural Environment*

Bernard Gadd (Hillary College, Otava, Auckland)

Cultural assimilation

In the teaching of English all the issues in multicultural education come to their focal point. And it is in the hands of the teacher of English that our society particularly and peculiarly places the apportioning of social justice among the youthful members of our multicultural, multi-social class society. And it is that English teacher, you and me, who is supposed to keep the price of that justice – that equality of opportunity, that social equity upon which we pride ourselves so much – high, so that it is simply too high a price for thousands of our young people to pay.

For the price that our society – through all of us – demands is assimilation: cultural assimilation wholly or at the least assimilation whilst one is in the process of learning in school, out of your own cultural and linguistic group and assimilation into another group.

Oh no, you may well be saying, not that old stuff again, teachers have gone past all that. Multiculturalism is quite the recognized thing now. Well, maybe I had better spend a few minutes to convince you that, sure, a lot of the rhetoric, the new cliches, the 'in' platitudes of educational talk voice a multicultural sentiment – but the day-to-day realities of school and classroom and examination and textbook stand square upon an unaltering demand for considerable uniformity among, for conformity of being within, the children we teach.

Certainly the demand for assimilation into the supposed mainstream culture comes to us in a somewhat different form than it did in the crude past. It comes chiefly in the form of an expectation that, however much the school and the community extend toleration to the varied cultural traditions of its members, in the actual teaching situation all students ought to learn in much the same ways, ought to respond to much the same range of materials, ought to be able to learn through and in more or less the same kinds of English. And any child who gives evidence of finding these expectations difficult to comply with is diagnosed as demonstrating a learning or a language problem that various programmes or teaching strategies can and should remediate. I think I could offer the current English as a Second Language bandwagon as a good example of what I

*Abridged, by permission, from *Teaching English: Selected Papers from the first NZATE Conference*, Stockton House, 1982.

mean, where even New Zealand-born, native English speakers of Maori or Pacific Island or Dalmatian or working-class European descent may find themselves diagnosed as requiring structured language programmes or the like to teach away their variants of English which express their ethnic or social identity. And other similar children are being diagnosed as requiring special slow-learner or bottom-stream or vocationally oriented or specific learning deficiency courses, or special pre-school or early intervention programmes. I want to make it quite clear that such programmes *are* assimilationist wherever teachers or psychologists or others interpret the expression of the child's ethnic identity as revealing some sort of educational deficit or disadvantage. It is assimilationist wherever it is assumed that the normal child cannot learn in the school because of the English he speaks (I am not at the moment discussing specifically ESL needs), or because of the way he customarily interprets experiences and learns. Our schools are full of special classes made up of people whose only – or major – educational 'problem' is their membership of a minority ethnic or socioeconomic grouping.

This kind of soft-sell assimilation – assimilation with sympathy and good intentions – got its boost into educational respectability with the inauguration of one of America's mass solutions to a social problem, Project Headstart. It identified socioeconomic and ethnic minority status as the cause of the existence of learning patterns, attitudes, expectations and aspirations displaying 'clearly observable deficiences which lay the pattern for failure'. The Project then states the issue as the educational planners see it – either the child assimilates culturally and socially whilst at school to the mainstream, or the school fails him.

This view – assimilate or fail – won instant academic and bureaucratic and political respectability in this country [New Zealand] and has continued to receive support ever since. Professor J.B. Pride wrote in 1973: 'The more proper target in my view, is that of a harmonious biculturalism and bidialectism, in which the school, as part of the educational system, is the accepted place for standard English.' And there we have it – this is the way the demand to assimilate the youngsters we teach comes to us English teachers, comes from those who in the same breath proclaim their attachment to the multicultural ideal. You will notice that this view demands that the entire concept of biculturalism be reinterpreted to mean your own culture at home, mine (as teacher) at school. The professor's words would, I'm sure, be taken as entirely acceptable uncontroversial orthodoxy by thousands of teachers. And yet, here is James Sledd of the University of Texas looking back in 1969 over several years of what the professor had advocated for us. Sledd says: 'In fact the complete bidialectal, with undiminished control of his vernacular and a good mastery of the standard language is apparently as mythical as the unicorn – no authenticated specimens have been reported.' And he goes on to term the whole idea of enforced bidialectism 'the linguistics of white supremacy' – and believe me, Texas is a good place to judge that issue from.

And yet nearly ten years after Sledd wrote, Jane Ritchie was writing of her project for Maori pre-schoolers: 'Our over-all aim was clear. The children were to be prepared for school entry . . . . Standard English is the currency of opportunity. Respect for Maori cultural differences does not and need not mean elevating the oral communication register to pre-eminence. In our view, not to teach the children the language of the schools because of well-meaning concern for their home or ethnic background and speech is a form, albeit unconscious, of racism. Correct language is an instrument of power in our society, and though a child may talk in one way at home, a child who is going to succeed in the school system must achieve mastery over the school language.' The child must be, that is, a bidialectal.

I think maybe some teachers who are finding it hard to sympathize with or fully grasp the view that I'm presenting, which is that to demand linguistic and learning conformity among students is to demand cultural assimilation, may nevertheless have been somewhat disturbed by the archaic and simplistic notions expressed in that statement about the place of oral language, about the easy confidence that there is a readily identifiable form of correct language that is invariant throughout the schools – and the assumption that those who dissent from one's views are racists. And this may in turn cause some unease as to the quality of thinking that has gone into Project Headstart kinds of approach to ethnic and socioeconomic differences among students, a kind of thinking that sees it as a legitimate and achievable task to mould the child to the school while apparently believing one can do this and leave the rest of the child and her culture as they were.

Maori views

I have so far attempted to present to you the idea that the demand for a linguistic standard among children is one of the major ways the education system expects the English teacher to carry out a policy of ethnic or cultural or socioeconomic assimilation. If I have not been persuasive or clear enough, perhaps I could offer to you the perceptions of informed Maori educators as to whether they see, and their children experience, a pressure towards cultural asimilation. Ranginui Walker in 1975: 'Educators have assumed that the possession of middle-class skills and values will enable a person to function successfully everywhere and at every level of life.' And he notes that this is not so, saying later, 'the former policy of using schools as an instrument for homogenising and assimilating its component elements into what is presumed to be the mainstream by those who hold power needs to be revised. . . . We can no longer afford a monocultural education system because the stakes are too high, the survival of pupils and the sanity of teachers.' The McCombs committe in 1976 begs that the adaptation of schools towards more cultural inclusiveness 'should not be treated as a pious hope'. And last year the National Advisory Committee on Maori

Education reported that we were at 'a critical moment' in ethnic relations in school and community. And it said, 'We should rid ourselves of the notion that only those schools which are mutli-racial should be multicultural.' And yet that report itself talks of Maori children being 'weak in English language skills' and requiring 'a sound command of English in the classroom', sounding to my ear a little close to those who, in demanding a common English for all, are demanding at the same time a common school culture for all – which suggests the difficulty we have in examining our educational assumptions, and how deep is the expectation of a single kind of education and a single standard of educational excellence.

Maybe the final and convincing demonstration that we are only too little ahead of our predecessors in this matter of cultural assimilation in the schools is to be found in the fact that our education system still insists on a public examination for fifth formers which acts as a gate to further education and to employment, and which is demonstrably ethnically biased. The latest official statistics available to me relate to the 1979 School Certificate examinations and reveal that Maoris (the sole ethnic minority for whom statistics are kept) are still passing at about half the rate of total candidates; that the gap in English between the all-candidates and the Maori pass rate was 24.5 per cent, and that even in the Maori examination there was a 1 per cent gap to the disadvantage of Maori candidates.

The price is too high

Now the point of all this is not just to convince you that cultural assimilation is what our schools and the system itself are aiming to do, but to urgently persuade you that social justice in the form of equal educational opportunity for all that is only available at the price of assimilation is justice set at too high a premium. In my next set of comments I want you to see that this expectation of assimilation within the classroom is quite simply an expression of ethnocentrism, of cultural and linguistic arrogance, is a monstrous demand by those with the power to enforce their wishes upon our society that everyone else should subject themselves to *their* definitions of what it is to be human, or to be a New Zealander. To do this I want to set before you my reasons for claiming that the price is too high.

First of all, this demand displays too meagre an understanding of what ethnic identity is. I'm taking it that we all accept that we belong to a complex and changing social–cultural entity which is New Zealand society. And every New Zealander belongs to this entity, there is no escaping its pervasiveness, there are no pockets anywhere wholly of some other culture. But it is not a unitary culture in the sense of an utterly uniform culture. Sharing a style of upbringing and their continued association together, whole groups of people share in variants of our common culture. These groups are what I'm calling ethnic groups, and from them come our individual ethnic identities. And scores of thousands of New Zealanders in fact share not only in the common culture but also, to some extent, as part of their distinctive New Zealand ethnic identity, share in quite other cultural traditions, modified to fit New Zealand patterns, e.g. Maori Greek. I suppose it is especially members of minority ethnic groups who are most conscious of the difference between the various groups of New Zealanders. In short, our individual ethnic identity is our unique expression of the particular strand or variant of our common culture that we share with our nearest and dearest. Our ethnic identity is to a large extent, and not only socially, our definition of ourselves. And it is our ethnic group that gives us the language or languages we normally speak in the particular forms we use. (Maybe this is oversimplified, but in Britain it seems to be your social class that hands you your kind of English, in America it's your region, but with us it seems to be your ethnic group, and if you change that you tend also to alter your ways of using English.) The ethnic group we are reared in hands on to each of us its customary ways, its values, its attitudes, its patterns of child rearing, its links with the past. But much more importantly, it is from our ethnic background that we derive the inner charts of reality that we live by, our deepest perceptions, our preconceptions and basic assumptions, the approaches to reality that remain at the core of our identity whatever we may become during the rest of our lives. Therefore the demand for some form of ethnic assimilation is implicitly and explicitly to tell the individual: the kind of being you are, the things you have been raised to cherish, your forbears, your view of life, are in this classroom disprized, rejected, negated, are no good, are no go here. Believe me, the child may find it hard to feel that you really can like him if you apparently disapprove so heartily of his essential being.

Assimilation shows faulty understanding of relation between language and self

The demand for assimilation in the classroom further assumes that the human self is not an integrated whole but is fractionable – that you can change one part without in some fashion altering the whole. But surely one thing we have learnt in recent years is that language cannot be isolated from the rest of us, language is our self expressing itself, communicating with itself and with the world of which it is a part. You just cannot alter the language of a child at school without affecting in some way also his self-perception, the perception of him by others; because language is also an expression of group belonging, of attachment, of loyalty. Furthermore, you cannot alter the language without interfering somehow with the underlying pattern of reality that language both communicates and constructs. In short, the theory of bidialectism – a language variant for home and one for school to put on and off with your school uniform – is radically simplistic and naive. No wonder Sledd doubts if it can at all succeed.

Assimilation is not necessary socially or culturally

But to approach the entire question of assimilation from another tack:

many members of our ethnic minorities do not see the necessity for this assimilation. They notice that all New Zealanders share common political, social and economic systems, mass media, the impact of our nation's history and geography and international relations. That we all share one way or another in the prevailing range of lifestyles and in the assumptions these draw upon, and in the national language. Increasingly conscious of the extent to which they share all these with their fellow-citizens, members of minority groups are questioning why, then, they cannot have equality of education with their fellow-citizens. And, further, they observe that even assimilation into the majority ethnicity does not necessarily bring with it happiness, security, status or even a job. Indeed, minority members may perceive more acutely than their teachers what their society will allow them to be and do, and may be very sensitive to covert racisms, ethnic prejudices and stereotypes. And they may observe in their fellows who have crossed ethnic borders, a lingering sense of loss, a sense of isolation from roots, an uneasiness – even a conflict – within the self. Alistair Campbell, the poet, reflecting upon just such a personal anguish, has written of a feeling of a need for forgiveness: 'Forgiveness is a journey from despair along a path my ancestors approve – I must go back and with them make my peace – Forgiveness is a journey into love.'

Assimilation is linguistically not necessary

But when all is said and done, why on earth is it supposed to be necessary to change the child's language? When people say some standard form of English is necessary for academic success, what do they mean? Linguists such as Halliday have been telling us for years that, 'There is no evidence whatever that one language, or one variety of a language can be more efficient than another' (Halliday et al., 1964). Of course students have to learn the vocabulary and the framework of theory and assumptions of a discipline. But these are very limited goals, readily accomplishable without a wholesale attack on a child's language and therefore on his or her very being. Or are the people who talk of what academic success requires of our language caught in a mental trap that assumes that since the public examinations and their close relatives, the normed language tests, score Maoris and Polynesians and working-class children lower, that the fault must lie within these children rather than with the tests and the testers? And therefore that instead of carrying out a relatively straightforward procedure of making tests and exams more ethnically and linguistically inclusive, these people prefer to set about the enormously difficult task of altering the children until they match the assumptions and expectations of the testers and examiners. Or is it that the people who advocate the standard English in the classroom mean that you can't expect an employer to give you a job unless you speak like he does? All I can say to you on that score is that I don't see it as my job to reinforce any prejudices or hang-ups the business world may have – that simply makes our jobs as teachers more and more difficult in the long run. And nor do I see it as my job to plot a child's life in advance and determine the sort of English that will be most useful in his or her future life. If students want to enter jobs with linguistic franchises, such as teaching or broadcasting, they can adapt *themselves* from forms 5 or 6 onwards, having laid a good educational basis beforehand, and having a sound self-confidence.

A matter of values

We have reached at last the heart of the matter – which is a matter of values. Either you value every ethnic identity, either you see in ethnic and linguistic diversity a resource of richness, of differing perspectives, of potential new insights and new creativity as these differing mentalities meet in discussion, in debate, in literature – or else you think your own ethnicity, your own self is the norm for all mankind. This is what the continuing debate about multicultural education is about: we not only respect, but we actually use in our educating, we allow into every aspect of the curriculum the ethnicities of all our students, or we insist that there is only one way to be a student. We either teach children to value only their own particular ethnicities, or we go out of our way in *all* our schools to teach children to respect others, to learn to live with others, and we encourage them to want to learn about other kinds of lives New Zealanders lead. We either aim to provide an education that makes sense to all its students, or we limit true education to the ethnically chosen.

The crisis is now

I would be lying if I claimed that the multicultural adaptation of education and of the schools will lead to the promised land, flowing with the milk of shared human kindness and honey of sweet teacher–pupil relations, and the soft grass of pedagogic ease. There's nowhere like that on earth.

But let me end with the bluntest warning. If we choose to go on as now, mouthing multicultural platitudes and living ethnocentric realities in our daily teaching, Northern Ireland, Watts, South Africa, Wounded Knee, Notting Hill shall all of them come out of the TV screen and into your classrooms. As the National Advisory Committee on Maori Education Report said, the crisis in our ethic relations is *now*.

And the English teacher has a central role to play, dealing as we do directly with our students' selves. And we must demand more help from the Department, including a clean break with its existing apartheid organization of help – separate help for Maori, for Polynesian, for Asian students, and no working conception of multicultural education whatsoever. But of course our immediate task is to find ways to help each other. I wish you well. *Kia ora koutou katoa, e hoa ma.**

* Maori 'greeting to all present'.

188

Reference

Halliday, M.A.K., McIntosh, A. and Strevens, P. (1964) *The Linguistic Sciences and Language Teaching*, London, Longman.

22   A Lot of Talk About Nothing*

Shirley Brice Heath (Associate Professor of Anthropology and Linguistics, School of Education, Stanford University)

Inside a third-grade classroom described by the principal as a class of 'low achievers', several pairs of children are working over tape-recorders in dialogues with each other. One small group of children is dressed in costumes performing 'Curious George' scenes for a few kindergarteners who are visiting. Yet another group is preparing illustrations for a story told by one of their classmates and now being heard on tape as they talk about why their drawings illustrate the words they hear. A lot of talk about nothing? Why are these children who presumably lack basic skills in language arts not spending their time with obvious instruction from the teacher in reading, writing and listening?

These are students in the classroom of a teacher–researcher who has adapted information about the oral and written language experiences of these children at home into a new language arts curriculum for school. She has developed for her children a program in which they spend as much of the day as possible talking – to each other and the teacher, and to fifth- and sixth-graders who come into the class one-half hour each day to read to small groups. This teacher has thirty children and no aides; she enlisted the help of fifth- and sixth-grade teachers who were willing to have some of their students write stories for the younger children and read to them several days of each week. The kindergarten teacher helps out by sending a few of her children for the third-graders to read to each week.

Talk in the classroom is about personal experiences, stories, expository textbook materials and, perhaps most important, about their own and others' talk. Their teacher gives no reading or writing task which is not surrounded by talk about the content knowledge behind the task and the kinds of language skills – oral and written – needed to tackle the task.

Since the beginning of the year, the teacher has asked visitors from the community into her class to talk about their ways of talking and to explain what they read and write at home and at work. The children have come to think of themselves as language 'detectives', listening and learning to describe the talk of others. Grocery clerks have to use many politeness terms, and the questions they ask most often of customers require only a yes or no answer. On the other hand, guides at the local nature museum talk in

* Reprinted, by permission, from *Language Arts*, vol. 60, no. 8, November/December 1983; Based on research reported in full in *Ways With Words*, by Shirley Brice Heath, Cambridge University Press, 1983.

'long paragraphs', describing what is around them and usually asking questions only at the end of one of their descriptions. The children have also learned to analyse their talk at home, beginning early in the year with a simple record of the types of questions they hear asked at home, and moving later in the year to interviews with their parents about the kinds of talking, reading and writing they do at their jobs.

The teacher in this classroom comments on her own talk and the language of textbooks, of older students, and of the third-graders themselves during each day. 'Show and tell' time, usually reserved for only first-graders, occurs each day in this class, under the supervision of a committee of students who decide each week whether those who participate in this special time of the day will: (i) narrate about an experience they or someone else has had, (ii) describe an event or object without including themselves or another animate being, or (iii) read from their diary or journal for a particular day. The children use terms such as *narrative*, *exposition*, and *diary* or *journal* with ease by the end of the year. Increasingly during the year, the children use 'show and tell' time to talk, not about their own direct experiences, but about content areas of their classroom. Also by the end of the year, the children are using this special time of the day for presenting skits about a social studies or science unit. They have found that the fifth- and sixth-graders can offer assistance on these topics, and planning such a presentation guarantees the attention of the upper classmen. By the end of the year, most of these children score above grade level on reading tests, and they are able to write stories, as well as paragraphs of exposition on content areas with which they feel comfortable in their knowledge. This is clearly no longer a class of 'low achievers'.

Teachers as researchers

All of these ideas sound like pedagogical practices that many good teachers bring intuitively to their instruction. What was different about the motivations of this third-grade teacher for approaching language arts in these ways? The teacher described here was one of a group of teacher–researchers who co-operated with me for several years during the 1970s. I worked as an ethnographer, a daily participant and observer in homes and communities similar to those of the children in their classrooms, studying the ways in which the children learned to use oral and written language. As I studied the children at home, the teachers focused on their own language uses at home and in the classroom. We brought our knowledge together for comparison and as the baseline data from which to consider new methods and approaches in language arts.

We do not need educational research to tell us that different types of attention spans, parental support systems and peer pressures can create vast differences among children in the same classroom, school or community. But what of more subtle features of background differences, such as the amount and kind of talk addressed by adults to children and solicited from children? How can teachers and researchers work together to learn more about children's language experiences at home? And what can this knowledge mean for classroom practice?

For nearly a decade, living and working in three communities located within a few miles of each other in the south-eastern part of the United States, I collected information on ways in which the children of these communities learned to use language: (i) Roadville is a white working-class community, (ii) Trackton is a black working-class community in which many of the older members have only recently left work as sharecroppers on nearby farms, (iii) the townspeople, black and white residents of a cluster of mainstream, school-oriented neighbourhoods, are school teachers, local business owners, and executives of the textile mills.

Children from the three groups respond differently to school experiences. Roadville children are successful in the first years of the primary grades. Most Trackton children are not successful during this period, and only a few begin in the higher primary grades to move with adequate success through their classes. Most of the mainstream children of the townspeople, black and white, are successful in school and obtain a high school diploma with plans to go on to higher education. Children from backgrounds similar to those of these three groups make up the majority of the students in many regions of the south-eastern United States. They bring to their classrooms different patterns of learning and using oral and written language, and their patterns of academic achievement vary greatly.

Intuitively, most teachers are aware of the different language background experiences children bring to school, but few means exist for providing teachers with information about these differences and their implications for classroom practice. Recent development of the notion of 'teacher-as-researcher' has begun to help bridge the long-standing gap between researcher and teacher. This approach pairs the roles of teacher and researcher in a co-operative search for answers to questions raised by the teacher about what is happening in the classroom and why. Answering *why* questions more often than not calls for knowledge about the background experiences of both children and teachers. Thus, researcher working with teacher can help bridge yet another gap – that between the classroom and the homes of students.

Throughout most of the decade of the 1970s, I worked in the Piedmont Carolinas with teachers in several districts as research partners. Together we addressed the questions teachers raised during the sometimes tumultuous early years of desegregation and ensuing shifts of curricular and testing policies. These teachers accepted the fact that language was fundamental to academic achievement, and their primary concerns related to how they could help children learn to use oral and written language in ways that would being successful classroom experiences. They asked hard questions of language research. Why were some children seemingly unable to answer straightforward questions? Why were some students able to give elaborate directions and tell fantastic stories on the playground, but unable to respond to assignments calling for similar responses about lesson materials? Why did some children who had achieved adequate success in their first two or three years of school begin to fail in the upper primary grades?

In the 1960s, social scientists had described the language habits of groups of youngsters who were consistently failing to achieve academic excellence. The teachers with whom I worked were familiar with these studies, which had been carried out primarily in black urban areas. Most accepted the fact that children who spoke a non-standard variety of English had learned a rule-governed language system and, more over, that these students reflected learned patterns of 'logic', considerable facility in handling complicated forms of oral discourse, and adeptness in shifting styles. But knowing this information about language learned at home did not answer the kinds of questions noted above about classroom performance. Neither did it provide for development of improved classroom materials and practices.

Ethnography of communication

Late in the 1970s, as some language researchers tried to describe the contexts in which children of different cultures learned to use language, they turned to ethnographic methods. Participating and observing over many months and even years in the daily lives of the group being studied, these researchers, who were often anthropologists, focused on oral and written language uses. My work in Roadville, Trackton, and among the townspeople centred on the children of these groups as they learned the ways of acting, believing and valuing around them in their homes and communities. Following the suggestions of anthropologist Dell Hymes, who first proposed in 1964 that ethnographers focus on communication, I lived and worked within these three groups to describe where, when, to whom, how, and with what results children were socialized as talkers, readers and writers. The three communities – located only a few miles apart – had radically different ways of using language and of seeing themselves in communication with their children.

Roadville parents believe they have to teach their children to talk, and they begin their task by talking with infants, responding to their initial sounds as words. They respond with full sentences, varying their tone of voice and emphasis, and affectionately urging infants to turn their heads in the direction of the speaker. As they talk to their infants and young children, they label items in the environment, and as children begin to talk, adults ask many teaching questions: 'Where's your nose?' 'Can you find Daddy's shoes?' Adults fictionalize their youngsters in talk about them: 'He's a little cowboy; see those boots? See that cowboy strut.' Parents read to their children and ask them to name items in books, answer questions about the books' contents and, as they get older, to sit quietly listening to stories read to them. Parents buy colouring and follow-the-number books for their children and tutor them in staying within the lines and colouring items appropriately. All of these habits relate to school practices, and they are transferred to the early years of reading and writing in school. Yet, by the fourth-grade many of these children seem to find the talking, reading and writing tasks in school foreign, and their academic achievement begins to decline.

In nearby Trackton, adults immerse their children in an ongoing stream of talk from extended family members and a wide circle of friends and neighbours. Children become the responsibility of all members of the community, and from birth they are kept in the centre of most adult activities, including eating, sleeping or playing. Adults talk about infants and young children, and as they do so, they fictionaize them and often exaggerate their behaviours and physical features. They nickname children and play teasing games with them. They ask young children for specific information which is not known to adults: 'Where'd that come from?' 'You want what?' By the time they are toddlers, these children begin to tell stories, recounting events or describing objects they have seen. Adults stop and listen to their stories occasionally, but such stories are most often addressed to other children who challenge, extend, tease or build from the youngsters' tales. By about age 2, children begin to enter ongoing conversations by actively attracting adults' attention with some physical gesture and then making a request, registering a complaint, or reporting an event. Very quickly, these children are accepted as communicating members of the group, and adults respond directly to them as conversational partners.

Most of these children first go to school with enthusiasm, but by the end of the first half of the first grade, many are coming home with reports that their teacher scolds them for talking too much and working too little. By the third grade, many Trackton children have established a record of failures which often they do not break in the rest of their school careers.

After hearing from me how children of these communities learned to use language, some of their teachers agreed to work with me to study either their own uses of language with their pre-schoolers at home or those of their mainstream friends. They found that when talking to very young infants, they asked questions, simplified their sentences, used special words and changed their tone of voice. Moreover, since most of these mainstream mothers did not work outside the home while their children were very young, they spent long hours each day alone with their pre-schoolers as their primary conversational partners. They arranged many outings, usually with other mothers through voluntary associations, such as their church groups or local social memberships.

These teachers' findings about mainstreamers' uses of language with their pre-schoolers indicated that they and the Roadville parents had many language socialization habits in common. Parents in both communities talked to their children and focused their youngsters' attention at an early age on labels, pictures in books and educational toys. Both groups played with their children and participated in planned outings and family recreation with them. Yet mainstream children and Roadville children fared very differently in their progress through the middle primary grades.

A close look at the home habits of these two groups indicated that a major difference lay in the amount of running narrative or ongoing commentary in which mainstram parents immersed their young children. As these youngsters pass their first birthday, mothers and other adults who are part of their daily network begin to provide a running commentary on events and items surrounding the child. In these commentaries, adults tell the child what is happening: 'Mummy's going to get her purse, and then we're going to take a ride. Mummy's got to go to the post office.' As soon as the child begins to talk, adults solicit these kinds of running commentaries: they ask children what they are doing with their toys, what they did when they were at some one else's house, and what they had to eat on a trip to the grocery store. These requests for running descriptions and cumulative accounts of past actions provide children in these families with endless hours of practice of all the sentence-level features necessary to produce successful narratives or recounts of experiences.

In using their own experiences as data, children begin their developmental progression of story conventions and narrative structures which they will be asked to replay in school from the first day of school through their college courses. They learn either to use an existing animate being or to create a fantastic one as the central actor in their stories; they take these actors through events in which they may meet obstacles on their way to a goal. The scripts of the stories that the children have heard read to them and the narratives that have surrounded them and storied their own and others' experiences are replayed with different actors and slightly different settings. Gradually children learn to open and close stories, to give them a setting and movement of time, and occasionally, even to sum up the meaning of the story in a moralistic pronouncement ('He shouldn't have gone without his mother'). Some children move from linking a collection of events related to one another only by their immediacy of experience for the child to tying a story togther by incorporating a central point, a constant goal or direction, and a point of view which may not be that of the child as experiencer and narrator.

When children are very young toddlers, parents both talk of and ask children about events of the here-and-now: the immediate tasks of eating, getting dressed, and playing with a particular toy or person. Of older toddlers, adults increasingly ask questions about events that occurred in the past – tasks, settings and events that the child is expected to recount from memory. These recountings are, however, then interpreted by adults or older siblings in a future frame: 'Do you want to go again?' 'Do you think Billy's mother will be able to fix the broken car?' Questioners ask children to express their views about future events and to link past occurrences with what will come in the future.

In many ways, all of this is 'talk about nothing', and adults and older siblings in these mainstream households model and elicit these kinds of narratives without being highly conscious of their having a didactic purpose or a heavily positive transfer value to school activities. Yet when teacher–researchers examined closely the instructional situations of the classrooms into which these children usually go, they found that, from first-grade reading circles to upper-primary social studies group work, the major activity is producing some sort of commentary on events or objects. In the early primary years, teachers usually request commentary in the form of labels or names of attributes of items or events ('What did the boy in our story find on his walk?'). Later, the requests are for descriptive commentary ('Who are some community helpers? What kinds of jobs do they do for us?'). Gradually the requests are mixed and students have to learn when it is appropriate to respond with labels or features (brief names or attributes of events or objects), fantastic stories, straightforward descriptions, or interpretations in which they comment on the outcome of events, the relative merits of objects, or the internal states of characters.

A closer look

On the surface, these summaries of the early language socialization of the children from these three communities support a commonly held idea about links between language at home and at school: the more parents talk to their children the more likely children are to succeed in school. Yet the details of the differences and similarities across these three communities suggest that this correlation is too simple. Trackton children hear and take part in far more talk around them than the children of either Roadville or the townspeople. Yet, for them, more talk does not have a positive transfer value to the current, primary-level practices of the school. Roadville children have less talk addressed to them than the townspeople's children. Yet, from an early age, they are helped to focus on labels and features of items and events. They are given books and they are read to by parents who buy educational toys for their children and spend many hours playing with their toddlers. As the children grow older, these parents involve their children in handicrafts, home building projects, and family recreational activities such as camping and fishing. Both Trackton and Roadville parents have strong faith in schooling as a positive value for their children, and they believe success in school will help their children get jobs better than those they have held as adults. Yet neither Roadville nor Trackton children manage to achieve the same pattern of sustained academic success children of townspeople achieve with relatively little apparent effort. Why?

A primary difference seems to be the amount of 'talk about nothing' with which the townspeople surround their children and into which they socialize their young. Through their running narratives, which begin almost at the birth of the child, they seemingly focus the attention of their young on objects and events while they point out verbally the labels and features of those that the child should perceive and later talk about. It is as though, in the drama of life, these parents freeze scenes and parts of scenes repeatedly throughout each day. Within the frame of a single scene, they focus the child's attention, sort out labels to name, and give the child ordered turns for sharing talk about these labels and the properties of the objects or events to which they refer; adult and child thus jointly narrate descriptions of scenes. Through this consistent focus, adults pull out some of the stimuli in the array surrounding the child and make these stand still for co-operative examination and narration between parent and child. Later occurrences of the same event or object are identified by adults who call the child's attention to similarities and differences. Thus townspeople's children are not left on their own to see these relations between two events or to explore ways of integrating something in a new context to its old context. These children learn to attend to items both in real life and in books, both in and out of their usual locations, as they practise throughout their pre-school years running narratives with adults.

In much of their talk, mainstream adults ask 'What do you call that?' 'Do you remember how to say the name of that?' Thus children are alerted to attend to the particulars of talk about talk: names, ways of retelling information, and ways of linking what one has told with something that has gone before. Thus, mainstreamers' children hear a lot of talk about talk and are forced to focus on not only the features and names of the world around them, but also on their ways of communicating about that world. From the earliest days of their infancy, these habits are modelled repeatedly for them, and as soon as they learn to talk, they are called upon to practise similar verbal habits. Day in and day out during their pre-school years, they hear and practise the kinds of talk in which they will display successful learning in school.

The teacher in the third-grade classroom described at the beginning of this chapter recognized that her students needed intense and frequent occasions to learn and practise those language uses they had not acquired at home. She therefore created a classroom that focused on talk – all kinds of talk. The children labelled, learned to name the features of everyday items and events, told stories, described their own and others' experiences, and narrated skits, puppet shows and slide exhibits.

Many classrooms include such activities for portions of the day or week; others provide some of these activities for some children. A critical difference in the case given here, however, and one driven by a perspective gained from being part of a research team was the amount of talk about talk in this classroom. School-age children are capable of – and can be quite proficient at – stepping back from and commenting upon their own and others' activities, *if* the necessary skills are modelled and explicated. In this classroom, and in others which drew from ethnographic data on the home life of their students, teachers and visitors to the classroom called attention to the ways they used language: how they asked questions, showed politeness, got what they wanted, settled arguments, and told funny stories. With early and intensive classroom opportunities to surround learning with many different kinds of talk and much talk about talk, children from homes and communities whose uses of language do not match those of the school CAN achieve academic success. A frequently heard comment, 'Talk is cheap', is, in these days of bankrupt school districts and economic cutbacks, perhaps worth a closer examination – for more reasons than one.

Editor's References

Beckett, S. (1966) *Molloy*, London, Jupiter Books.
Bruner, J.S. (1971) 'The process of education revisited', *Phi Delta Kappan*, September.
Bussis, A.M., Chittenden, E.A. and Amarel, M. (1976) *Beyond Surface Curriculum*, Colorado, Westview Press.
Empson, W. (1961) *Milton's God*, London, Chatto & Windus.
Gusdorf, G. (1965) *Speaking*, trans. Paul Brockelman, Northwestern University Press.
Langer, S.K. (1953) *Feeling and Form*, London, Routledge & Kegan Paul.
Polanyi, M. (1969) *Knowing and Being*, London, Routledge & Kegan Paul.
Vygotsky, L.S. (1971) *The Psychology of Art*, Cambridge, Mass., MIT Press.
Vygotsky, L.S. (1978) *Mind in Society*, Cambridge, Mass., Harvard University Press.
Whitehead, A.N. (1932) *The Aims of Education*, London, Williams & Norgate.
Wilde, O. (1956) *Poems and Essays*, London, Collins.
Winnicott, D.W. (1971) *Playing and Reality*, London, Tavistock Press.

AAA. 5233   7-9-90

Davison
PE
65
E52
1984
c. 2

0 00 02 0484773 5
MIDDLEBURY COLLEGE